Critical Acclaim for *The Making of a Quagmire*

"The book was invaluable to me when I went to Vietnam in 1966; and it remains invaluable today as a unique first-hand account of the period 1962–1963 in South Vietnam. . . . Halberstam gives us both an analysis of events and the texture of the time in Saigon."

> Frances FitzGerald, Pulitzer Prize–winning author of *Fire in the Lake: The Vietnamese and the Americans in Vietnam*

"In the voluminous literature on America's Vietnam war, Halberstam's is one of the very few first-hand records to emerge as a classic. . . . The vividness of this enterprising and courageous correspondent's account will still grip the attention of any reader. . . . Halberstam's knowledgeable assessment of the U.S. record is so devastating that the reader will soon appreciate why he so discomfited the Kennedy Administration, and why that President took the controversial step of trying to get *The New York Times* to pull him out of Vietnam."

> George Mct. Kahin, Cornell University

"As was the case in 1965, the book still deserves the widest possible audience. It is as fresh and stimulating as when it first appeared. Halberstam's capacity to cut through the illusions and self-deception that characterized American and Vietnamese behavior in the early 1960s still makes a fascinating story. . . . Students will use the book to make connections to more recent events in Central America and the Middle East."

> Robert Dallek, University of California at Los Angeles

Also by David Halberstam:

THE NOBLEST ROMAN
ONE VERY HOT DAY
THE UNFINISHED ODYSSEY OF ROBERT KENNEDY
HO
THE BEST AND THE BRIGHTEST
THE POWERS THAT BE
THE BREAKS OF THE GAME*
THE AMATEURS
THE RECKONING: The Challenge to America's Greatness
SUMMER OF '49

*Published by Ballantine Books

THE
MAKING
OF A
QUAGMIRE

David Halberstam

BALLANTINE BOOKS • NEW YORK

*Grateful acknowledgment is made to the following for the permis-
sion granted to use copyrighted material in this volume:*
Articles by Robert Trumbull, Homer Bigart, David Halberstam
and Peter Grose. © Copyright, 1947, 1962, 1963, 1964, by The
New York Times Company. Reprinted by permission.
Excerpts from *Time* cover stories: "The New Frontier" and
"SOUTH VIET NAM—To Liberate from Oppression." © Copyright,
1950, 1962, by Time Inc.
Excerpt from "Last Act in Indochina" by Graham Greene. Re-
printed from *The New Republic*, May 16, 1955.
Article by Marguerite Higgins. © Copyright 1963, by New York
Herald Tribune Inc.
Portions of this book have previously appeared in *Commentary,
Esquire* and *Harper's Magazine*.

Library of Congress Catalog Card Number: 65-11258

ISBN 0-345-35777-9

This edition published by arrangement with Random House, Inc.

Manufactured in the United States of America

First Ballantine Books Edition: January 1989
Third Printing: March 1991

For my mother, Mrs. Blanche Halberstam,
and in memory of my father,
the late Dr. Charles Halberstam

Just remember one thing: there are no dumb Asians.
—Advice to the author from Robert Trumbull, Old Asia Hand and *New York Times* correspondent in Southeast Asia—September 3, 1962

Author's Note

This book is a reporter's story, and as such it belongs as much to those others who were there: Mert Perry, Neil Sheehan, Nguyen Ngoc Rao, Mal Browne, Ray Herndon, Horst Faas, Peter Arnett, Pham Xuan An, John Sharkey, Nick Turner, Francois Sully, Vo Huynh, Ha Thuc Can and Charley Mohr.

Luck—or lack of it—makes a lot of difference in a reporter's career. A good friend of mine named Neil Sheehan, who covered Vietnam with style, enthusiasm and remarkable accuracy for United Press International, was virtually ordered to take a vacation near the end of October 1963. Sensing an imminent coup, Sheehan protested vigorously, but his Tokyo office, noting that for the past nine years Vietnam had lived on the brink of imminent coups, insisted nonetheless. When the coup came, in November, Sheehan was in Japan—and this probably cost him a Pulitzer Prize. The incident did not ease his innate suspicion of desk men.

There is, however, something to be said for *good* luck in failing to get big stories. On one occasion I missed a major story and it probably saved my career.

The time was September 1961, and I had just gone overseas to the Congo for the *Times* on a six-month assignment to spell the exhausted Henry Tanner. (Tanner knew he needed a rest according to the yardstick of Congo coverage invented by still another *Times* colleague, Paul Hoffman, who had noted earlier: "The time to leave this place is when all white people begin to look alike.") I was just twenty-seven years old, and incredibly eager. I had always dreamt of being a foreign correspondent, and had worked my way toward that goal: after college, a job on a paper in Mississippi, then four happy years on the Nashville *Tennessean*, then suddenly a job in Washington with the *New York Times*, and even more suddenly, it seemed—after only six months in the bureau—a chance to go to the Congo for the *Times*. I carried a portable typewriter belonging to the *Times* (which I was to leave in ruins behind me, much to their dismay), a trench coat (the countries I was to visit were always too hot and muggy for wearing it), some Abercrombie & Fitch bush clothes (of very limited value, since you were more likely to be shot at if you wore them) and a vast variety of small stomach-disorder pills (always the wrong kind).

I arrived in Leopoldville, reported from there for three weeks and then went to Elisabethville in Moise Tshombe's Katanga just in time to watch the United Nations start military operations in an attempt to end the Katanga secession. (The UN later denied this and claimed it was simply rounding up white mercenaries, but the truth of the matter was that it tried to end the secession and bungled the job.)

For five days the fighting between the UN forces and the Katangese continued. It was a remarkable story: exciting and dangerous, a small but very nasty street war, where reporters were shot at by both sides, and by civilians as well. As one of my colleagues in the Washington bureau later said, it was obviously more dangerous to be a reporter than a participant. The sounds of the war were magnificent: the Katangese were given to taking their new automatic weapons, pointing them up in the air, and firing away. One burst would provoke—or scare—another Katangese and he might fire off a long burst of his own; which might provoke a third Katangese . . .

The reporters had come to own a fleet of broken-down automobiles, pock-marked with bullet holes, and we drove in constant fear of their inevitable collapse while we were under automatic-weapons fire. Most of the cars were vintage Volkswagens, and there is nothing quite so frightening as sitting cramped in one of them with four other people, driving down a solitary street and hearing bullets come at you.

The cable to the outside world had been cut on the first day;

filing was a shambles. We smuggled copy out with any frightened tourist who was hoping to escape down some eroded African road, or we hopefully passed a bulletin to a ham-radio
operator. But three British colleagues and I had managed to
make other arrangements. In the early hours of the first day of
fighting we had cornered a Belgian pilot and had chartered his
light plane; we had quelled his inhibitions with an awesome
amount of money, and we had turned the Katanga secession into
our own commuter war. On the first night we flew out of Elisabethville to the barren little town of Ndola in the Rhodesian
copper belt, a lean and hard land reminiscent socially and ra-
cially of the hill country of northeastern Mississippi. Ndola had
some saving graces: the marvelous global link of British Empire
communication; old colonial efficiency; a penny a word to your
office in London—giving you a priceless feeling of security in
knowing that the copy you sent would arrive safely in a disbe-
lieving Western world, and would not remain mysteriously, collecting dust in the back of some African cable office.

Then it was to bed in Ndola, in a cramped hotel over the
railroad yards, where the chugging of the early-morning trains
always entered my dreams as machine-gun bursts; then to a
bad breakfast of runny eggs made worse by runny nerves; then
the commuter flight back to Elisabethville; then once more to
the thinning ranks of Volkswagens to find out first-hand how the
pockets of fighting had changed. Those days were particularly
pleasant for me because I was the only American correspondent
in the group, working among extremely talented British colleagues; in such a war this singularity made me feel somewhat
like a bit player from Evelyn Waugh's *Scoop*.

We managed this for four days, arriving promptly at 10 A.M.
and spending the day chasing Katangese and Belgians and Irish
and Swedes and Indians in order to extract a semblance of the
truth and of the various languages and dialects. *(We are fighting
back bravely;* or, *It is a great day for all black men;* or, *The
Katangese have attacked us again and have provoked us once
more. We are, however, being strictly nonaggressive,* went the
varying stories of both sides. "If no one is attacking nobody
else," one reporter remarked, "then where are all those dead
people coming from?")

At 4 P.M. each day we would stop by the so-called "Grand" Hôtel Leopold Deux to scoop up our colleagues' copy, and then rush once again to the Elisabethville airport. At one point en route some snipers came very close, and I asked Peter Young-husband of the London *Daily Mail* what nationality they were. "Indians," he answered. I asked him how he could tell. "Too close to be Africans or Swedes," he said.

On the fourth day we landed at the Elisabethville airport as the single Fouga jet fighter in Moise Tshombe's air force came by and dropped a bomb. It caused a good deal of excitement and panic, and some of the South Americans who were stationed at the airport as transport pilots immediately petitioned to go home. I was nicked by shrapnel, and the Fleet Streeters had a marvelous time writing about it because it allowed them to feel they were in the heart of combat. "I wasn't hit, but David Halberstam of the *New York Times*, who was right next to me, was wounded," one of them wrote, "and my typewriter case was shattered." (One of this man's colleagues assured me that this was the fifth time his typewriter case had been shattered, and that stories like this helped greatly at the end of the month when it was time to file expense accounts.) Later in the fighting the UN by chance mortared the hotel room of Cyril Ainsley of the *Daily Express*. Ainsley was out at the time and only heard about it belatedly; by that time one of the other Fleet Street men had already filed, claiming that it was *his* room which had been hit— thereby, he said, staving off a cable from his desk saying, WHY YOUR ROOM UNMORTARED?

Incidents like this helped balance what fear the assignment provided. At the end of each day we would remind the increasingly nervous Belgian pilot how much money he was making, then get full speed up on the take-off, fly about two feet above the runway so that the plane could not be seen and at the last minute turn upward suddenly at about an 80-degree angle to avoid possible Katangese anti-aircraft fire. This was really an unnecessary precaution; the Katangese had anti-aircraft guns, but despite the pleading of the white mercenaries they refused to use them. As one Katangese officer said, "If the guns are fired, the UN will know where we are."

Day after day we went on like this, with mixed feelings: the fear of going into that city, and the pride in coming out each day with a story. In between we adjusted as best we could to the never-never land of Katanga, a country whose unique qualities can be summarized by the story of what happened to an Associated Press photographer named Horst Faas. Horst was arrested by the Katangese and first accused of being a Swede (because he spoke some English), then an Indian, and finally an American. Poor Horst, fearing for his life, pleaded that he was a German, that the Americans had bombed the Germans and killed "almost as many Germans as the UN is now killing Katangese." As a result he managed to come up with exclusive photos of UN prisoners being held by the Katangese. The UN, rather than being pleased with the first evidence that the prisoners were still alive, became angry with Faas and claimed he was a right-wing German agent in league with the Katangese. Horst later went to Vietnam, where his fine photographs often revealed aspects of the war that the Americans wanted left unseen, and consequently, by late 1963, the American brass was insinuating that he was a Communist agent, and that the AP in Saigon had been infiltrated. Thus Horst had completed the cycle.

But our precarious life as commuters could not last. On the fifth morning the Belgian pilot rebelled; the bombing of the airport had taken place the previous morning, the French pilot of the Fouga had warned him away, and our man had had enough. He refused to fly back to Elisabethville, and we were grounded.

By that time, of course, the press corps had swelled considerably. Reporters and television teams were coming in from all over Africa and Europe. We who had been in on the original fighting enjoyed the mystique of being considered old-timers; we had been there, and we had The Word. So we all sat around trying to plan our return to Katanga. The main route was out; there had been several ambushes along the way already, and the Katangese troops and some of the irregulars who were doing some bushwhacking along the way were considered very dangerous. But there was a back way—or so the maps indicated; the relationship between African maps and African landscape is extremely haphazard. This road went to the little border town of Kipushi, where the Union Minière had a plant and where our chances for safe entry were much greater.

By this time there must have been fifteen of us, and five cars. We decided to organize a caravan, primarily for reasons of safety. In the Congo one or two persons traveling alone can disappear relatively easily; with a caravan there may be some ugly moments with an armed guard, but more likely than not, he will bring a group of Europeans to a higher authority. At least this had happened many times in the past.

So the caravan was organized and everyone went around buying candles, canned food, whiskey, loaves of bread, and cigarettes—some of the latter to be smoked, but mostly to be used in trading with the African border guards.

At four o'clock the next morning we set off from Ndola. It was a journey into misery. No one actually knew where we were going, we were not really sure we wanted to get there, and we were frightened. Again and again we became lost. Several times cars broke down; knowing the way we drove, knowing Katanga and knowing the roads, the Ndola counterpart of Hertz was sending his worst cars to the front. It was the dry season; the first car traveled dust-free, but for the rest of us it was terrible. Covered with a thin red powder and coughing that bitter copper-country dust, we looked as if we had all been made up for some high school play about a family of redheads. It also seemed like a trip without end; during that whole interminable morning we averaged about ten miles an hour.

At 1 P.M., bitter and exhausted but finally convinced that we were on the right route and that we were two-thirds of the way to Elisabethville, we stopped for lunch—which meant opening a few cans of tinned beef or sardines and drinking warm beer. Terry Spencer of *Life* carried a radio, and we had managed to get the aerial high up in a tree by the time the BBC came on. When you are covering a major story in that part of the world, you are often completely cut off from other aspects of the event. If you are in Leopoldville you may have no knowledge at all of vital developments either at the UN in New York, or in Washington—or even in Elisabethville, since news from a Congolese city had to go all the way to the Western world before it could be relayed back. Thus, the BBC was often the only contact

with the outside world. There was something reassuring about
its imperturbable tones; listening to the BBC news about the
Congo it was often impossible to relate its calm and stately
phrases to the events we had just been seeing.

From the evidence of the broadcast that afternoon we were
still the top story (reporters always live in fear that *their* catastrophe will be superseded by someone else's). Suddenly there
was a bulletin: "Secretary-General Hammarskjöld is flying from
Leopoldville to Ndola to meet with President Tshombe there."
Ndola? Ndola was eight or nine dusty hours behind; we had just
left it. The news seemed like the cruelest joke of the year. The
fifteen of us all looked at one another, trying to figure out what
to do. For some the decision was automatic: the wire-service
men would have to turn back and cover the most important part
of the story. For others, like Spencer and Lee Griggs of *Time*,
the decision was equally simple: *Life* would want Spencer's pictures of the fighting, and *Time* would want background color
material from Griggs. They would go ahead.

For me it was a more complex decision. The meeting in Ndola
was almost surely front-page stuff ("NDOLA—Secretary-General
Hammarskjöld and Secessionist President Moise Tshombe of
Katanga began high-level talks here tonight over the future of
the Katanga secession . . ."). But knowing high-level meetings,
and in particular knowing Tshombe's reputation (Moise was always good for at least four days; he believed there should be an
element of grace and style to African palavers, and that he should
threaten total breakdown of the talks at least twice), I felt there
was likely to be little substance in it. The first day there would
be nothing but preliminaries, or what Horst calls "the handshake." (He is convinced that if Eisenhower arrived in Europe
to see Adenauer and punched the Chancellor in the nose, and
he, the photographer, got an exclusive photograph of the act, he
would be told by his office, "Yes, that's very nice, but where's
the pic we need—you know, the handshake?")

So I made up my mind to keep going to Katanga. I was
two-thirds of the way there, and the story in Ndola would be no
more than a quick front-page play; whereas if I continued into
Katanga I could work early the next day, cover the situation in
Elisabethville, leave early and get back to Ndola in time to cover

the Hammerskjöld-Tshombe talks. (As it turned out, I ended up with two stories under two different datelines). Then I could cover Ndola and stay there until the *Times* moved another man into the area.

It is surprising how quickly you can think of all the options in a situation like this. So when the others turned to me, I gave them a note to send to my home office, explaining my plans and telling them to use the wire-service reports on Hammarskjöld-Tshombe. Six of us went on, and the rest headed back to the Ndola airport to wait for Hammarskjöld.

The rest of the trip was relatively pleasant. At the Kipushi border gate we caused a stir, but we managed to convince the guards that we were great friends of the free and independent State of Katanga and that we were there to tell the rest of the world about the story of Katanga's brave fight. The fact that we gave the guards four cartons of cigarettes proved that we were as good friends as Katanga could have.

I realize that the above sounds a bit cynical, but the fact is that if you are too scrupulously moral in Africa, you may be left at endless border posts. The guards, after all, are not going to read your copy. They can be extremely touchy and sensitive, however, and there is a fine art to handling them. The foremost practitioner of this was George Clay of NBC, a fine correspondent and a cool operator. Clay once bought himself a Polaroid camera and specialized in taking pictures of himself and the guard; he always left the picture with the guard, and today in hundreds of huts in Africa there hang photos of bearded Bwana Clay. (After this was written, George was killed in an ambush by rebel Congolese troops near Stanleyville. He was as usual in the center of action when he died. This senseless accident took away one of the great present-day correspondents, a man whose work was marked by bravery, wit, urbanity, tolerance and intellect.)

Beyond the border post we were stopped several times and threatened; this cost us time and more cigarettes, and we did not reach Elisabethville until after dark. Ours were the only cars moving around. Well, there *were* other vehicles: UN armored cars were moving around, and civilian cars filled with white mercenaries and automatic weapons were moving around—

running up on UN roadblocks and emplacements, blasting away and bugging out. We drove slowly, very slowly, fearing that if someone saw us moving too quickly he might fire. I remember one chilling moment. We were second in line, but then the lead car pulled over in order to let a reporter talk with a friend who was a white mercenary. Younghusband, who was our driver, was anxious to get to the hotel and pulled out into the lead. A Rhodesian photographer in our car suddenly started shouting, "Let them go first! Let them go first!" The implication was obvious: let them draw fire for us. Younghusband wanted to throw the Rhodesian out but he was restrained, and we finally made it back to the Leo Deux. There we were welcomed—both for the whiskey and for the evidence that there still was an exit to the outside world. That night, freed from the railroad yards and bothered only by the mortars, we slept very well.

The next morning there was a rumor that Hammerskjöld's plane was missing, but it was a rumor impossible to check out. We went to UN headquarters, where Conor Cruise O'Brien, the UN representative, was obviously worried (later we learned that O'Brien had asked Hammarskjöld to take him along and that Hammerskjöld had turned him down—a bitter personal and professional rebuff for the Irishman). No, O'Brien said during the outdoor press conference, the plane had not been heard from, and he had no late news. Just then the Fouga came over and strafed the press conference; everyone ran for cover. A moment later the reporters regrouped and the conference began again. "That's Mr. Tshombe's idea of a cease-fire," O'Brien said bitterly; as if it had overheard him, the Fouga came back and sent us into the ditch again.

When the conference was over, Sandy Gaul of Reuters and I looked at each other and nodded. We had better return to Ndola, and quickly. We suspected that Hammarskjöld almost certainly had crashed. We drove to Kipushi, where we saw some air activity, and we were told that there might be a light plane to Ndola. But there was no such aircraft. One light plane did arrive, bringing Godefroid Munongo, the Interior Minister of Katanga and an awesome figure. He was returning from Jadotville, where he had successfully negotiated the surrender of one hun-

dred and eighty Irish UN troops. He was beaming proudly as
he showed us the list of Gaelic names.

While in the Congo, I found Munongo the most interesting
and able man there. He is a sinister-looking man—always, it
seemed brooding from behind dark glasses—and he exuded an
aura of intrigue; mercenaries were regularly arrested who
claimed that they had defected in order to avoid participating in
suicide plots, engineered by Munongo, to assassinate local UN
officials. He is the grandson of a famous chief who had fought
the Belgians and the British, and he is immensely proud of this
heritage. Munongo was probably responsible for the death of
Patrice Lumumba, and more than likely was on the scene when
Lumumba died; for this and other acts he has earned the reputation among Afro-Asians as the Bad African. But to me he
symbolized Africa: brooding, making little attempt to hide his
contempt for the local Belgians who sought his favor, proud of
his heritage, ruthless and instinctively attracted to power.

I had always thought of the Congo as a place which destroyed
good men of good intentions, a place where only the sinister
could flourish and survive, and somehow the sight of the jubilant
Munongo waving the surrender list seemed to prove it. Hammarskjöld was missing, probably dead in a plane crash on a
peace mission which could not possibly have succeeded. At the
other end of the spectrum beamed Munongo—a man who was
one of the leaders and a vital factor in the secession which had
prompted Hammarskjöld to take that fatal trip, but who, if he
had been born a few miles to the east or south, might have been
a run-of-the-mill African nationalist. For the moment time
seemed to stand still, and the Congo story became as clear to
me as it ever would.

Sandy and I waited at the small airstrip for about an hour after
Munongo had left. Then we knew we couldn't wait any longer,
and we drove to Ndola instead. Normally I am a fairly careful
driver, but this time a story depended on speed, and we flew
around those narrow, twisting turns. What had been a fourteen-
hour trip on the way up took five hours on the way back.

Shortly after 7 P.M. we rushed into the Ndola post office.

There our colleagues who had covered the Hammarskjöld story briefed us on what had happened: the crash, what the site looked like, news of the one survivor. In turn we told them about the situation in Elisabethville; then we all sat down to write.

Three hours and three thousand words later we left the post office to talk and drink and eat. We were joined by Colin Frost of the AP, just in from London—"in time," he said, "to pull the greatest journalistic gaff of the age." He and others like him were still reeling from what had happened the night before. Most of the reporters had mistakenly believed they saw Hammarskjöld arrive at the Ndola airport. It is difficult for anyone who has not covered a place like Africa or Laos to understand how such a monumental blunder was not only possible but, given the circumstances, quite plausible. A year later I was to see Bernie Kalb, who for four years had covered Indonesia—a particularly vague country—for the *Times*. "I knew what had happened the moment I read about it," he said. No reporter who has ever dealt with the inconclusiveness of events in countries like this, the elusiveness of facts or the impossibility of checking them, will be surprised by the story.

The Congo is not a land where facts abound. In Leopoldville, for instance, the Congolese press offices were considered absolutely useless as a source of information; the United Nations, by and large, was not much better. At one point a UN spokesman had acquired a bad reputation for lack of integrity and honesty. It was a time of endless rumors about Katangese delegations visiting Leopoldville, and the reporters decided to ambush the spokesman. They created a mythical Katangese delegation, headed by an imaginary Katangese colonel named Kerala. At one briefing a reporter got up and asked if it was true that Colonel Kerala was in town. The spokesman said he had no knowledge of Kerala. The next day another reporter rose and asked about Colonel Kerala and his secret mission. Again the spokesman pleaded ignorance. On the third day, yet another reporter asked the same question. The spokesman shook his head, but after the briefing he summoned the three reporters aside, looked at them knowingly, and said, "Look, boys—he's here, and we know it, and we're watching him." Such were the voices of authority in the Congo.

All the problems of reporting under such circumstances came
to the fore that fateful night at the airport. The reporters gathering at the edge of the airport were kept off the field itself by
tight security precautions; as a result, they had to watch from
behind a wire fence several hundred feet away. It was dark, and
at the moment Hammarskjöld's plane was due, a plane *did* arrive. Some figures walked out on the field to greet a man getting
off the plane. The figure was about the size of Hammarskjöld,
and a reporter with field glasses said, "It's Hammarskjöld."
Someone else checked with a guard, and the guard—who, it
turned out later, knew no more than the reporters—confirmed
the identity. A Rhodesian Ministry of Information official was
also there and concurred. Then a big black car went by. There
was no press conference. Back went the newspapermen to report that Hammarskjöld had arrived safely. After all, planes
carrying famous men rarely crash, and since the plane had obviously landed—bringing, incidentally, a high British Foreign
Office representative who was to be the mediator in the discussions—the conclusion was inevitable. Consequently, some very
professional correspondents—men who had been top-flight reporters for a decade, and who had covered wars and revolutions
in many countries—did not hesitate to cable their papers that
Hammarskjöld had arrived safely in Ndola.

Out went the story, clacking across the machines in the world's
newsrooms. One reporter, oddly enough a correspondent for
the sedate and prestigious *Manchester Guardian*, not only had
Hammarskjöld arriving, but purported to give some of the conversation between the Secretary-General and Tshombe. Two reporters failed to file: Jerry Ratzin of Reuters and Cyril Ainsley
of the *Daily Express* were not convinced that Hammarskjöld
had arrived. Reuters did carry the report because it has a working agreement with the South African Press Association, and
the SAPA man put out the report. Reuters automatically picked
it up, and then killed it brief hours later because Friedl Ungeheuer, its alert young man in Leopoldville who had watched
Hammarskjöld take off, realized that something was wrong.
When he made a routine spot check on the incoming Reuters
wire at the Congolese radio station about two hours after the
plane had left, he read to his surprise that Hammarskjöld had

already arrived. Since Elisabethville is four hours away, this was patently inaccurate. Ungeheuer put out an immediate kill, thus getting Reuters off the story very early and scoring a major journalistic non-scoop. But for the others the kills came too late.

Ever since then—spared that night at the airport, spared that fatal mistake—I have wondered what I would have done in the same position. Reporters like to consider themselves reasonably honest men, and I have to admit that I would probably have made the same mistake. For my career the result would have been disastrous, for this is just the kind of blunder that is remembered.

All serious errors are fatal, but some are more fatal than others. It is possible for a reporter to be absolutely wrong in covering a country, to misjudge virtually every significant issue, to see a catastrophic series of events through rose-colored glasses—and still not be found out except by a handful of colleagues and a few skilled professional readers. Similarily, it is possible for a football player to miss endless blocks all afternoon during a game, even during a season, and not be spotted by the crowd. But let one ballplayer run the wrong way just once and his name is remembered forever.

At that time I had been overseas only briefly and had enjoyed remarkable luck. I had arrived in Katanga a few days before the fighting, and I had been the only American special correspondent on the scene when fighting broke out. I had gotten out ahead with my stories and had managed good communications despite considerable problems. I had in my pocket several congratulatory cables from my superiors, and I was still green enough to think that one *always* gets cables like these on stories.

But had I made that mistake—an error with catastrophic consequences on paper, but entirely plausible on location—all those pluses would have added up to less than zero. I would have gone down in *Times* annals as "Old Airport Halberstam." I might have been returned to Leopoldville quickly; certainly I doubt that the *Times* would have extended my assignment as a foreign correspondent from six months to two years.

I doubt that I would have gotten the prized Vietnam assignment; more importantly, had I been sent to Vietnam nevertheless, I would have been writing under a terrific cloud. I would probably have been under considerable pressure to be extra cautious not to stray from the official version of events there; I would have been forced to play the story much closer to the vest. And I would have made a marvelous target for all those opposed to realistic coverage of Vietnam; instead of repeating incessantly, as they did, that I and my colleagues were too young, they could have used my mistake as a weapon.

As a result of this scoop *manqué,* I went to Vietnam more cautious than ever, questioning even the obvious, and willing, if necessary, to come in second on occasions when I felt that I simply couldn't take a chance on information given me.

It was a good lesson—and of course, it never hurts to be lucky.

II

Early in 1962, while I was still in the Congo, I began to hint to the *Times* that I was interested in an Indochina assignment. After ten months in the Congo I'd had enough; despite all the front-page stories, there was, as the late George Clay put it, less there than met the eye. At the same time the American military build-up in Vietnam was taking place, and it sounded exciting and very much a part of our times. Again and again in the Congo I had run across men who had served in Vietnam and who told fascinating stories about it. Clearly those forces which were only slightly at issue in the Congo were in direct confrontation in Vietnam; there a hot war was taking place in the postcolonial embers, and the West was trying to learn to use the Communist tactics against the enemy.

On the one hand Edmund Gullion, the American ambassador to the Congo, who had served in Vietnam during the last days of the French, would tell me of the political difficulties of the Western position there; on the other hand Tshombe's white mercenaries, many of them former members of the Foreign Legion, would relate their view of the war. Quite apart from a great affection for the Vietnamese people, these men retained an eerie fascination for the techniques of the enemy.

The request for a transfer to Vietnam also meant that I was

15

trying to bug out of the Congo with honor, for there was no disgrace in trying to go to a hot war. Basically, however, Indochina sounded far more substantive than the Congo, and in this I was right. I found it more stimulating and exciting making the inside pages for the first six months in Vietnam than I ever had in making the front page in the Congo. I was tired of the Congo: tired of hearing UN spokesmen claim they controlled areas they obviously did not control; tired of hearing the UN say before each major meeting that Tshombe could be trusted, and that it was the people around him—the Belgians and Munongo—who were causing all the trouble and who were the villains; tired of hearing Tshombe say that everyone else was a liar, and then learning that he was breaking his word; tired of feeling that the Congolese cared less about their country than white people did. In fact, I was tired of all Congolese except for my house boy Philomon, who was decent and honorable.

One night in June of 1962 I had dinner with a British major stationed with Nigerian troops in Luluabourg, and he explained some of the reservations many of us felt.

"You have dinner with the local head of Kasai Province," he said, "and he's a terribly charming and engaging chap, and very articulate. He sits there and outlines all the problems of his people, and he tells you about their economic needs and their political problems, and how they need trained people and outside help and more dedication. And he does it well, you know—it's very touching. And just about then the dinner breaks up, and it's been so very moving that you go back to your room and in your own Western way you sit there and worry about them and try and find solutions—while he's gone off for a beer and a woman."

There was, I thought, more than a little truth to this story. It was all very well to sit back and rationalize about why the Congolese had such problems and how much the Belgians had short-changed them educationally, but in the year 1962 it did not make working or living there any easier. In those days the London *Daily Express* was sending in a fresh man every three months, and while there is a great deal to be said for tenure in most situations, a year in the Congo is a very long time.

I knew that Homer Bigart, the *Times* man in Saigon, was there only on a temporary tour and wanted to come home. In May of 1962 I began to nudge Manny Freedman, our foreign editor, about the possibility of a Vietnam assignment. If Homer was leaving Saigon we ought to replace him with a young, unmarried reporter, was the way my reasoning went. Manny, who'd had a hard enough time filling the Congo job before I took the assignment, was in no great hurry to shift me and thereby necessitate a search for a new white hunter. He replied predictably, stressing the benefits of the Congo.

So, off I went on a third trip to Katanga. Elisabethville was my favorite African city; the climate was good (there were even fireplaces in some houses); and Tshombe lived there, adding style to the situation ("Who is this man Adoula, the Prime Minister, who wants me, Tshombe, the President, to come and visit him? He is not a man of good heart, Adoula. At first he fooled me because I am generous, but now I understand him . . .").

Besides, on my previous two trips to Elisabethville, fighting had broken out almost immediately after my arrival. It nearly broke out the third time too; two armies—the UN and the Katangese—controlled the city, and there was a constant squabble over who was crossing the other's roadblocks. When such an argument developed one morning, Munongo sent ten thousand broom-carrying African women to challenge the UN roadblock. It was one of the funniest—and most dangerous—scenes I have ever seen; wave after wave of women charged up the hill against the outnumbered Indian UN troops. I watched the encounter with a major from the Rajputana Rifles, who took it all philosophically. First he offered tea to the leaders of the Congolese women; then, seeing his troops pounded with brooms, he said, "They are doing to us just exactly what we did to the British. Time marches on."

One extremely well-dressed young Katangese was carrying an anti-American sign. Although there was a considerable amount of anti-American feeling because of the U. S. support of the UN, this was the only sign of its kind at the demonstration. Another reporter and I went over to ask the African what he had against the Americans. "Because," he answered, "their engineers were the ones who told the Belgians there was copper in our land in the first place." Never underestimate the sophistication of the African.

But even the sight of Munongo's girls storming up the Indian hill failed to stir me. I had already become war-weary in the Congo.

The *Times* wanted a long magazine piece on Tshombe, and Moise had jumped at the chance. I suspected that Michel Strulens, Tshombe's Belgian public relations representative in New York, must have told Tshombe that I represented the last hope for a free Katanga, because when I arrived in Elisabethville I was deluged by all sorts of people trying to do things for me—free rooms, a car at my disposal, and so on; I was the President's personal guest. I thanked them and said the *Times* did not permit this. I was even invited to several parties where Katangese and Swedish officers were decked out in great assortments of ribbons. (The press corps had long since decided that the number of medals an officer wore was in inverse proportion to the number of wars his country had participated in. One enterprising *Daily Express* reporter had asked a high-ranking Swedish officer about his medals; some of them, he learned, had been bestowed by the Germans in World War II, for successfully helping them to cross the country, once on their way in, once on their way out. Since the *Express* was both violently anti-UN and violently anti-German—it commonly refers to World Wars I and II as the First and Second German Wars—this made a fine story.)

Social life in the Congo was always somewhat faster than an outsider might imagine; the Congolese and the Katangese liked the idea of going to parties, and the various foreign representatives had little else to do with their time. Even in the worst and most dangerous days in Stanleyville right after Lumumba's death, when the Eastern Bloc nations had taken over, there was a party almost every night. The British consul, who was one of the two Westerners living in Stanleyville in those dark times, told me later about his daily life. It began each day, he said, with a knock on the door. He would answer the knock and immediately be seized by a bunch of Lumumbist goons in Army uniforms under the command of a young captain. The captain would direct a ten-minute beating, and destruction of his papers. Then the consul would be carried bodily out of the hotel, taken out of town, lined against a wall and given a last cigarette while the goons aimed their rifles at him. At the last minute the captain would give him a reprieve; he would be tossed like a sack into the back of a truck and delivered back to his hotel. There he would spend the rest of the day nursing bruises and patching cuts, and by seven o'clock he would be sufficiently recovered to go to the evening's reception, to be held at, say, the Russian embassy. Midway through the reception he would look across the room and see the young captain who commanded the daily beatings. The captain would break into a disarming smile, wave and say, *"Ah, Excellence—ça va?"*

The Katangese receptions lacked some of the primitive charm of the ones in Stanleyville, although politically they were incongruous enough; it was a common sight to find Tshombe obligingly autographing Katangese franc notes for the Swedes, and toasting the Indians on their Independence Day ("It was an Indian trader who taught me the meaning of independence . . .").

Strulens must have told Tshombe that he had personally arranged for an article in the *Times* and that I had been flown in from New York especially, for when I entered the President's office General Norbert Muke, the Katangese supreme commander, who had arrived earlier, was kept waiting outside. (By that time I had grown cynical enough to suspect that perhaps Tshombe always kept poor old Norbert waiting out there so that reporters would think that they took precedence over the supreme commander.)

When I entered his office Tshombe seemed disappointed. "Oh," he said, and his face dropped, "I know you." Then, remembering that this was not good public relations, he smiled and quickly added, "You are an old friend. You have seen many of our wars here." From then on it was the usual lyrical interview, the saga of the Tshombes against the world: enemies were everywhere; the Belgians wanted to crush them; the Belgians were cruel, but the Tshombes would overcome; they fought back; the Belgians knew they must treat Tshombe with respect.

As he talked, Tshombe's face was like a stage drama in which he played every part—looking, as a friend of mine noted, like a black Fernandel. On the UN: "They have always lied to me. They would lie to me today if I would see them." On his close political associates: "Munongo is a coward—he is not as brave as Tshombe." On the Americans: "They are imperialists and they are spilling African blood. Why don't you warn them that what they are doing is wrong?"

It was a virtuoso performance, lasting for more than four hours, and all the time I kept wondering if Muke were still waiting. Later I was worried about having filed the quote about Munongo over the local wires, for he read the daily file carefully.

Two days after the interview all the Westerners attended Katanga Independence Day—an occasion that was something of an embarrassment for the UN, which technically controlled the city and which was committed to a firm stand against the secession. There we watched the Katangese para-commandos march with their goose-stepping stride and obvious pride in their paratroop badges; none of them had ever made a jump, but they assured us that it would be no problem because they had good pilots. Then the Katangese national anthem was sung lustily, including the last line in which the faithful pledge to defend the fatherland "with the teeth." Overhead two UN Saab jets patrolled the airway and served warning that time might be running out. It occurred to me that the lead to my story should be: "Secessionist Katanga Province today celebrated its second, and probably last, Independence Day . . ." This proved accurate: in December of 1962 the Katangese and the UN fought again, and the secession ended.

* * *

It was peaceful in the Congo that night, but things were already growing hotter in Algeria, to which independence had recently come and where there was a threat of civil war. Two days later, while I was in Rhodesia doing the Tshombe piece, I got a cable asking me if I would go to Algeria by the first plane. North Africa at that time was not a reporter's idea of a sinecure, but at least it was different from the Congo; I was ready to go. The next day, however, the Algerian revolt fizzled and I was told to stay on the spot. I was also requested to write a long summary weekender piece on the Congo after two years of independence.

The dateline on this article was July 28, and it was to be the last long piece I ever wrote on the Congo. Rereading it now, I realize that it sums up how I felt about the country at the time:

> What has been decisively and incontestably proved in the Congo over the last 25 months—at the estimated price of $10,000,000 a month—is that if the Congo problem is given enough time and cash and effort and thought, it will not go away.
>
> Similarly there are corollary rules: Moise Tshombe, if given enough time, will demand more time. If the Congolese leaders are allowed to meet together in their own way to settle their own problems according to their own demands, they will settle nothing, with the further corollary that if there are any non-Congolese aides or advisers at hand, any settlement will be bitterly rejected and repudiated from all corners as being essentially a foreign affair, an unworkable, impractical product of non-Congolese minds.
>
> Finally, if your economy is very bad and you continue to pay some 40,000 fifth-rate troops first-rate salaries, your economy will tend to worsen.

I spent the weekend in Salisbury and then flew to Nairobi on the way back to Leopoldville. Nairobi was everything Leopoldville was not; it is a lovely city with a temperate climate and good-looking women. The contrast confirmed my impression that it is all right to send a reporter to the Congo as long as you don't let him out. But you let him sample the outside world and find out about such things as razor blades, whiskey, paperback books and women, he becomes depressed about going back. The more I saw of Nairobi, the lower my spirits sank. Bob Conley, the *Times* man there, graciously showed me his palatial new residence, thereby further lowering my morale.

But that night I received a cable from New York, saying that there was an opening in Southeast Asia, with a base in Saigon. Was I interested? New York never heard from me so fast, and I flew back to Leopoldville to gather my papers in preparation for switching countries, continents and colors.

Leopoldville was sharply changed; white women were coming back, and the swimming pools were lined with girls in bikinis—a far cry from the days thirteen months before when the few UN girls working there had dates for weeks ahead. The bars were filled with Belgians, they had reopened their embassy in the city, and Belgian drivers were again honking their horns impatiently at the Congolese. The UN briefings had dwindled from two a day to one a week. An American public relations firm was handling public relations for the Congolese—building their image, I suppose. The press corps had dwindled, and no self-respecting bar could be supported by it. I sensed among my colleagues a difficulty in trying to operate under such quiet conditions, without the hazards and preoccupations of crisis. The Congo, after all, had been most bearable when there was no time to rest or to think. Now the press corps had time to be despondent.

Friedl Ungeheuer and I went across the river to a Chinese restaurant in Brazzaville for a last dinner. The owner, an oldtime Indochina hand, served us the spring rolls which are a Vietnamese mainstay, and when Friedl told him that I was going to Saigon the poor man nearly burst into tears. He talked about Saigon at great length; eighteen months later, explaining Saigon to Peter Grose, who was to be my successor there, I found myself using virtually the same words.

The dinner elevated me, but depressed Ungeheuer. He and Grose—who at that time was the AP man in the Congo—and

I had worked closely for more than a year; we were good friends, and we were all about the same age—twenty-six or twenty-seven. Friedl felt destined, he said, to spend the rest of his life in the Congo; perhaps he would teach Grose's and my children how to cover it. But within a year he was working for Reuters in New York, and shortly after that for *Time* in Paris.

The next day I flew to Geneva for a short vacation. There I exchanged letters with Homer; I was, I wrote him, immensely proud to be following him. If I had harbored any doubts about the atmosphere in Saigon, Homer's reply would have relieved me of them. "It is not an easy assignment, but I think you will find it more pleasant than the Congo," he said, "and the food is better than in New York."

"[X]," Homer wrote further, "is honest, so protect him. The city is full of American spooks trying to silence the few honest Americans who will level with correspondents. Never reveal your sources of information."

I was warned, and I was on my way.

III

I arrived in Saigon at a time of singularly bad feeling toward foreign correspondents. Francois Sully, the *Newsweek* correspondent in Saigon and for seventeen years a resident of Indochina, had just been ordered out by the Vietnamese government—or rather by Madame Nhu. Several official protests about the expulsion had failed, and though at first the American authorities had referred to the banishment as a misunderstanding which would soon be cleared up, it became clear that there was no misunderstanding at all. According to the unofficial explanation, Sully was being expelled because he had offended Madame Nhu in a *Newsweek* article: a quotation from Madame Nhu about the Vietcong ("The enemy has more drive") had been used under a photo of her Paramilitary Girls' organization—a cadre which she usually referred to as "my little darlings," and whose members drew better pay than the Government soldiers in the field. Cables from *Newsweek*'s highest executives, pointing out that Francois had nothing to do with writing captions, were of no avail.

The campaign against Sully had gone according to the prevailing style. At first there was criticism in the local, controlled press—some of it personal, some of it political. "The colonialist journalist Sully was seen on the Rue Catinat eating Vietnamese rice," went one particularly good story—implying that Sully was not only telling stale lies about the country, but was virtually taking food from the mouths of starving Vietnamese. Then the Women's Solidarity Movement, controlled by Madame Nhu, called for Sully's expulsion. Sure enough, an official announcement of the expulsion was made.

Francois thus became something of a hero to many Vietnamese. In a store he was stopped by two young girls and asked for his autograph; later in the day when he went by to pay his taxes, amounting to several hundred dollars, the local official smiled, shook his hand, called him a true friend of Vietnam and said there would be no tax collection.

The night I arrived in Saigon there was a farewell party for Francois in the *Newsweek* room at the Caravelle Hotel. The most striking quality about the gathering was an atmosphere which reminded me strongly of my working days as a reporter in Mississippi: we all seemed to be outsiders. There was no one there from the mainstream of the American embassy or the American military mission—just as in Mississippi comparable gatherings of reporters never included the leaders of the Chamber of Commerce, the mayor or a local legislator.

The expulsion of a colleague is a serious business for reporters, for it questions their very *raison d'être* and it puts a gun at their heads. In this case the arbitrariness and malice of the decision made it even worse. An expulsion like this means that every reporter must make basic and personal decisions about how much he *can* write without being expelled, and how much he *should* write in order to fulfill his obligation to his readers. Since Sully's departure was followed shortly by that of Jim Robinson of NBC, and since we all soon began to receive a variety of personal warnings from Government agents, the threat of expulsion hung over all of us, and each man had to employ his own personal form of self-censorship.

In this circumstance the reporter draws his own line and then tries to walk it. This line is a combination of what he knows, of what he thinks the traffic will bear and of what he feels must be told. For instance, in such a climate as prevailed in Vietnam at that time, he would try to avoid writing stories that were likely to have an emotional effect on the ruling family (Madame Nhu was married to the President's brother Ngo Dinh Nhu); quite apart from the consequences, such a piece would only skirt the serious issues of the country. Similarly, the reporter would hesitate to jeopardize his position in Vietnam during, say, the Cuban missile crisis, since whatever he wrote would probably be overshadowed by those fateful events. One of the most difficult decisions for me was to write highly critical military exposés about the Mekong Delta during the newspaper strike in early 1963; I realized that my reports would have minimal readership and that the risk of expulsion was great, but I also felt that they had to be written.

The line is a difficult one to follow, and it has to be played entirely by instinct. After all, a reporter gleans a certain amount of background knowledge by covering a country for several months, and this is lost to his paper if he is expelled. Eventually a reporter makes a decision that the story is important enough to risk expulsion; to a degree I did this in the spring of 1963, as I mentioned above, in writing about the deterioration of the military situation in the Delta, and I followed this by reporting very frankly the Buddhist crisis in June, when it became clear that the Government lacked the capacity to handle the conflict.

What was perhaps even more disturbing than Sully's expulsion itself was the reaction of the highest American officials to it; clearly they were not a bit unhappy to see Francois go. He was, as one of the highest embassy officials at the time told me, just a *pied noir*, a derogatory phrase implying that he was something of a half-breed. He had caused trouble for the American mission; they felt that he had written solely about negative aspects of the country, and that his reporting reflected a doomsday attitude at a time when there was an official policy of optimism.

As far as most American officials were concerned, Francois was a Frenchman, and they suspected that like many of the French in Vietnam he wanted to see all Americans fail there too. After all, the French had lost in Vietnam and it would hurt French pride to see the Americans succeed. This was true of many Frenchmen in the country at the time, who were basically unsympathetic to the American commitment, even though their commercial interests would suffer if it failed. But this was not true of Francois; Sully was a highly Americanized, lively and funny Frenchman who cared desperately about the country. In writing me, Homer had said, "He is so hard-working and good-natured that you have to forgive his bias—he doesn't think we are any better than the French."

What was disturbing to me on my arrival was that none of the American officials was talking about the substance of Sully's stories. Yet his fellow newsmen considered his sources very good, particularly his military information. He often heard of Government defeats before other reporters; indeed, he was told of events which his sources were afraid to tell the President, Ngo Dinh Diem. This did not increase Sully's popularity at the Palace, and since he angered Diem and thus made the embassy's life more difficult, it seemed to me that the embassy protests on his behalf were largely perfunctory.

It had become clear to me very soon after my arrival in Saigon that the relationship between the American mission and the American press in Vietnam was quite different from any other in the rest of the world. In Vietnam there was a sharp and unfortunate polarization of the press reporting on the one hand, and the official position on the other. This was no overnight development; nor was it, as was claimed later, a product of the Buddhist crisis, for that was still eight months away. (Curiously, it was the Buddhist crisis that finally cost the Diem government the support of most of the remaining members of the American community and impelled them to take the viewpoint of the reporters.)

The existing dichotomy had been a long time in developing. It began at the time of the Indochina war in the late forties, when French officials, and then American officials, spoke optimistically about the war against the Vietminh, and the reporters reserved their judgment. Indeed, one of the first shots was fired by Robert Trumbull, the *New York Times* correspondent in Indochina at the time, who wrote an exceedingly pessimistic and stunningly prophetic story from Saigon in early 1947, just a few weeks after the war had begun—an account which immediately aroused the ire of French officials, who felt Trumbull was trying to sabotage them. (Ironically, sixteen years later Trumbull, then chief of our correspondents in Southeast Asia, was still around to see other officials predict similar victories and criticize other reporters.)

His story began;

SAIGON, January 27—It is difficult to see how France can achieve a military victory in Indochina in a reasonable length of time, even with the promised reinforcements and with superior arms.

France faces a clever foe. It is a foe that employs elusive guerrilla tactics over a vast area and fights to the last man when occasionally pinned down. There will probably always be more armed hostile Annamese in Indochina than there are Frenchmen.

When cornered, the Vietnamese are probably among the world's fiercest fighters. They remind one of the Japanese on the Pacific islands who battled to the end, inflicting maximum casualties before dying themselves.

The Vietnamese, in defense of their ideals, however gently these may be expressed, fight like savages. We know that the fate of a Frenchman who falls into their hands alive is not happy . . .

The Vietnamese are clever saboteurs. They cut vital highways with tremendous hand-dug pits, carefully carrying away the dirt from the hole so that the French forces must forage for filler material. When the Vietnamese sever a railroad line, as they have done in scores of places, they take away not only the tracks and ties, but also the gravel roadbed . . .

In any stand-up fight in which artillery could be employed, the French, with what armament they have, would undoubtedly be victorious every time. But the Vietnamese do not fight that way. Against superior odds they retreat, leaving nothing behind but ashes and ruins. By night they return in small bands again and again, making life uncomfortable for the foe.

The French hold important positions in Tongking—Hanoi, Haiphong and Haiduong—and keep uneasy control of the road from Haiphong over which Hanoi receives its meager food. But the countryside is in the hands of the Vietnamese. There seems no present prospect of a change in this situation.

Then, ironically, in a short piece tacked to the end of this (we call it a "shirt tail" in the business), was a story quoting Vice-Admiral Georges Thierry d'Argenlieu calling the war in Indochina "another battleground between the Western democracies and Marxism." The story went on: "He [d'Argenlieu] said it struck him as very strange to see the American press supporting Communism in Indochina, as he expressed it, when the American press was strongly opposing Communist influence in other areas of the world."

The split between the American press and the American officials in Vietnam continued throughout the bitter years of the Indochina war and it continued to exist during the war of the Vietnamese government against the Vietcong. Faced with this historical blindness to the efficacy of guerrilla warfare, newsmen had become increasingly dubious, until by the time I arrived the feeling was strong, bitter and personal. Although the embassy occasionally chided the Ngo government for its attacks on the press, such high officials as Ambassador Frederick Nolting, Jr., General Paul Donal Harkins and the CIA station chief John H. Richardson were basically more sympathetic to the Vietnamese Government viewpoint. They felt we were inaccurate and biased; they thought the war was being won, and they longed for control over us. "The American commitment," said an embassy white paper prepared in January 1963 for General Earle Wheeler, Chief of Staff of the Army, "has been badly hampered by irresponsible, astigmatic and sensationalized reporting."

The polarization had become more pronounced as the United States stepped up its commitment to a new high in monetary and military aid and prestige, and as our activities became more and more involved with that of a suspicious, unresponsive and archaic family dictatorship. American officialdom in Vietnam became enthusiastic boosters of the Government; in fact, they were part of the Ngo team. As virtual participants in the struggle, they were in sharp contrast to American missions throughout the rest of the underdeveloped world.

In most underdeveloped countries there is a fairly simple relationship between the American embassy and the American reporter, and it is based largely on a degree of mutual confidence, respect and sophistication. There is not likely to be any vast lingering dispute between the two groups, or any radical difference in interpretation of events. For instance, an American reporter arriving in a country in Africa will see officials of the U.S. mission almost immediately. From them he will usually get a fairly detached view—albeit an American one—on the local government, its relations with the United States, with the Eastern Bloc and with its neighbors. The reporter will also have a list of names of a few lower officials in the mission considered to be knowledgeable, perhaps with a mark indicating the individual's candor and likely viewpoint. Thus the reporter will inevitably hear the local American line.

In the Congo in 1961 and 1962 the line went something like this: Prime Minister Adoula is better than most people think, and really better than you might expect in a place like this. Secondly, don't be fooled by Tshombe's stand of anti-Communism. He is an anti-Communist, but he is also following a policy which he hopes will turn the rest of the Congo over to the Communists, so that his Katanga secession will thereby look even better to the West.

There was a considerable amount of evidence to support this viewpoint; for instance, Tshombe's deputies were always voting with the radical left in the Assembly in an attempt to topple the moderate government. It was a sensible viewpoint, well worth printing—though it was far from the whole story. Actually, it was also part of the American policy to portray Tshombe in a bad light; this took the form of trying to make him look like just another tribal leader in Katanga—when in fact he had far broader support—and to minimize his considerable charm and real ability.

It is the reporter's responsibility to take all such facets into consideration. Thus, when I wrote the long magazine piece on Tshombe for the *Sunday Times Magazine*, the State Department was so unhappy that it sent a cable to the USIS man in Leopoldville, complaining that the piece was too sympathetic and suggesting that I be talked into doing an equally sympathetic piece on Adoula. The State Department often makes the mistake of thinking *Times* reporters are *its* reporters.

In addition to visiting local American officials in a new country, the reporter will also check with other embassies to get a non-American view. There *is* an American view overseas, and it is desirable that there should be; still, for better or worse, it is usually influenced by the Cold War. We have come to think in terms of the Cold War because we have so much responsibility for it; yet many countries in the world want no part of the struggle between East and West and are quite suspicious of us, and may well not confide in our representatives to the degree that they will in officials of some lesser power who can play a more fluid role. In Africa, for instance, the Israelis and Canadians were often knowledgeable, with small missions of highly talented people. The Israelis were a particularly good source of information; they had a real surplus of professional technicians to send overseas, and the Africans were very much aware of the Israeli struggle for independence and of the lessons to be learned from it.

In Asia, on the other hand, the Australians were often good sources; historically they know a good deal about the area, they send their top people to Asian countries, they lack the colonial stigma of the British and they can move around more freely than Americans.

In general, a relationship of mutual respect exists between ambassadors and reporters in most underdeveloped countries; if anything, reporters—and *New York Times* reporters in particular—may be treated too well. A reporter must always be aware that an ambassador in a small country which has no immediate crisis may view the press as the best way to break through State Department channels and get his country and its problems to the White House at breakfast.

But in Vietnam these relationships simply did not exist. The split between the reporters and the mission was basic; it had foundered on the policy itself. It was not, as some were later to claim, the result of a bad press policy, or poor handling of the press, or inept news management. News management cannot turn a bad government into a good one; from time to time it can hide the story of, say, one military defeat, but in the end it cannot conceal the fact that an enemy with superior drive and motivation is gaining ground.

The split between the American press and the American mission was very much the product of our country's traditional free-

doms and attitudes. There was a conflict between these and the
pressures of the Cold War, which often pushed the United States
into complicated, difficult and essentially alien situations. We
reporters were the heirs of a traditional American freedom: the
right of a journalist to write what he sees, whether the news is
good or bad for his own country. We did not have to worry
about the alternatives of policy making. The ambassadors and
generals, on the other hand, were the heirs of a new dilemma:
the discord between this country's traditional instincts, and its
duties and responsibilities in the Cold War.

Our commitment to the Diem regime changed drastically in late
1961, after President Kennedy had sent General Maxwell D.
Taylor to Vietnam on a special mission to see what could be
done to keep the country from falling to the Communists. From
the position of a relatively cool backstage backer with only about
six hundred advisors in the country—a relationship not too different from many others throughout the underdeveloped world—
the United States had gone operative. It committed itself fully
to Vietnam, and placed its prestige in Southeast Asia at stake—
and in the hands of the Ngo family. This position, moreover,
put the Kennedy Administration in jeopardy; a "Kennedy War,"
and a losing war at that, could have an influence in the next
election. In October of 1961 we decided to increase American
troops in advisory and supporting roles to over sixteen thousand, and to boost our economic aid to one and a half million
dollars a day. Yet in so doing we were tied to the Ngo family;
the United States could be no more politically sophisticated, no
more aggressive, no more sensitive or responsive than the Ngo
family.

Not only were we getting deeply involved in a situation where
we could be no more effective than the established government,
we were making a major commitment during a crisis in whose
making we had played only a minor part. Moreover, we were
making it at a time when the war had already been under way
for a long time and when there were really few new ideas or
panaceas left for a very tortured country.

True, Vietnam had become vital to our national interest at

the time of the 1961 commitment, but during many of the formative years that culminated in the crisis it had had very little priority at all; it had seemed far away. In the years immediately after World War II, when the struggle for Indochina began, U.S. attention was not focused on Vietnam: America was primarily concerned with trying to promote economic recovery in Western Europe and to establish a stable Japan. The question of change in the vast colonial empires of our Allies was very remote. President Roosevelt had been somewhat interested in Indochina; he believed that if the French resumed colonial control after the war, the results could only be disastrous. But Roosevelt died in early 1945, and Truman was less interested in Southeast Asia, simply because other issues were more pressing. In this vacuum the French returned to business as usual in Indochina.

The Vietnamese are not a phlegmatic people, and for centuries they have revolted against their oppressors. Bright, sophisticated people, traditional warriors, they have never accepted the rule of outsiders. During the thirties there was an increasing subsurface desire for independence; the defeats the white man suffered at the hands of Asians at the beginning of World War II simply accelerated these hopes. With victory for the Allies in sight, the Vietnamese had hopes of some sort of independence, perhaps at first as part of a French union. The French quelled these hopes, but they could not dampen the desire for independence; it simply became a matter of who would exploit nationalism most effectively.

It was not the West. Instead it was Ho Chi Minh, an old Bolshevik and the brilliant leader of the Vietnamese Communist Party. Ho ("Uncle Ho" to the peasants)—a thin slight figure, with a wisp of a beard, who looks like any pedicab driver in Vietnam—performed his mission brilliantly. He dissolved his own Vietnamese Communist Party in order to secure a broader base for a Communist-nationalist movement. Communist goals and Communist figures became secondary; emphasis was placed on a popular front. The cause was a national and patriotic one, and it camouflaged the hard-core Communist apparatus. Many nationalists joined who were not Communists; others who opposed the Communists were liquidated, sometimes by the Vietminh (which means, literally, Viet nationalist), sometimes by

the French. Slowly but steadily the anti-Communist nationalism
of Vietnam was strangled and destroyed; by the end of the war
with the French it was never to be a serious force again.

At first the French considered the Vietminh nothing but
peasant-bandits, and they consistently underestimated their
strength, dedication, leadership and ability. Ho went to Paris in
1946 to make a last desperate appeal for some political concessions, but the French were unbending; they did not sense as
quickly as the British the changes that were coming over the
colonial world. As for the United States, the brand-new world
of anticolonialism, postcolonialism and neocolonialism was
something it would discover belatedly in the late fifties.

In 1946 the French Indochina war began. There were many
instances of great gallantry, but the bravery of the individual
French soldier in fighting the war exceeded the motives of the
French government. Asians were on one side and white men on
the other, and though many Vietnamese did fight and die for the
French they were never offered any real incentive. One of the
cruelest ironies in Vietnam today is an inscription like the following, which can be seen on countless Vietnamese tomb-
stones: NGUYEN VAN DAN—MORT POUR LA FRANCE.

The French were confident about the outcome of the war.
They had elite troops and the finest of weapons; they had tanks
and airplanes. For them, the enemy was *les jaunes*, ''the yellow
ones.'' But though they lacked the equipment, the Vietminh at
least knew what kind of war was being fought. They had discipline, absolute political superiority and a knowledge of the land
and of the people; above all else they had a cause. They also
had developed techniques of guerrilla warfare similar to those
which Mao Tse-tung was using so effectively against the Chinese
Nationalists. Gradually, in small actions at first, they began to
ambush French troops, to capture French weapons and turn
these over to their own elite troops—who would thereby capture
more. The French controlled the highways and the cities; the
Vietminh controlled the people. The French moved during the
day, and the face they presented was always a military one;
the Vietminh moved at night, lecturing the people, distributing
medicine, promising land reform, reducing rents, teaching some
of the youngsters to read and write, promising a better society.

The Vietminh troops adhered to the strictest discipline, as the Vietcong do now, in dealing with the population. Severe punishment was meted out for such offenses as the rape of peasant women or for lesser infractions like the stealing of peasant pigs; often the troops worked by the side of the farmers in the field. Whereas the French had a limited military intelligence network, every farmer became an agent for the Vietminh. In the colonialists' eyes every Vietnamese was a potential spy.

The French would hold static points; if it took fifty soldiers to man an outpost, the Vietminh could not successfully mount an attack with fifty of their own troops. But knowing exactly where the French would be they could attack with two hundred or two hundred and fifty men, and in the end they would capture fifty more weapons. "Is the enemy strong? One avoids him," wrote Vo Nguyen Giap, the Vietminh military commander. "Is he weak? One attacks."

Slowly the insurgents gained strength. They used classic guerrilla techniques, emphasizing political education, always trying to confuse the enemy about the extent of their forces in any area. Eventually the French came to rely more and more on air power and napalm. This terrified the Vietminh, but it failed to deter them, for the war had become a great national cause, a war to force the white man out of Vietnam. To a young Vietnamese with any drive there were only two choices: either he joined the French, was paid money and fought to keep the French in Vietnam—taking a chance that they might some day leave; or he joined the so-called People's Army to drive them out. For a generation of inspired young Vietnamese the choice was clear.

One of the real problems of South Vietnam today is that a vast percentage of the vital, able people of the country became deeply involved with the Vietminh before they realized the full extent of its Communist role; by the time they did, they were so far along that they remained committed to what was to become the Hanoi government, in North Vietnam.

But politically the French gave the Vietnamese little. The best they offered was the discredited playboy Bao Dai. Writing of him in a cover story in May 1950, *Time* reflected the Western mood and attitude:

It is Bao Dai's mission and the U.S.-French hope to rally his countrymen to the anti-Communist camp of the West. In this undertaking he needs time. "Nothing can be done overnight," he says. He needs time to organize an effective native government, train an army and militia that can restore order in the village, win over the doubtful fence-sitters among the intelligentsia. Besides a military shield he also needs a display of winning strength and patient understanding by Western allies. As a national leader Bao Dai has his weaknesses, and largely because of this he does not enjoy the kind of popularity achieved by India's Jawaharlal Nehru . . .

In the early fifties the French were still predicting imminent victory, backed now by the Americans, who were their silent partners and were giving military and economic aid. Our military echoed the optimism of the French, even while the Vietminh strengthened their rural control. By 1952, Giap had divisions of troops, and was growing stronger. In the field, the French line officers' respect for the enemy continued to grow.

In 1954 the end came, militarily and politically. The French, seeking a set-piece battle, found themselves encamped at Dienbienphu, a fort deep in the mountains near Laos, reachable only by air. There the French high command hoped the Vietminh would attack, there they would break the back of Giap's forces. The French conceded the high ground to the enemy, and were dug in down in a valley. They believed that the Vietminh could never bring artillery and anti-aircraft guns to the site—and even if they did, they could not use them properly.

On March 13, 1954, the battle began. The French clearly were outgunned; the Vietminh had not only the high ground but the artillery, and they knew how to use it. The French artillery commander committed suicide the first night, and very soon the outcome of the battle became a foregone conclusion. The French fought bravely, but there was no way for them to be reinforced; planes bringing in air supplies ran into concentrated anti-aircraft fire from perfectly camouflaged positions, from guns which had been brought in piecemeal, on the back of coolies. The French lost sixteen thousand two hundred men—captured or killed—and they lost a war.

The day after Dienbienphu fell the Geneva Conference began.

It resulted in another Vietminh victory: the partitioning of the country, with the northern, industrial half going to the Vietminh. The French Indochina war had been what might be called a popular war, and its political legacy to the West was appalling; the Vietminh, who garnered almost all the talented people of a generation, was identified in the public mind as the side which drove the French out. Today Ho Chi Minh remains the closest thing to a national hero in both the North and the South. When Vietnam was divided in 1954 the North had the sense of dynamism, the leadership, a form of government whereby men rose through their ability, and an ideology which made the system work. In the South there was only the residue of that eight-year war.

South Vietnam was disorganized; there was no governmental authority; all anti-Communist feeling was identified with the French; the Vietminh were viewed by the people as liberators; the people were tired of war; the whole administrative structure was riddled with the worst kind of corruption practiced by the French and imitated by the Vietnamese—a legacy which is still a major problem. Any leader hoping to set up a stable government in the South would have to be both anti-French and anti-Communist, and eight years of fratricidal war had depleted the country of almost any qualified potential leader. The ruler of South Vietnam, Emperor Bao Dai—the corrupt playboy and French puppet—summoned Ngo Dinh Diem from his monastery in the United States to take over the country. Diem had been Minister of the Interior under the French in the thirties and belonged to an artistocratic, highly influential Vietnamese family. A reluctant United States also backed Diem; in the ashes of postwar Vietnam there was no one else capable, and no one else who wanted the job. The significance of Diem was not so much what he was, but where he came from—the fact that to find him, officials had to look outside the country. It was a time of human bankruptcy in South Vietnam and Diem was the one straw for a grasping America. The Saigon intellectuals were discredited for what had often been a dilettante attitude during the Indochina war; many of the other educated Vietnamese in Saigon were what became known as "Saigon bourgeoisie"—more French than the French, corrupt and weak. No real anti-Communist military hero had emerged during the years that the Vietnamese had fought alongside the French against their fellow countrymen; the political alternatives were largely war lords, gangsters or discredited puppets. Diem it had to be.

In those days the Americans were not unaware of the difficulties ahead. Many in the American mission at the time were against Diem; others recognized his numerous failings, but admitted that there was no other choice. In 1955 General Lawton Collins, President Eisenhower's special envoy to Vietnam, argued strongly against Diem, claiming that he was aloof, obstinate, suspicious and unwilling to accept American advice. His reports were countered by those of Colonel Edward Lansdale, the chief U.S. intelligence agent in Saigon at the time. Lansdale, who a few years before had played a vital role in the Philippines in defeating the Huk guerrillas and had helped bring Ramon Magsaysay to international prominence, sent his reports directly to Allen W. Dulles, then head of the CIA. Lansdale persuaded Dulles that he must support Diem; in turn, Dulles influenced his brother, then Secretary of State. (Ironically, nine years later several key associates of Lansdale who were still in Saigon played a vital role in Diem's downfall.) Thus, on what is known in the boxing world as a split decision, began the uneasy relationship between Diem and the Americans.

IV

After I had been in Vietnam for a few months, Madame Nhu granted me an interview.

The Americans, she said, were very silly in their attitude toward President Diem. They always wanted him to go out and mingle with the people, and wave to them and shake their hands and do those things which the Americans themselves like to do. But the President, she said, was very shy, and he could never do this; he would feel foolish and he would never be able to hide this from the people. The Americans did not understand him, she said.

Ngo Dinh Diem had been a prominent nationalist in the thirties, a respected mandarin and public servant who had resigned his position as Minister of the Interior of Annam because the French had reneged on promises that he would be allowed to rule freely. He was a member of an aristocratic, old family, a devout Roman Catholic and an early and articulate anti-Communist—something rare in an underdeveloped nation where the Communists were in the luxurious position of being the social critics and of being identified with nascent anticolonialism. Because of Diem's reputation as a nationalist, Ho Chi Minh asked him to join Ho's popular front in

1945. Diem refused; the Communists had murdered his eldest brother, Ngo Dinh Khoi, and this had only further increased his hatred for them.

It is true that as a young man Diem was well known as both a nationalist and an anti-Communist, but although his country was undergoing a decade of insurgence he kept himself strangely apart from revolutionary feeling. The excitement of independence, the techniques of mass crowd appeal remained alien to him; his nationalism stemmed more from a sense of responsibility than from anything else. In his youth he had taken vows of chastity, and as an adult he led virtually a monastic life, both in Vietnam and later in exile, where he spent the vital years of the Indochina war. During the last two of these years he stayed at Maryknoll Seminary in Ossining, New York, and in this country he often met such Americans as Cardinal Spellman, Senator John Kennedy and Senator Mansfield. Over these years he had built up a reputation for personal bravery and integrity—matched by his stubbornness—and a preference for priestlike seclusion.

According to one story, an American once asked Diem's elder brother, Archbishop Ngo Dinh Thuc, why Diem had abandoned his earlier studies for the priesthood. "The Church was too worldly for him," Thuc is reported to have answered. Another anecdote is told by Denis Warner, the Australian correspondent. Warner said to a Vietnamese friend that Diem sounded too much like a priest to be brought back to Vietnam. "Not a priest," answered the Vietnamese. "A priest at least learns of the world through the confessional. Diem is a monk living behind stone walls. He knows nothing."

A year after Diem's return, Graham Greene, seeing the growing pressures on him, was to write in the *New Republic*:

> Diem is separated from the people by cardinals and police cars with wailing sirens and foreign advisers droning of global strategy, when he should be walking in the rice fields unprotected, learning the hard way how to be loved and obeyed—the two cannot be separated. One pictured him sitting there in the Norodom Palace, sitting with

his blank brown gaze, incorruptible, obstinate, ill-advised, going to his weekly confession, bolstered up by his belief that God is always on the Catholic side, waiting for a miracle. The name I would write under his portrait is the Patriot Ruined by the West.

Diem had returned to a fragmented and shattered country which no one else wanted. Everyone predicted that he would not last the year, but it turned out that he had been right and they had been wrong. Against vast obstacles Diem acted forthrightly and courageously in the early years of his government. He resettled nearly a million refugees from the North, most of them Catholics who had fled Ho's regime. When he decided to wipe out the gangster sects some of his advisers warned him against it; Diem seemed lonely and poorly prepared for conflict with such powerful enemies, and it was suggested that he make an accommodation. Instead, he crushed the criminal elements which had ruled Saigon through their control of gambling and prostitution and through their alliances with the French police; again *he* had been right and *they* had been wrong. In 1956, two years after his lonely arrival back in Saigon, there was much American enthusiasm for Diem; *Life* called him "the Tough Miracle Man of Vietnam," and the *Saturday Evening Post* labeled his country "the Bright Spot in Asia." The blurb for the latter piece read: "Two years ago at Geneva, South Vietnam was virtually sold down the river to the Communists. Today the spunky little Asian country is back on its own feet, thanks to a 'mandarin in a sharkskin suit who's upsetting the Red timetable.'"

Yet his early successes were misread by Diem and his family; they were not necessarily a blank check from the population, and they did not mean that Diem would always be right. He was successful in some of his ventures partly because of his timing. On his return from exile he was hailed as a man who had at one time stood up to the French; when he moved against the sects he was doing what most Vietnamese wanted, for they were tired of corruption and the sinister link between the law and Saigon vice.

But the challenges against Diem and his country were particularly cruel, unlike those faced by any other ruler in a new nation. Perhaps if he had governed another country in a less critical area, and one not as badly splintered and without such a tortured recent history, he might have emerged an entirely different figure. But the pressures of Vietnam simply forced him into the bosom of his family.

It was a large and forceful family. There had been Ngo Dinh Khoi, Diem's eldest brother (who was killed by the Communists); there was Ngo Dinh Thuc, the archbishop of Hué, who was venerated by Diem, first, because he was a priest, and second, because he was the only surviving elder brother; there was Ngo Dinh Nhu, the intellectual and Palace strategist, and closest to the President; there was Ngo Dinh Can, the unofficial governor of Hué, who ruled central Vietnam like a feudal war lord; and there was the youngest brother, Ngo Dinh Luyen, ambassador to England and formerly emissary to several other European countries, who was considered something of a playboy by the austere Diem.

Within the family, Nhu and his wife were the most powerful, largely because they lived in the Palace and were with the President all the time. In family decisions they often acted in concert with Thuc. Brother Can, who was considered by many Vietnamese and Americans to be the most realistic of the family, often clashed with the Nhus, and the only debates which took place in the National Assembly came when Can's deputies clashed with Nhu's deputies.

Diem held a deep-rooted suspicion of almost everyone but members of his own family, who shielded him from the outside world; he had a strong sense of his own moral righteousness, and therefore of his inherent right to rule. Some of these qualities were once virtues; they helped him to survive in the first years of what was, to all intents and purposes, a condemned government. But eventually these traits became accentuated and excessive; they made Diem a prisoner; they came to haunt both him and the people who had helped put him in office; and in the end they led to his downfall. He, who could never have been corrupted by worldly goods, became corrupted by power and pride.

* * *

Diem was a shy man. He had taken his vows of chastity when he was quite young, and he was ill at ease in the presence of women, always a little afraid even of his sister-in-law. He was a prodigious worker who labored sixteen or eighteen hours a day, taking his work to bed with him and waking up in the middle of the night to continue. He hated to delegate responsibility; he tried to run the country by himself and with his family—even down to the granting of visas. Consequently the administrative machinery of Vietnam became increasingly snarled year after year, and any attempt at regional initiative was frowned upon.

Diem and Ngo Dinh Nhu considered themselves the most able military tacticians in the country. They established strategy and moved divisions and regiments and battalions around, often without telling superior officers in the field. In addition, the brothers often switched priorities on major projects whimsically, so that the country's resources were constantly being squandered.

Like his brother, Diem believed he had a unique knowledge of the war being fought, but American and Vietnamese officers in the field, who were charged with the responsibility of trying to fight it, disagreed strongly. Again and again, commands dictated by the Ngo brothers indicated a lack of understanding of the military needs in a given situation; to make matters worse, their confidence in their strategy had been systematically bolstered by fraudulent after-action reports filed by frightened commanders in the field.

Despite the growing sense of alienation among his former aides and friends in the Government, and the bitterness these officials felt toward the Nhus, many of them retained a considerable amount of grudging respect for Diem, even when they were plotting his overthrow; there was still affection for his vitality and for his considerable charm. "Kill him the moment you take the Palace," one officer once told another as they were preparing for a coup, "or else he will start to talk and he will talk you out of it. I know him."

As the years went by, Diem became less and less of a

conversationalist and more and more of a monologist. Toward the end, a visitor was lucky to leave his office after a
six-hour interview. Sometimes the talks lasted ten hours, with
no break and with the visitor allowed to ask only one or two
questions. One old friend who saw Diem in 1963 was shocked
by this stream of words; he said later that he felt that Diem
was talking in a desperate attempt to keep the visiting American from questioning him—as if they both understood what
the questions would be about. Charley Mohr, then of *Time*,
became adept at handling Diem as a result of shepherding a
long list of *Time* VIP's into the President's office. The Mohr
theory was based on the fact that Diem chainsmoked; every
time the President lit a cigarette, Mohr would immediately
ask a question. Robert Shaplen of *The New Yorker* saw Diem
in 1962 and wrote: "His face seemed to be focused on something beyond me and beyond the walls of the Palace; the
result was an eerie feeling that I was listening to a monologue
delivered at some other time and in some other place—perhaps by a character in an allegorical play."

It is always a strange sight to observe a man paying homage
to himself; I had occasion to do so on one of the national
holidays. There are many holidays in Vietnam, for that troubled country celebrates liberation from a long series of
oppressions, but October 26 is a special one: it commemo-
rates the day in 1955 on which elections were held and the
population was allowed to choose between Diem and the puppet playboy Bao Dai. The people voted overwhelmingly to
elect Diem, though the election was typical of those which
were to follow in that the number of votes cast greatly exceeded the number of names on the electoral rolls.

The wide avenue along the Saigon River had been readied
days ahead of time, and traffic had been routed away. Armored amphibious personnel carriers, which were desperately needed in the Delta because of the wet season, had been
up in Saigon practicing for weeks, despite the anguished pleas
of American advisers. In many areas the war had come to a
virtual halt because vital units were practicing for the parade.

With so many troops present in Saigon, the possibility of a military coup increased, and countersecurity precautions were in full force. The threat of assassination was also present, so only carefully selected units were permitted to march. Uniforms were issued to the elite and predominantly Catholic Presidential Guard only on the morning of the parade, and members of the unit were carefully inspected before and after dressing, so that no unauthorized ammunition could be hidden away. In addition, their weapons were checked several times during the morning. Other elite units went through the same careful scrutiny. The day before, men with mine detectors had gone over the area where Diem would be. At key points throughout the city were presidential tank units, their crews in full battle gear, their motors running, their radios on.

Reporters who had applied for seats two weeks in advance and had submitted photographs of themselves were issued special passes. We were told to be in our seats very early in the morning. At 7 A.M., on our way to the parade, we noticed a curious phenomenon; the police were turning away thousands of people. It seemed unbelievable, but it was true; the public was not to be allowed to watch the ceremonies. The parade ground stretched for several blocks on each side of the presidential reviewing stand, and that entire area had been blocked off. Only select people were permitted in the area: foreign visitors, special guests, wives of official members of the Government, and hordes of security men. But the public at large could only see the paraders gather at the start. This gave an odd aura to the entire ceremony: one felt as if he were watching a movie company filming a scene about an imaginary country.

After the parade Ambassador Nolting was beaming over its success. Jim Robinson of NBC, who was in the process of being expelled from the country, pointed out that the public had been barred, but Nolting refused to believe him.

The parade itself revealed much about the country. Off to the south flew several formations of fighter bombers. They were not permitted closer because they had been forbidden to fly over the city since two of Diem's best pilots had bombed the Palace in February of 1962. In the parade itself were long lines of Nhu's blue-suited Cong Hoa Youth; they were, in fact, civil servants allegedly loyal to him, but few of them were young, and few of them, as it turned out, were loyal. Madame Nhu's Paramilitary Girls were there too, goose-stepping smartly, and armed with the finest new American carbines and submachine guns. Scattered throughout the crowd were scores of police and security men. Diem was there, but the Nhus were not; this was part of a family policy which prescribed that for security reasons Ngo Dinh Nhu, Madame Nhu and Ngo Dinh Diem should never appear together in public. Even when they flew to Hué for family meetings they went in separate planes.

Diem arrived after most people were in their seats, received several salutes, made a quick tour of the short parade route, heard his own personal song played ("President Ngo should live forever"), and then sat impassively. He was small, strangely younglooking in appearance, with a duck walk which bordered on a bustle. From a distance he looked somewhat like the Little King in O. Soglow's comic strip. A few minutes after the parade had started, it was all over. After weeks of preparation the armored personnel carriers could go back to fighting the Vietcong; the Government was through with honoring itself for the time being.

The Government and the population lived side by side in what was at best mutual apathy and indifference. In those days the most encouraging thing that could be said about Diem was that he stirred no strong emotions among his weary people. At one time they had respected and even liked him, but much of that good will had eroded as he became more identified with his family. The population did not hate Diem the way it hated his brother and sister-in-law, but it no longer trusted him or his government. If apathy was what the Communists wanted, the situation in Saigon was ripe for them.

For his part, Diem had little instinct for his people. He operated not out of a sense of partnership, common bond and mutual identification, which had proven so effective for the

Communists and for men like Prince Sihanouk of Cambodia, but out of a sense of duty, of religious feeling and a corresponding feeling of righteousness. The political result of all this was a leader who felt that he represented God to his people, who felt that he could do no wrong and had discharged his obligations if he remained morally and spiritually correct. Before becoming President, Diem wrote in an article: "The state is founded on the people; the mandate of heaven held by the sovereign is revocable if he proves himself unworthy thereof." He added: "A sacred respect is due the person of the sovereign . . . He is the mediator between the people and Heaven as he celebrates the national cult."

This curious sense of righteousness that was inflicted on his rather easygoing and tolerant people was not matched by any corresponding ideology on their part. There was almost no attempt to persuade the population to identify themselves in any way with their government. "A little good old-fashioned demagoguery," one American once said wistfully, "would do this government a lot of good."

Diem's ascetic life, his observance of his codes and his remarkable luck in escaping death several times and in finally achieving the presidency confirmed his belief in his divine role. Anyone who doubted him on any question was likely to be judged not on the merits of the disagreement, but on the fact that he defied and therefore blasphemed. Similarly, anyone whose personal life was judged to be morally inferior to his own was, despite other qualifications, dismissed as a person ill prepared to rule or lead.

Eventually, Diem's people knew him only as an outdated photograph; his trips to the countryside became increasingly rare, and more and more like inspection tours—the local officials alerted days in advance, the town carefully policed, and on the day of the visit the population lined up for hours in advance, standing at attention in the hot sun and wondering what all the fuss was about.

Diem's increasing aloofness brought him into continual conflict with American officials. They would urge him to change, to reform, to broaden the base of his government, to permit a political opposition. Each time there was a conflict the hard line would be taken by the Nhus, who opposed all compromise. The Nhus did not really trust the Americans; despite all our pledges, they did not believe that the American commitment to them, the family, was absolute enough. In these tugs of war the Nhus inevitably won; they understood Diem better, they were Vietnamese, they were his family and they knew that its survival came first.

The conflict came to a head during the abortive military revolt in November 1960; the paratroopers had in fact accomplished their coup d'état—and then they sat around negotiating terms with Diem. He promised a new and different government, but while they picnicked and dallied for one crucial night, Diem called in loyal troops and crushed the rebellion. There were several by-products of that evening. One was that a coup d'état would be far more difficult the next time, and that the Vietnamese would be more wary of attempting one. Another was that Diem's reputation for integrity became tarnished in the minds of many Vietnamese. He had promised to change the Government—virtually at gun point, to be sure, but a promise was a promise—and then he reneged.

Inside the Palace almost everyone had wavered and had suggested accepting the paratroopers' terms. Only Madame Nhu had rejected the idea of compromise and had insisted on fighting to the end; she had been right, Diem decided later, and her influence around the Palace rose sharply. "Up until then," she told me during an interview in 1963, "they had not taken me that seriously. But then they began to notice me, and began to worry when I said things."

Though the Americans did not sponsor the coup—if they had it would have been carried through during the hours when the paratroopers wavered—the Nhus considered them accomplices. At one point U.S. officials offered Madame Nhu safe-conduct to the embassy; in her mind this convicted them of participation. The Nhus were later able to use this incident to gather increasing power.

The ultimate result of the paratrooper rebellion was paradoxical. Diem's best and allegedly most loyal troops, led by a young officer who was so close to him that he virtually considered him an adopted son, had rebelled over the political oppression in Saigon and over the military conduct of the war. They were not glory or power seekers; they failed, in fact, because they did not seize power, because they did not know exactly what they wanted politically, because in other words, they were too naïve. Therefore, the final lesson that Diem learned was not that there were some true anti-Communist patriots who opposed him and that reforms were desperately needed; it was, rather, that conciliation was the way of the weak and inept. This was a lesson which was to haunt him in the Buddhist crisis.

The Palace became more suspicious than ever, and as Diem turned closer and closer to his family, the regime became less and less popular; the Government, once tolerated, became actively disliked. Everything that went wrong in Vietnam was blamed on the Nhus. Ngo Dinh Nhu controlled the secret police apparatus; therefore he had to bear the brunt of the hatred for a regime under which midnight arrests were becoming increasingly frequent, all political opposition was outlawed and dissent had been quelled. Madame Nhu, proud and vain, who had outlawed first divorce and then dancing, was delving into men's politics with sharp and ill-concealed arrogance, and she became the target of even more intense hatred. Nhu was primarily interested in control of the population; Madame Nhu was primarily interested in political power, and the population knew this.

The Vietnamese traditionally believe in strong families, and Diem was nothing if not a traditionalist. (In late 1963, when American officials in Vietnam were discussing what type of man would be the best alternative to Diem, one of them was asked for his ideas about a candidate's necessary qualities. "Well, first of all he should be an only child," he said.) As Diem was the first to realize, the Nhus were largely responsible for his ascension to the presidency in the first place. Back in the uncertain days of the early fifties when Diem was in exile, it was the Nhus who had lobbied successfully with other nationalists in favor of Diem. Nhu had formed his own party, the Can Lao, which was later to become a vast secret source of power in the country, and with it he had created the shaky little base which supported Diem when he returned in 1954. Henceforth Nhu and his wife were Diem's most ardent workers, for they felt they were working just as much for themselves. Thus, the test used by the Ngo government in evaluating a man became not what he had done for Vietnam, but what he had done for the Ngo family.

Moreover, Diem greatly admired his brother. Nhu was Western-educated, which Diem was not, and the President considered him a true intellectual. Nhu could make long and impressive ideological speeches, and he had devised his own political philosophy for Vietnam ("personalism," a confusing counterideology to Communism, which no one else in Vietnam ever understood). Diem considered Nhu the perfect Vietnamese: he was dedicated, he worked as hard as Diem himself and he was an intellectual.

I once asked a Palace official which of the brothers he considered more influential. The Vietnamese thought for a minute and then said, "Nhu, because he can always influence Diem, but Diem can never influence Nhu."

Ngo Dinh Nhu was a born intriguer. He delighted in spending vast amounts of time and energy to trick people into doing the simplest and most normal tasks. Though eventually this peculiar trait proved to be his undoing, it served him well for a long time; not only did he survive countless intrigues in Vietnam, but his reputation as a schemer discouraged many other plots. He was an arrogant, vain man, sometimes privately a little contemptuous of Diem, whom he considered to be his intellectual inferior. He told one reporter that he considered himself "the unique spine of the anti-Communist movement" in South Vietnam, and that the program would collapse without him. He once boasted to Charley Mohr and Dick Clurman of *Time* that he was the "only serious strategist of guerrilla war" in modern times, and then spent an hour describing his unorthodox techniques. (His plan called for Government troops to squat in Communist-base areas; these tactics were in fact used by hapless Vietnamese commanders with an unparalleled lack of success.)

In late 1963, when the head-on collision with the Americans appeared imminent, Nhu had apparently put out feelers to North Vietnam about the possibility of discussions. One American official who knew him well said that this sounded very much like Nhu: the man probably believed that he could work out some form of coalition government with the Communists, and that in the inevitable, concomitant double cross he would come out on top. "Just the idea of playing with the Communists would fascinate Nhu and make the negotiations worthwhile," the official said.

Nhu made no attempt to conceal his lack of interest in the needs of the Vietnamese people; he was an intellectual and an aristocrat, and they were not. Stanley Karnow, now of the *Saturday Evening Post*, recalls a long conversation with him after the abortive paratrooper coup. Karnow had been asking Nhu about charges of corruption, and Nhu had offered to show Karnow his bank accounts. "But even if you're not involved in corruption," Karnow said, "people believe you are, and that in itself is a political reality." To this Nhu answered, "I don't care what the people think."

Nhu had a thin, chiseled, handsome face; if Hollywood had cast a movie on Vietnam and the Ngo dynasty, it would have been perfect type-casting to have Nhu play himself. He was not an extrovert, and he performed poorly in front of crowds; when reviewing his Cong Hoa Youth he would raise his hand in a Fascist-like salute and they would raise theirs in response, but his heart hardly seemed to be in it. He was a violent anti-Communist, but he was fascinated by the Communists and their methods. He came to mimic their techniques, and again and again to adapt them to his own needs; indeed, the Can Lao Party was modeled after the Communist Party. He also tried to create the equivalent of Communist cadres, and his long, boring speeches were filled with references to them.

Madame Nhu shared her husband's fascination for the enemy and believed that the Government would do well to adopt some Communist methods—particularly in regard to the foreign press. She once suggested to a press conference that the foreign correspondents form a committee to decide each day on "a common line to follow." She proposed Joseph Alsop as a man who would be helpful in determining the line. The other correspondents decided that this might be a wise choice from her point of view, but felt that their editors might not be receptive.

The obvious result of the Nhus' fascination with Communism was a government which in many ways was patterned after the Communists'. One Frenchman who also knew the Hanoi government very well called South Vietnam "the only Anti-Communist People's Democratic Republic in the world," while a member of the Vatican delegation once said, "All they need to do is change the flags, and overnight South Vietnam would be a Communist country."

Under Nhu, the men who rose to power were of a kind. They were from the same geographical area and of the same religion as the Ngo family; more importantly, they were men who were at home in the daily intrigue of Saigon, men who concentrated more on petty Palace conspiracies than on the long-range needs of the country, men who had little sense of the needs of the peasants, but a highly developed feel for the Palace winds, men who understood the vast security systems of the country and who had little compunction about telling the brothers anything they wanted to hear. Thus the family became surrounded by officials who resembled Nhu and Diem in all minor and petty qualities, but who lacked the major talents of the two brothers.

Eventually South Vietnam became, for all intents and purposes, a Communist-type country without Communism. It had all the controls, all the oppressions and all the frustrating, grim aspects of the modern totalitarian state—without the dynamism, efficiency and motivation that Communism had brought to the North. It was a police state, but it was unique in that its priorities were so haphazard; as a result, it was hopelessly inefficient. It was likely to pick up people for the wrong reasons; it had a strong enough police force to shake the loyalty and allegiance of the population, but not efficient enough to make them truly afraid.

To a large degree all of this could be traced to the Nhus: to them, running a government was largely an intellectual exercise; the form and fun of it mattered as much as the result.

Madame Nhu in particular ruled by impulse. The traditional sentimental songs were one of the few things that the average soldier, clutching his cheap transistor radio, enjoyed in his pathetic life. But to Madame, such songs were the product of a weak and decadent society, not sufficiently anti-Communist, and she banned them all. The Vietnamese generals, proud men engaged in an exacting war, were treated at the Palace like house servants, lackeys in her personal control from whom she demanded the most complete and petty kind of obedience.

Madame Nhu was a strikingly beautiful woman, and she was well aware of it; yet she looked too perfectly manicured, too much like someone who had just stepped out of a beauty shop, to be leading a country at war. Her speeches rang with appeals to sacrifice, but there was nothing about her which gave any indication of sacrifice. To me she always resembled an Ian Fleming character come to life: the antigoddess, the beautiful but diabolic sex-dictatress who masterminds some secret apparatus that James Bond is out to destroy. She liked power, and it showed; once in an interview she told me, "People say I am a woman of intrigue, but that is not true. People who intrigue are people without means, and I am a woman of means." She hated the American press, but she loved all the trappings of the personal interview: the long list of American correspondents going through the elaborate procedure of requesting a private audience; the personal letters addressed to her explaining precisely what they wanted to ask; the correspondents finally arriving—and being kept waiting; her own dramatic entrance, and their paying homage before asking their questions; tea being served by little male servants who bowed and scraped so low that the gesture resembled some form of medieval torture. (In this connection it is interesting to note that public ceremonies at which her

Paramilitary Girls performed were always highlighted by ju-
jitsu contests in which the girls defeated the boys.)

In contrast to Diem, who was shy and ill at ease in public,
and Nhu, who often seemed indifferent, Madame Nhu had a
real zest for the ceremonies of leadership. She was the only
one of the family who walked the way a dictator should walk—
with flair and obvious enjoyment, trailed by a line of atten-
dants—turning slowly first to the right, then to the left in
acknowledging the crowd. It was always a virtuoso performance, and a reporter watching felt this was the way Mus-
solini must have done it.

Once Neil Sheehan decided to test Madame Nhu's vanity.
In early September of 1963, at a time of total censorship right
after the Buddhist crackdown, Madame decided to hold a
small press conference. She told the assembled reporters that
she was just a housewife and a mother, that her husband and
Diem never discussed politics with her—indeed, chased her
away whenever the subject came up. After emphasizing this,
she also told the reporters that she could not be her usual
frank self "because my husband told me to be very cautious
with the press." At this time Madame was personally cen-
soring all stories about herself, so Sheehan, carefully wrote
his lead as follows: "President Diem's beautiful and *powerful*
[italics mine] sister-in-law, Madame Ngo Dinh Nhu, today
said . . ." He then followed with the quote about her husband warning her to be more cautious. When the story
was returned the word "powerful" was left in, but she had
crossed out the reference to her husband's warning and had
written: "Madame Nhu herself said she had decided to be
cautious . . ."

Madame Nhu had complete faith in herself and her cause,
and little use for anyone who in any way contradicted or
doubted her. Her tongue was sharp and agile and it spared
no one, not even the Pope. "Poor Pope," she once told Charley Mohr, commenting on the *Pacem in Terris*, "he pleases
everyone on earth with this encyclical. But how is this possible? Even God is challenged by the Devil. If something
pleases everyone, it can be exploited."

Madame was the true believer—that is, she had complete

confidence in herself and, by extension, in the right of the Ngo family to rule. The responsibility of everyone else, Vietnamese, American, private and general, was to understand this and get in line. She also had the complete fearlessness of the true believer. If she had been in Saigon when the final coup took place on November 1, 1963, she would never have allowed the brothers to leave the Palace. (On the other hand, the new junta would have had a terrible problem in trying to keep howling mobs from lynching her. As it was, crowds smashed a giant statue that she had created in her own image, and ran howling through the streets with the pieces.)

Every Vietnamese, afraid of her and angered by her and her power and regulations, passed on every scurrilous rumor about her. They believed that she owned all of the six thousand tiny taxis which roamed Saigon's streets; they believed that she owned most of the downtown bars in Saigon; they believed all sorts of nasty rumors about her personal life. She herself was well aware of this. During a prolonged series of interviews for a *Time* cover piece, she told Charley Mohr, "If any man is promoted and he is not too ugly, it is immediately said, 'A protégé of Madame Nhu's.' "

In August, 1963, NBC had a television interview with Madame during the Buddhist crisis. When she insisted that the cameraman be her own staff member, NBC agreed, and soon after the tape had been received by the New York office they contacted the NBC man in Saigon, asking who had made the tape, "because they really must hate her." They explained that every time Madame had said something about having liked the Buddhists when she was a little girl, the Vietnamese cameraman had flashed to her long, tapered fingernails digging cruelly into the side of her chair.

It was typical of the decaying spirit of the times in Vietnam that men contented themselves with scurrilous attacks on the person of Madame Nhu, rather than with concern for the real problem: her power. For she wielded an enormous influence, in the same way that a strong-minded wife exercises control in a family business. She was a fiercely determined, extremely practical woman with none of the intellectual pretensions of the Ngo brothers; she was vigorous—two decades

younger than Diem, a decade younger than her husband—
vital and uncompromising. She felt that both men were too
unworldly, too intellectual and too removed from reality; they
needed, she felt, someone to watch over their interests. Diem,
she told me in an interview, "is terribly scrupulous—much
too scrupulous. He is always worried." Her husband, she
added, "is very intellectual, but it is not really a handicap.
Like all the Ngo family, he is very cultured."

Madame's greatest strength was her consistency and her
determination. Her credo was very simple: the Ngo family
was always right; it should not compromise and it should
ignore criticism. Critics would be convinced sooner or later—
and if they were not, they must pay the consequences. During
the Buddhist crisis, for instance, she argued that the population would remain loyal to the President only if he stood up
to the Buddhists and crushed them. What made her particularly strong in family council was that in effect she was the
conscience of the family, that in their hearts the brothers believed what she was saying; as a result, she could destroy all
opposition arguments advanced by the Americans or the one
or two Palace aides who still maintained some independence
of thought, because she always took the line that Diem and
Nhu wanted to hear.

After Henry Cabot Lodge had just arrived in Vietnam, his
wife asked a veteran American in Saigon to describe Madame
Nhu and her power. The American gave an appraisal similar
to the above. "Yes," the ambassador said when he had finished, "that's exactly what her mother told me when we talked
in Washington."

Madame had an almost mystical feeling about the Ngo
family, and she talked constantly of how cultured they were.
She ordered Vietnamese press officers to refer to her as Madame Ngo, although Madame Nhu was the accepted usage.
She once told me with a perfectly straight face that it was
absurd to call the family a dictatorship; after all, she said,
every member had a free voice at family councils.

* * *

Step by step Madame Nhu and her husband shut Diem off from the rest of Vietnam. Dr. Tran Kim Tuyen, head of the secret police network, saw the paratrooper coup as the final warning to the Government and at great risk he wrote a long, carefully documented report for Diem, analyzing what had happened and what it portended for the future. Dr. Tuyen traced much of the trouble to Madame Nhu, and he warned that if the Government were to survive, Madame's role and power must be curtailed. After Nhu had shown the report to his wife, the influence of Dr. Tuyen, who had been the most brilliant member of the Palace staff, was effectively ended.

All power emanated from the Ngo family, in part through their vast series of subsurface networks of peculiar nomenclature. (When Dr. Tuyen headed the secret police, he held the title of "Director of the Political and Social Research Service of the Presidency.") The generals with political influence and power were not those with long titles and distinguished records, such as General Duong Van Minh, military adviser to the President, or General Tran Van Don, commander of the Army of Vietnam. The military who counted were those who had command of troops in the areas around Saigon; they had power because they were trusted not to participate in coups and would, indeed, help stamp them out. Throughout both the military and civilian establishments, a main source of power was the Can Lao Party, controlled by Nhu: a man might be a colonel, but if he was not a member of the Party and, say, a major was, it was the major who really exercised power.

At one time there were thirteen different secret police organizations, controlled by different members of the Government. Many of these police did not know one another, and we reporters took advantage of this. Neil Sheehan would send a young photographer named Nguyen Thai into otherwise impossible situations; Thai, dressed like a secret policeman—in open sports shirt, simple slacks, and dark glasses—blended in perfectly with the others and used the same kind of small camera they employed. Each secret policeman thought Thai was a member of a rival organization and he was always accepted as such. He took excellent photographs of situations from which other photographers were barred, and he became an important source of news about the secret police. (Ironically, his only dangerous moment came at a demonstration by medical students against the Government; the students, believing that he was an agent, took off after him, and he barely escaped.)

By 1961 the power of the Nhus was immense. Imagine Diem as the President of the United States; in such a situation Nhu would have controlled all the country's newspapers, headed the CIA, the FBI and the Congress, served as Attorney General and Secretary of State, and written all the reports the President saw. What Diem knew of the outside world was what Nhu wanted him to know; what he saw he saw through Nhu's eyes; the people he met he met only after Nhu had approved them. Once, in 1961, Diem called in a corps commander, hauled his maps out and described a major operation he envisioned just north of Saigon in D-Zone, a major Communist base. When Nhu heard that this major operation was being planned, he summoned the division commander and ordered him not to commit his troops because he did not want them to leave Saigon at that time. The division commander called his superior, the corps commander, who, in a dilemma, went to see Nhu and said he couldn't countermand Diem's plan. Nhu finally devised a solution; he ordered the corps commander to deploy a couple of battalions to D-Zone and then send in phony information to Diem. The operation took place as Nhu had ordered, and of course it was reported to the President as fully successful.

Nhu had created the Cong Hoa Youth in his own image. He ran the Army's security systems, and he pitted one faction against another. Madame Nhu had her groups too: the Women's Solidarity Movement, regarded as an apparatus for family espionage, and the Paramilitary Girls. It was also clear that Nhu planned to use the strategic hamlet program, which was designed to separate the peasants from the Vietcong, as a means of controlling the population, in particular the young people. When the war had ended successfully, Nhu would emerge as the most powerful man in the country.

This strange triumvirate ruled over a government that had no parallel. There were elections, though no opposition candidates were permitted; there was a legislature, but it was the rubber-stamp kind, whose only real function was to legislate between representatives of brother Can in the central region and brother Nhu in Saigon; there was a cabinet, whose ministers had responsibility but no power and who lived in mortal fear of Madame Nhu.

The election returns of South Vietnam would have staggered the imagination even of the Communists in the North. In the 1963 Assembly elections, Nho Dinh Nhu, representing Khanh Hoa Province, received 99.98 percent of the vote, while Madame Nhu, running as a candidate from a district in Long An almost totally controlled by the Communists, received 99.4 percent. When I asked her about this later, she said, "I am becoming a popular figure, which is very encouraging because I have no public relations."

In 1961, at the very vital point in the history of Vietnam when the Americans made their major commitment and praised Diem at every opportunity in order to improve the relationship, political disintegration lurked beneath the unrest on the surface. The three main power factions in the country were all shaky. First, the family depended on its growing police power, which in turn was making the rest of the population increasingly unhappy and the Americans increasingly nervous. Second, the Army's loyalty was dubious, despite the elaborate lengths the brothers had gone to in order to control it. Promotion on the basis of personal loyalty rather than ability, the use of informers, the banishment of men of integrity and initiative, and the domination of all strategy had not made the Army more loyal; these methods had merely brought about a tenuous control, and badly compromised and diluted a military force which was in a fight to the death with a tough enemy.

The third source of power was the Americans, seen as a potential danger by the suspicious Nhus, who tolerated the Americans only as long as they did everything the family wanted. Therefore, the increase in the U.S. role was offset by stronger efforts to minimize American influence and to keep the Americans out of the vital area of policy making.

Thus, a government was fighting a complicated war, suspicious of its own army and attempting to minimize its effectiveness; at the same time remaining suspicious of its major ally and attempting to minimize its influence.

It was not a happy time in Vietnam, despite all the surface optimism. Some Americans thought the answer lay in separating Diem from the Nhus—that Diem was good and the Nhus were bad, and that therefore everything could be solved by dividing the two. But anyone who dealt with the Government knew that this was an impractical solution; as Ambassador Nolting told one friend, "Trying to separate the members of that family would be like separating Siamese twins."

V

A short time after I had arrived in Saigon I was having lunch with Doug Pike, a member of the U.S. Information Service mission and one of the brightest Americans in Vietnam. Pike, who had spent a good deal of time in Asia, was a specialist on psychological warfare, and was making an ill-fated attempt to impress on both the Government and the American military the importance of psychological warfare in a struggle like this.

That day he was in a less than enthusiastic mood. He had just been to see an American general about coordinating some additional "psy-war" teams into the Government program. The general had looked at him coolly and displayed contempt for "psy-war." "We're here to teach 'em to kill Communists," he said. Pike argued for a few minutes, got nowhere, and then reminded the general that the French had killed perhaps a million soldiers fighting under the Vietminh banner during their war.

"Didn't kill enough then," said the general. "We'll teach 'em to kill more."

Following the French debacle in 1954, the United States started on the long, tortured road of its own policy in Viet-

nam. Previously we had gone along with the French and had
acquiesced in their policy; now it was to be our primary
responsibility. This was during the first Eisenhower Administration, in the days of John Foster Dulles' policy of con-
tainment. Dulles made the basic decision to try and hold
Vietnam, believing—rightly—that it was the key to a large
part of Southeast Asia. If the Vietnamese, who are perhaps
the toughest people in Southeast Asia, fell to the Communists, the pressure on the other shaky new nations there would
be intolerable.

United States foreign policy—at least until recently, and
certainly in regard to underdeveloped countries—is not an
orderly matter in which the policy maker sits back and tries
to decide which of the many options he likes best, searching
in particular for like-minded nations led by like-minded governments. Rather, it is too often a matter of expediency, with
the United States trying hurriedly to carve out some sort of
policy which fits its traditional view of what a foreign nation
and a foreign ruler should be, at the same time satisfying the
demands of its national and international security. The original problems in the Congo, for instance, cannot be traced to
any basic decision this country has made during that nation's
brief history; indeed, the specific acts and decisions by the
Kennedy Administration were very enlightened. The trouble
there lies primarily in the chaos which existed in the Congo
at the time of independence: a nation without any trained
leadership; a mutinous, ill-trained army; a constitution which
was totally unsuitable for such a vast embryo; the Belgian
decision to make a man like Patrice Lumumba prime minister. In the virtual anarchy which followed independence, policy making was equivalent to pinning the tail on the donkey:
a matter of luck and instinct.

Throughout the world during the fifties, when colonial empires were collapsing, the United States was trying as best it
could to help pick up the pieces; too often we had to rush in
and provide a last-minute policy for a country about which
we knew very little and in the shaping of whose future we
had played a remarkably small part. Too often, by the time
we became interested, the options were limited and the

chances for flexibility were gone; the only diplomacy that
could be employed was the good old-fashioned firehouse kind.
Again and again we were forced to resort to surface solutions;
the deep-rooted conditions were by then far beyond our control.

The nine years of the Diem regime were marked alternately
by excessive optimism, constant mutual suspicion, continu-
ous political unrest, vast American military miscalculation,
economic aid that did not reach the peasants, training and
preparation for the wrong war—and no preparation for what
was the predictable war. After we had entered Vietnam we
tended to disregard every lesson the French had learned; by
the early sixties our generals had begun to sound like *their*
generals; our self-deception had begun to match *their* self-
deception.

Diem had misjudged the Vietnamese people's acclaim for
the popular reforms he brought about when he first came to
power, but the real optimists in this situation were the American military officials in charge of the Military Assistance and
Advisory Group (MAAG) in Vietnam. The Communists had
prepared their cadres in the South, but had not yet made their
challenge. The Americans, just finished with the Korean War,
were remarkably ignorant of the nature of the French Indochina war. They still retained the Korean War psychology;
they believed that if the Communists struck it would be by a
traditional border crossing, a stab at the Seventeenth Parallel.
Therefore they trained the Vietnamese Army conventionally,
and they virtually ignored guerrilla and counter-guerrilla
techniques. They were openly contemptuous of the French
experience; to them, the French simply had not fought well
enough.

Not only did the chiefs of the American mission consistently fail to take the enemy seriously, they did not understand the political aspects of the war. They fawned over those
Vietnamese who conformed to their own image: crew-cut
Vietnamese air-borne officers, fairly bursting out of their uniforms, parachute insignia on their chests, and dropping oc-

casional words of American slang. "How good is the
individual fighting man?" Peter Kalischer, then with *Col-
lier's*, asked General "Hanging Sam" Williams in 1956.
"Man for man," answered General Williams, "they're as
good as the Vietminh now." He went on to tell Kalischer that
the officer corps was being built up, and that American mobile offensive tactics had replaced the French doctrine of static
strongholds.

This was to become a familiar tune in Vietnam. The Americans kept repeating it, but the plan never materialized. After
seven years, in late 1963, with most of the lower Camau
peninsula already under Communist control and the few remaining outposts nothing but suicide traps, Neil Sheehan and
I wrote stories which pinpointed how this strategy was not
being followed. A very able American lieutenant colonel,
relatively new to the country, took exception to our stories,
pointing out that he had just finished a long and detailed plan
for doing away with the posts, and that his Vietnamese counterpart had accepted it. Neil told him that we had heard a lot
of American officers say exactly the same thing, and that we
would believe it when we saw the outposts come down. The
colonel listened, and then nodded his head regretfully.

An indication of the American blindness to the military
situation was this comment, in the summer of 1959, by Major
General Samuel Myers, deputy chief of MAAG, who said,
referring to the enemy by the name used during the French
Indochina war, "The Vietminh guerrillas, though constantly
reinforced by men and weapons from outside, were gradually
nibbled away until they ceased to be a major menace to the
Government. In fact, estimates at the time of my departure
indicate that there were a very limited number of hostile individuals under arms in the country. Two territorial regiments, reinforced occasionally by one or two Army
regiments, were able to cope with their depredations."

For four key years, from 1955 to 1959, the Americans and
Diem marked time. They had failed to prepare for the kind
of threat that even the most cursory study of the Indochina

war would have shown was most likely. The Government had failed to extend its authority to the villages; prodded by the Americans, it had made a stab at land reform, but because of Diem's own conservatism and lack of interest, the program had failed badly and had given the enemy rich opportunities for political subversion among the peasants. Local Government militia in the villages were badly trained and were still depending largely on the old French outpost psychology.

In late September of 1959, two Government battalions were searching for an estimated forty guerrillas in the Plain of Reeds, southwest of Saigon along the Cambodian border. Instead, they were ambushed by two enemy companies. The fire fight lasted fifteen minutes; twelve of the Government regulars were killed, and the rest surrendered their weapons. The second Indochina war had officially begun, though few people realized it at the time. From this time on, the enemy was to be known as Vietcong, which means, literally, Vietnamese Communist.

The new Indochina war was not a spontaneous uprising from the South. It was part of a systematic and calculated conspiracy on the part of the Communist government in Hanoi to take over the South. But it was the most subtle kind of conspiracy, for though Hanoi directed the war, set its pace, controlled its overall strategy and on the international front articulated the propaganda aims of the Vietcong, it did not in those days send North Vietnamese troops to fight in the South. Rather, the *face* of the war was of a purely indigenous uprising: the troops were Southerners, and captured weapons were usually employed. Some of the Southerners might have been trained in the North and might have served with the North Vietnamese infantry before infiltrating back to the South in the early sixties to serve as battalion or cadre commanders in the new struggle. In this type of conspiracy, Hanoi was aided by the frontiers of South Vietnam: the incredibly rugged Laotian border, and farther south, the Cambodian—a vague and aimless boundary separating South Vietnam from a neighbor more sympathetic to the insurgents than to the established regime. The failure of the Government to attempt even the most fundamental antiguerrilla techniques made the nature of this terrain relatively unimportant. Had the Government been more effective, the borders might have been more significant; successful insurgencies in Greece, Malaya and the Philippines depended, among other things, on isolation of the rebels. (In 1964, according to reliable intelligence reports, the Vietcong not only increased the number of infiltrators, but by the latter part of the year Hanoi was reportedly sending North Vietnamese into the South.)

The pace was stepped up early in 1960; the Vietcong started a systematic attack on Diem's village officials, designed to undermine what little Government authority existed. Forty village chiefs were killed the first week and many arms were captured. Two types of village chiefs were targets: the bad and corrupt, because in killing them the Vietcong looked like benefactors to the population; and the able, who represented threats to the enemy because they were effective representatives of the Government.

To the Vietcong, terror was an act of discrimination. They also made schoolteachers a prime target; hundreds were murdered. Between 1959 and the end of 1961 the Government was forced to close six hundred and thirty-six schools, either because of intimidation, or because the Vietcong were using them for propaganda. Again and again the story was the same: brutal murders, decapitation of village officials and teachers in front of an entire village; hidden Vietcong cadres coming slowly to the surface. These spotlighted the corruption of officials, and by wholesale murders demonstrated that a government which could not protect its own officials certainly could not protect its people.

The Government troops, trained and poised to repulse a crossing at the Seventeenth Parallel, were totally unprepared for an enemy who stole the countryside away at night. Diem, proud and aloof, refused to recognize that insurgency existed in 1959 and 1960, because that would have been a reflection on the Government. For a long time his administration would not admit that a war existed; the Vietcong movement was written off as isolated banditry. Government casualties soared (some estimates place the number of civil servants and teachers murdered between 1959 and 1961 at over ten thousand)

and so did arms losses. This produced an ever-quickening spiral, for as Vietcong arsenals grew, so did their capacity to strike and to capture more weapons. "Ngo Dinh Diem," said one enemy propaganda tract at the time, "will be our supply sergeant."

In late 1960 some American officials were still pretending that the situation in South Vietnam was healthy, that the revolt was primarily the work of disorganized bandits. By mid-1961, however, the Government position in the countryside was extremely shaky. The Vietcong were threatening to take over the entire rural Delta, and they appeared to have all the drive and momentum. The Government Army was ill prepared to fight back; it was disorganized, it lacked the mobility to catch the elusive guerrillas; its morale was extremely low, for it saw the enemy as the successor of the erstwhile victorious Vietminh, and thus believed that it was fighting men who were ten feet tall. The Army lacked leadership and it lacked a will to fight. According to a friend of mine, "in those days, when you woke up in the morning you didn't know whether or not you would have a country left."

In October 1961 the Taylor mission set the stage for the major American build-up and for the second step in the American commitment to Diem. It came at a time when the Diem government, difficult and isolated in 1954, had become almost paranoiac in its touchiness. It was reduced to police-state methods for survival, and it had grown more and more suspicious of its major ally—particularly following the abortive 1960 paratrooper revolt, which the Nhus still believed was planned by the Americans. Increasing numbers of small groups of nationalists who had been drawn to Diem in 1954 and who had liked his early rule now found him impossible to work with. If they were talented, they quickly ran into conflict with the family; as a result, many of the best people around him were leaving. Of course their departure made Diem more suspicious than ever and tended to make him rely more and more on his family, particularly on the Nhu branch—which was exactly what the Nhus wanted.

Seeing former supporters turn against him, Diem relied increasingly on the Nhus and on police-state techniques for control. As a result, more and more members of his own government and the population turned against him; the more frequently this happened, the more Diem relied on police methods. The Army was rife with political favoritism and security networks; personal loyalty, rather than merit or bravery, were the keys to promotion. This is not unusual for an underdeveloped country, but South Vietnam was an underdeveloped country fighting for its survival; it could ill afford such luxuries.

It was against this background that the Kennedy Administration was forced to make a deliberate—and once again limited—choice in late 1961. It could back out of South Vietnam entirely—which would virtually turn Southeast Asia over to the Communists and might have disastrous repercussions in the next presidential election. It could search for another leader—but because of Diem and the Nhus, no national hero had been allowed to emerge. Moreover, Diem was a tantalizing figure in that he always seemed better than his government. Was the Government corrupt? Diem was a paragon of integrity. Was the Government unjust? Diem always seemed a model of personal justice and honor.

Finally, 1961 was also the year of the Bay of Pigs, the Berlin Wall and the deterioration in Laos; a change of government might backfire, and the Administration could not stand another major international bungle at that time. It could send U.S. combat troops into Vietnam, but were the American people prepared to subscribe to such a war? Besides, American combat troops would create exactly the same situation as the French had; they would be white men fighting Asians on Asian soil, and they would turn the entire population in favor of the Vietcong.

There was one other alternative: the United States could step up its own commitment to a point just short of combat. It could help the country to help itself, could send in advisers, helicopters, fighter bombers, and pilot trainers and pilots. It could, in fact, do everything but give the Vietnamese the will and desire to win.

This decision was made, and the reasons were relatively simple: there was nowhere else to go.

The key man in making this choice was Maxwell Taylor. As such, he was in fact a representative of what is known in Washington as the "Never Again Club," a Korean legacy—a phrase meaning that its members never again wanted to place American combat troops on the mainland of Asia without atomic weapons. Above all else, Taylor wanted to keep American combat troops out of the Vietnamese jungles. He and others like him shared a feeling that this was not America's war. Thus, the commitment was in effect a booster shot, but it was one step short of actual combat, and it was made in full knowledge of the limitations of the government on which it was being superimposed.

In effect, the Taylor mission reported that the war could be won, and could be won under the existing government—provided that a huge retraining program oriented the Vietnamese military away from conventional warfare to new concepts of flexible counterguerrilla warfare. The study called for greater mobility of the Vietnamese Army by giving them helicopters and amphibious personnel carriers. It recommended aid programs designed to break through the frustrations of Diem's overly centralized and personalized government and to bring aid down to the peasants. It suggested a series of reforms: broadening the base of the Government; taking non-Ngo anti-Communist elements into the Government; making the National Assembly more than a rubber stamp; easing some of the tight restrictions on the local press.

Above all, the people and the Government itself had to develop a relationship of mutual trust. All of this, Taylor and his advisers hoped, would end what was perhaps the worst characteristic of the Government: corrupt local officials constantly telling peasants that they had not seen those abuses which were in fact taking place before their very eyes. For the Vietnamese peasant there was no redress from official bungling or corruption, because even when Diem knew an official had acted improperly or incompetently he would not replace him, lest he lose face. To dismiss a man would show that Diem had erred by choosing that official in the first place.

Thus, while Diem was not corrupt, he tolerated corruption; while he himself was not necessarily cruel or unjust, he tolerated cruelty and injustice. Friends of mine who saw the Taylor report consider it a brilliant analysis of the ailments and symptoms of a very sick country.

The U.S. Administration and its representatives in the field believed that by all-out support of the Diem government we could change its attitude toward its own people and persuade it to make changes it had been unwilling to make on its own. The problem, however, was very simple: the Ngo family wanted American aid, American equipment and some American troops, but it did not want American advice.

It was emphasized by Ambassador Nolting that support of the Government must not be half-hearted. The ruler's peculiar psychological make-up—and therefore the character of the Government itself—demanded that support must be full and enthusiastic and without quibbling. Only this, Nolting was convinced, could influence Diem.

But there was a flaw to this argument. An unresponsive government which has been receiving considerable American aid and not listened to American advice, and which then is given even more aid because it has repeatedly failed in its mission, is not apt to be more amenable to suggestion later on. Predictably, the reverse took place: the Ngo government became more convinced than ever that it had its ally in a corner, that it could do anything it wanted, that continued support would be guaranteed because of the Communist threat and that after the commitment was made, the United States could not suddenly admit it had made a vast mistake.

Although seven years and two billion dollars of American aid had previously been spent in the face of steadily increasing enemy strength, the American material aid recommended by the Taylor mission—the helicopters and the men to fly them—began to arrive in January of 1962. At the same time the Americans began to talk about some of the promised reforms. Almost immediately Ngo Dinh Nhu unleashed a violent anti-American campaign in the controlled press. After a few days of this—plus sulking on the part of Diem—the Americans decided not to push for reforms; they would back Diem strongly and hope that the sheer force of military equipment would help to turn the tide. So, the Americans began to give in to the Ngo family on virtually everything. Having failed to get reforms, our officials said that these reforms were taking place; having failed to improve the demoralized state of the Vietnamese Army, the Americans talked about a new enthusiasm in the Army; having failed to change the tactics of the military, they talked about bold new tactics which were allegedly driving the Communists back. For the essence of our policy was: *There is no place else to go.*

When reporters began to file stories which tended to show that the policy was not working, its authors, President Kennedy and General Taylor, clung to it stubbornly. At least part of the explanation for this apparent blindness is that although they knew things were going wrong, they felt that the alternatives were worse. The psychosis of the American position had been evidenced by none other than Lyndon Johnson, then our Vice-President, who visited the nation in the summer of 1961 as Kennedy's personal representative. Johnson praised Diem lavishly as an Asian Winston Churchill. On the plane out of Saigon a reporter started talking to the Vice-President about Diem and some of his faults. "Don't tell me about Diem," Johnson answered. "He's all we've got out there." Of course the Ngo family understood this perfectly well; the Americans were their main support, and the brothers had long learned the fine art of handling American diplomats.

By the time Maxwell Taylor arrived in Vietnam on his first trip in 1961, the options available to the United States were already limited; to a remarkable degree we were the victims of recent history—not so much a history that we had made as a history that we had ignored. In early 1964, Dang Duc Khoi—the former information officer for the Vietnamese government who had fled the country in August 1963, a step ahead of Nhu's secret police—was asked about the possibility, suggested by the French, of a neutralized Vietnam. It was too late for neutralism, Khoi said. There was no such thing any more in Vietnam; the enemy was too real and the game had been played too long. "But I wish," he continued, showing as much bitterness as I had ever seen a Vietnamese permit himself in public, "that the French had been as interested in a neutral Vietnam seventeen years ago as they are now. Then we could have been neutrals."

He was right, of course; the vital decisions in Vietnam had been made long ago, back when it was still called Indochina.

In September of 1962, General Taylor visited the country again, and spoke optimistically about improvements in the military situation. But despite reporters' urgent questions at a press conference he shied away from discussing political changes; these had been shoved aside. Because of this, the Ngo family, still suspicious of basic American intentions, was convinced that it had handled the Americans properly; they went on doing business as usual, reassured that no American administration would dare tamper with it because of the danger of the Communists. ("The chief export of this country," a British friend of mine said at the time, "is anti-Communism.")

Bernard Fall, the noted French authority on the Indochina war, was permitted to visit North Vietnam in 1962 and was granted an interview with Pham Van Dong, the Prime Minister. The interview was published in the fall of 1962, and for those of us working in the South it had a haunting quality. Dong spoke patronizingly about Diem. Poor Diem, he said, he is so unpopular that the Americans must give him aid. But that makes him more unpopular, so the Americans give him even more aid, and that makes him even more unpopular. Fall interrupted to say that this sounded like a vicious circle. "No," said Pham Van Dong, "not a vicious circle. A downward spiral."

With the increase in American equipment and American participation, more American reporters arrived as well. They saw little of the alleged new enthusiasm for the Government. They heard American officials talk of reforms, but they saw such reforms were shelved after Nhu fomented the anti-American attack in the newspapers. They would pick up their American papers and read Washington-inspired stories about new experts on guerrilla war, about special Washington staffs on counterinsurgency, about books being rushed into print to inform the American public about counterinsurgency. Then these reporters would go out into the field and see the same tired old Government tactics, the same political commanders in charge, the same waste of human resources.

Yet American policy was still consciously optimistic—the idea being that if the Americans expressed enough optimism, Diem would come to trust them and be more receptive to their suggestions. In addition, a sensitive Administration back home wanted to hear that it was winning the war. But the reporters were more cautious in their judgment; they were reluctant to join in the chorus not only because of the country's tarnished past, but also because of what they saw in the field.

Homer Bigart said that the American officials were dressing up the same faces and techniques with "gimmicks." In July 1962 he wrote:

> Unfounded enthusiasm for sentry dogs prompted a worldwide recruitment of German shepherds. The United States Advisory group wanted 1,000 dogs, but procurement was impossible. Only about 200 are currently in South Vietnam or in the pipeline. Most of the dogs that reached South Vietnam are sick. Of the five dogs assigned to the Seventh Division, four were sick and so was their trainer.
>
> It was reported that they needed three months to adjust to the tropics. Meanwhile, someone discovered that each dog required $1.20 worth of frozen horse meat a day; a Vietnamese soldiers gets by on 19 cents' worth of rice.
>
> Gadgets will not win this war, and neither will war dogs.

Again in July, in his final article, he wrote that although there had been some military improvement, victory was remote. "The issue is in doubt because the Vietnamese President seems incapable of winning the loyalty of his people . . . Visions of ultimate victory are obscured by the image of a secretive, suspicious, dictatorial regime. American officers are frustrated and irritated by the constant whimsical meddling of the President and his brother Ngo Dinh Nhu in the military chain of command.''

The conscious policy of optimism on the part of the American mission extended to an attempt to manipulate the news through visiting VIP's. Some general or official would arrive in Vietnam, would spend one day in Saigon being briefed and meeting the Ngo family, and another day or two in the field inspecting selected strategic hamlets and units. Then he would hold an airport press conference in which he would say that the war was being won, that the people were rallying to the Government, that he had been impressed by the determination of President Diem, who was a great leader. The policy was partially successful, but according to a State Department white paper in January 1963, it "had tended to make reporters cynical.''

The American line of "cautious optimism" went something like this: there is a slow, inevitable tide running and it is running in our direction. The people are rallying to Diem; to be sure, he isn't a popular leader, at least not in the American sense, but he is respected. The Government—well, the Government is difficult, and it is naïve to expect a democracy in this part of the world. (This reasoning neatly obscured the difference between a strong and dictatorial government which can guide its population, and this aloof, inefficient, self-defeating dictatorship whose population was more or less in quiet rebellion.) As for reports about troubles in the Army, anyone who criticizes the Army is saying that the Vietnamese won't fight, and this is insulting to a brave ally.

The result was an outward rigidity and orthodoxy at the top that was unique among American missions overseas. Admiral Harry Felt, the commander of all American forces in the Pacific, summed up the attitude eloquently when, at a press conference in Saigon in late 1962, he became angered by a question from Malcolm Browne of the Associated Press, and snapped, "Why don't you get on the team?''

The reasons for the press dispute when I arrived in South Vietnam were symbolized by the personalities of Nolting and

Bigart. It would be hard to find two men more different. Nolting is a Virginian, a gracious and considerate former philosophy professor who since World War II had been a career diplomat. He had never been in the Far East before, and he had a desire to take what the Vietnamese government was telling him at face value. If he was shown a piece of paper saying that local officials were going to do something, he was satisfied that it would be done. Though he had served in a major role in NATO, he had never been much involved with reporters before and he had almost no conception of the working press. He once told Peter Kalischer that Diem was popular in the countryside. Kalischer was staggered, since he knew that this was where the Vietcong was strongest and the Government weakest, and from then on he no longer regarded the ambassador as a serious source of information.

Nolting could not understand that reporters wrote what they saw; once he said to me, "You're always looking for the hole in the doughnut, Mr. Halberstam." He worked extremely hard, but he was caught in an almost impossible situation with an ally who would not match his efforts.

Still, Ambassador Nolting's position would have been more acceptable if he had not fed the fire himself. He kept saying that the war was being won and he was pressuring his subordinates to tell him only the good news, thereby cutting off reliable lines of communication. He had to believe that American policy was more successful than in fact it was, so that he could reassure Washington. In a cover story on General Harkins in May 1962, *Time* said:

> Nolting has probably done more than anyone else to persuade Washington to stick with Diem. He knows all of Diem's familiar shortcomings—his authoritarian rule, which has thirty thousand political prisoners under arrest, his inability to delegate authority, his refusal to allow any political opposition, the excessive powers vested in his family. But Nolting sees no alternative to Diem, insists accurately that he is a man of personal honesty, high courage, and deep dedication. In Washington last January, President Kennedy bluntly asked Nolting whether we could win with Diem. His reply: "Yes, but it will be difficult."

Yet in following this policy Nolting came to remind me of some white community leaders I had known in Mississippi and Tennessee, men who—at a time when their communities were about to blow up in racial disorder—reassured me that all was well, that the Negroes were satisfied with the status quo, that the problem was entirely the work of outside agitators and that writing about it would only make the situation worse. These men had no contact with the Negro community except for what their maids or hired people told them, and they went on believing what they wanted to believe, while in the meantime a restless community grew angrier and further estranged.

Sometimes during those months I used to wonder what would have happened if someone like Edmund Gullion had been ambassador to Vietnam. Gullion seemed to me to be the epitome of what an American diplomat should be. He always tried to find out exactly what was happening in the country where he was posted, and he had a reputation for being blunt both with the State Department and the White House. This frankness was tolerated at State and permitted at the White House because Gullion personally had President Kennedy's respect; he had gained this in part when, as a high political officer in Indochina, he had frankly told visiting Congressman Kennedy in 1951 that the French were not winning the Indochina war and could not win it under the present circumstances. Gullion convinced Kennedy both that American policy should be changed and that he was a young diplomat who was willing to speak out despite what the rest of the mission was saying. I still find it hard to believe that Gullion would have deluded himself or his superiors very long about what was happening in Vietnam at the time.

Nolting's job was difficult, but it was made even more difficult by the almost psychotic preoccupation of Diem and his family with the Western press—the one element operating in Vietnam, other than the Vietcong, which they could not control. Diem resented any criticism of his family; since his family was in fact his government, he became angry at a wide assortment of stories. Diem and the Nhus believed that the American press was Communist-infiltrated; paradoxically the Nhus also believed that some of the reporters were CIA agents and part of a vast underground American conspiracy against them. Diem devoted time and energy to reading what the American reporters were writing about him, far beyond what could be considered the understandable sensitivities of a leader whose country is engaged in a difficult war. When reporters filed their stories at night, copies were immediately taken to the Palace. The next morning, when the incoming AP and UPI wire stories arrived in the country, all dispatches dealing with Vietnam were stamped "Top Secret" and brought to the Palace. When the first Buddhist monk burned himself to death, Diem was convinced that this act had been staged and paid for by an American television team—despite the fact that there had not been a single television man on the scene. He mentioned this suspicion to Nolting; the ambassador assured him that it was not true. Apparently Nolting did not make any headway, however, for two months later Diem made the charge publicly—a sad and revealing insight into the paranoia of the Government.

Every time we wrote something that Diem disliked he was convinced that American officials had deliberately leaked it to us. (Actually, the source was often one of his own supposedly loyal Palace intimates.) Nolting did his best to keep us from finding out anything which might reflect on the Government, but the city was filled with dissident Americans and Vietnamese who talked freely; it is a national Vietnamese characteristic that they cannot keep a secret. But though Nolting was a part of the closed society, he could not—unlike Diem, who could control the Vietnamese press—muzzle the American press, could not get reporters on the team.

The prototype of a non-team player is Homer Bigart. (It was he who coined the classic summation of American policy in Vietnam: "Sink or swim with Ngo Dinh Diem.") He had failed to make the team in Greece, in Turkey, in the Congo, in Korea, and on the way he had picked up two Pulitzer

prizes for it. He enjoys great prestige and most colleagues
are in awe of him. He is no scholar; if he reads books it is a
well-kept secret, and his proficiency in foreign languages can
be summarized by his reply to a French colleague who once
offered him a cigarette: "Je ne smoke pas." He is not one
of the new breed of reporters—Harvard or Yale, and a Nieman fellowship—but he sheds light wherever he goes in the
world by writing simply, incisively and lucidly. Bigart appears to go at his job in the manner of a police reporter and
nothing more, but behind this façade is a remarkable sensi-
tivity to events and men. "All Homer has is a form of portable
ignorance," one colleague once said. "He shows up knowing
little, and then finds out everything." He professes to be a
simple and naïve man, but he has had thirty-five years of
experience in sensing trouble and decay, and in finding the
weak links. He seems to know when people are lying before
they themselves do.

  In Saigon, Bigart was fifty-five years old, and his stomach
bothered him. But in what was essentially a young man's
assignment—a relentless, ruthless grind under tropical conditions—Homer simply outworked every young reporter in
town. The embassy officials who had accused Sully of being
a *pied noir* and the rest of us of being too young were obviously awed by Bigart's reputation. Eventually officials even
tried to discount his reporting because of his age. Poor old
Homer, the line went, he's too old to get on helicopters and
he's sour because his stomach hurts.

  At a news conference in April 1962, visiting Secretary of
Defense Robert S. McNamara professed to be a friend of the
press and asked if the working reporters had any complaints.

  Homer rose and said, "Mr. Secretary, we're not getting
enough news."

  McNamara was startled and thought for a moment. "Well,
Mr. Bigart," he finally said, "that's not my impression. My
impression in Washington every morning is that you're getting a great deal of news—a very great deal."

  "Yes," said Homer, "but I'm having to work too hard for
it."

  In a situation like the one in Vietnam, Bigart had vast advantages. All his life he had dealt with governments which were hiding things and with officials who were trying to make bad situations seem better. Nolting once asked a reporter, "Why don't you people give President Diem the benefit of the doubt?" But men were dying and the nation's prestige was at stake, and there was no longer time to give anyone the benefit of the doubt. The result of this conflict was great bitterness; Homer had been the recipient of most of it, but it extended to other reporters as well.

When Bigart left Vietnam, there was a mutual sigh of relief from him and from American officials. Indeed, the first day I was there Jacques Nevard of the *Times* and I had lunch with an official who gave us a good story. Later I asked Jacques if this happened regularly. "No," he said, "it's the first time he's ever told me anything. They're making a play for you— and they're very, very glad that Homer's gone."

VI

When I first arrived in Vietnam, AP photographer Horst Faas and I greeted each other with the enthusiasm befitting liberated Congo hands. "You'll like this country," he said. "It's everything the Congo is not. Most of all you will like the Delta. It is south of here." (Horst is a very specific man. Sometimes his observations on skirmishes were delayed for precious moments while he gave an exact description of, say, how a wounded soldier had been bandaged.)

I asked Faas why I would like the Delta.

"Because it is like nothing you have ever seen. There is the farmer, his wife, the rice they have, the coconuts, the pineapples and oranges, the ducks and chickens, the dogs and pigs, the children fishing in the canals and riding the water buffaloes." Horst pronounced it "boofalows." "It is like a page out of the Bible." Then he added, "All the war is going on down there. Very much shooting. Much more than the Congo. Much more dangerous. You know how the Congolese are." He did an imitation of a Congolese soldier hiding behind a building and sticking his weapon around the corner and firing. "They are not like that here," Horst said.

When I first went to the Delta I saw that Horst was right: this was what the war was all about. The soil of the Mekong River lies rich and flat and green just south of Saigon. This area comprises only about a quarter of all South Vietnam, but most of the peasants in the country live there, about 80 percent of the country's agricultural resources are there, and when I arrived, most of the war was taking place there. Unfortunately, a major part of the Government's military effort was going into the central highlands and also into the central coastal region, where the Ngo family came from and whose population they trusted.

The Delta is difficult country to fight in: it consists mainly of paddies, swamps, canals and bogs. It is marvelous outlaw country; historically it has served as the hiding place for bandits. Yet its natural richness, its abundance of fish, rice and other food makes it easy country for guerrillas; the Ngo family's attempt to starve the enemy into submission had about as much chance of success as an attempt to deny a glutton food in an American supermarket.

At the end of September 1962 the optimism which pervaded the American mission in Saigon was strikingly absent in the Delta. There the enemy was gradually utilizing the cadres he had built up painstakingly during the eight years since the end of the Indochina war; he was fighting well and showing drive, resourcefulness and ingenuity. The guerrilla war fluctuates constantly; in the Delta young American officers serving as advisers were immediately thrown into the most complex and difficult situations imaginable. Also, the limitations of the Diem government—the problems and handicaps it imposed on field commanders, and the kind of leaders it chose for key areas—stood out even more conspicuously in the Delta.

The advisory mission placed young American captains and lieutenants down at the battalion level. It meant that at every level the Americans had as a counterpart a Vietnamese officer, hopefully passing on this country's vast background of military experience, trying to make the troops more aggressive, cutting down on mistakes, fighting the war the way we believed it should be fought. We also had men at regimental and division levels—and sometimes with companies—all the way to the top at the Palace. (It was the belief of the men in the field that it was at the very top that the advisory effort was failing, and that if the Palace had really wanted its own officers to listen, the word would quickly have come down and the American advice would have been followed.)

At that time the Delta was divided by the Bassac River into two military areas. In the lower half, the Twenty-first Division was operating in the toughest part of the country, a territory which included the entire Camau peninsula, an area under Communist domination since before the French Indochina war. Here Government troops were isolated, and they rarely controlled more than the ground under their feet at any given time. The Seventh Division was in a more vital spot, in the upper half of the Delta, where the provinces were the richest and most heavily settled; approximately 25 percent of the South Vietnamese people lived in this area. But more important than its population was the fact that this was an area up for grabs; the Communists were not as strong here as they were in the lower Delta, but they were making an effort, and up until that time they had possessed the military initiative. However, there had been some recent Government successes, and when I arrived in 1962 the two forces were virtually stalemated, the Communists matching their greater discipline, political mastery and fighting ability against the Government's superior weaponry.

In those early days of my Vietnam assignment I was trying to decide how to evaluate this perplexing war. How do you add up thirty minor engagements each day, almost all of them in places you've never been to, and with no substantive information to cast light on the significance of the situation? It was very quickly obvious to me that the story could not be covered from Saigon briefing rooms, despite all the multicolored arrows on the maps. The Seventh Division struck me as being as good a litmus paper of the war as any: the problems were all there, the Government had a fair chance and it was unlikely that things could go badly there and well elsewhere, or vice versa. Besides, My Tho, the division headquarters, was only forty miles south of Saigon on a good road, and we reporters could drive down, talk with friends and participate in operations.

This proximity proved invaluable on two occasions. The

first was the major battle at Ap Bac, early in 1963, when all
the reporters hopped into cars and drove down to the site,
thereby seeing what the military was trying to conceal and
getting out with the story far ahead of official channels. The
other time came in July, August and September of 1963, when
the Pentagon, which was down on me in particular because
of my pessimistic reporting of the Delta, was trying to monitor my sources. During those months the public information
officers were keeping a highly inaccurate record of where I
had been and what operations I had been out on, but since I
could slip quietly down to the Delta and talk unobserved to
old friends among the American and Vietnamese officers, this
surveillance was pointless.

By the end of September 1962 there was growing concern
over the direction of the war in the upper Delta, despite the
fact that the Seventh Division had turned in what Saigon considered impressive victories. These were six consecutive engagements in which a total of more than a hundred Vietcong
had been killed. To a large degree these victories were the
product of the infusion of American aid. Helicopters, fighter
bombers and armored personnel carriers had given a shot in
the arm to Vietnamese regulars, and nowhere was this more
noticeable than in the Seventh Division. (To a degree the
changes in the use of the helicopters mirrored the ever-
increasing American involvement. At first they were nothing
but transport aircraft designed to ferry Vietnamese troops
into battle, carrying two light machine guns for self-defense.
Then, in late 1962, the armed helicopters arrived, with four
mounted machine guns and sixteen rocket pods; they were to
escort the unarmed helicopters into battle and were not to fire
until fired on. But this was too dangerous—it gave the enemy
too many opportunities—and the rules of engagement were
further broadened. By mid-1963 the armed helicopters were
often serving as fighter planes, carrying out strafing missions.)
     But the American officers felt that the victories were de-
ceptive. When the Government troops in helicopters had come

upon the Vietcong, the guerrillas, surprised and panicky, had been flushed out and then were mowed down either by the fighter planes or by the armored personnel carriers. But the Government troops still did not use their rifles, and those U.S. advisers who had dealt with the Communists before felt that this luck could not last, that the enemy would soon change its strategy. They also realized that the new equipment was giving the men a false sense of security, and in addition they were worried because the troops were not fighting at night, were not using counterambushes against the guerrillas, were not waging psychological warfare against the enemy. All that the Government troops had done so far was to seize a momentary advantage because of the new weaponry—and they had even failed to exploit this fully.

The Americans were also worried about the unwillingness of Colonel Huynh Van Cao, the division commander, to risk casualties in battle; this was in direct contradiction to American advice. In essence, American military strategy is based on infantry offense, on the theory that their forces will in the long run expose themselves to even heavier casualties if they do not attack continually. But the Vietnamese were hesitant about this for political reasons; it was known that commanders who suffered heavy casualties incurred Diem's wrath. For that reason Cao was doing most of his killing by air and artillery; militarily he was really trying to get something for nothing.

Lastly, the Americans were disturbed by the fact that despite these successful battles there were as many guerrillas in the Seventh Division area as ever before; the Vietcong were having no trouble in recruiting or in replenishing their ranks. When I first went to My Tho I talked with some of the senior officers about this. It was true, they said, and very disturbing. At the beginning of the year there had been approximately five thousand guerrillas in the tactical zone; in the following nine months Government forces had killed an estimated five thousand Vietcong, and yet there were still approximately five thousand guerrillas in the tactical zone. This meant that there had been no real change in the basic politico-military situation in the area.

* * *

On October 3, 1962, I made my initial trip to the Delta. Because that particular excursion made a lasting impression, and because what I learned on the first military operation I accompanied was later to prove significant, I shall describe that field trip in some detail.

When I arrived I asked one of the senior officers if we were in real trouble in the Delta.

"No, we're not in bad trouble here—not yet, anyway," he said, "but we've got us a lot of war. We'll give you plenty to write about down here."

Two days earlier, elements of a crack Vietcong unit, the 514th Battalion, had ambushed a group of Catholic volunteers and had killed forty of them. Now there were reports that the 514th had been seen in western Dinh Tuong Province, and the division was about to go after them.

Since this was my first operation, Lieutenant Colonel John Paul Vann, the division adviser and one of the brightest young officers in Vietnam—he was later to become a major source of controversy—assigned me to his best unit, a battalion whose adviser was Captain Ken Good, a thirty-year-old West Pointer from Hawaii. Good was exactly what an officer in his position should be: thoughtful, intelligent, diplomatic, decisive, brave and candid. Three months later he was killed at Ap Bac by a sniper bullet, and his death hit all of us very hard.

That night the officers went over the battle plan in the briefing room. The Americans were far from satisfied with it; they felt that it left too many potential escape hatches for the enemy, and that we were covering too much territory.

I can still remember certain details of that night: shaving (so that I wouldn't have to in the morning), and a careful check on essentials like my boots, extra socks and mosquito repellent. I felt like a boy preparing for the first day of school.

I belong to a generation of Americans who were too young for Korea, and thus fortunate enough never to have experienced organized war. I had seen fighting in Katanga, and though one session with live machine guns and one visit to a field hospital make a lasting impression on the participant, I was sure that they were very different from the full-scale war I was about to see.

I shall always remember the scene at the small Tan Hiep airstrip at My Tho the next morning—that morning and the many mornings afterward when I went out on other operations. What greeted me was a miniature D-Day. The ARVN (Army of the Republic of Vietnam) forces were lined up in small squads all over the airstrip. The men looked very tiny and patient and were in full battle gear, wearing helmets and carrying American-made weapons—all designed for bigger men. Jammed into packs were bags of caked cold rice and bottles of *nuoc mam*, the rotten-smelling fish sauce they use on food. They seemed to be unusually lighthearted; except for their attire they could as easily have been traveling *en masse* to Saigon for a well-deserved furlough as going into battle.

Vietnamese soldiers are among the most likeable people in the world. Peasant-tough and peasant-shrewd, fooled by little, they evaluate what they see so simply that a bad officer never fools his men and a good officer is always loved. Now they stood at ease, some listening to their transistor radios (the great status symbol in Vietnam; transistor radios are to Vietnamese soldiers what dark glasses are to African politicians), some singing sentimental songs.

The Americans were the nervous ones, for getting the helicopters there on time, loading the troops into them and directing the copters to the right place was their responsibility. This sounds relatively simple until you discover that every rice paddy looks like every other one. Since the helicopters were a little late, I started to take pictures to keep busy, but in the midst of this activity I suddenly got the shivers; privately I hoped that the delay meant the mission had been aborted. But when I asked one of the officers about this, I suspect he understood my thought processes, for he smiled and said, ''No, there's nothing at all wrong. They're on their way. You can relax—you'll get your story.''

Suddenly the choppers appeared on the horizon, like a plague of giant grasshoppers coming out of the night. After they had landed there was no time for me to hesitate, only time to try to get into the right one, scramble aboard, hold on to my hat (the sign of a tenderfoot is that he is always losing his hat to the swirl of the helicopter blades), and follow the squad inside. These were old H-21 helicopters, tired remnants of the fifties, banana-shaped, bugged by mechanical problems, but surprisingly sturdy and durable. They were piloted by some of the toughest young men in the world, who might refer to their ships bitterly—"an accident looking for a place to happen," one officer called them—but who would take quick umbrage if any layman was critical of them.

The squad of soldiers was delighted to have me with them. In part this was probably because it meant that their Vietnamese officers would treat them a little better, but the fact that all Americans in Vietnam are regarded as mobile cigarette-vending machines might also have had something to do with my welcome. (Actually, offering cigarettes to the men was mere reciprocity, for the Vietnamese troops were usually more than willing to share their meager rations; they are among the most generous people on the face of the earth.) But beyond these considerations, I sensed the squad's pride in having someone else share this terrible war which had been going on so long, an American who would die if they died.

The soldiers kept grinning and reached out for my arm to feel the hair on it: completely smooth-skinned people, they are awed by the amount of body hair Westerners have, and one of their favorite games is to pull it. Other members of the squad were sitting on the floor of the copter, shaving; they did this by using tiny mirrors and tweezers, pulling out the few hairs on their chin one by one.

There were two ways helicopters flew over the Delta: very high or very low. We flew high for the first ten miles, then low, right above the treetops, for the last half mile or so. Pilots called this flying "map of the earth," and the advantage was very simple: the guerrillas could hear the aircraft, but because of the trees they couldn't see them until too late. It is an exciting, spine-chilling business.

We sped over startled farmers, one of the oldest professions scanned by one of the newest. Earlier in the war the

Vietcong had told the farmers to run away when they saw
helicopters; the farmers had run, and of course gunners had
drawn the wrong conclusion and fired on them. But now the
farmers had learned, and they froze whenever they saw
the aircraft. Later I was to notice that they never looked at
the helicopters; as far as they were concerned the aircraft did
not exist.

Now, as we skimmed across the paddies, our gunner suddenly opened up with a burst, and a farmer fell down. Later
the pilot asked him what he had seen, and the young man,
who was very inexperienced, claimed that he had seen the
farmer go for a gun. But the pilot and I had been watching
too, and we were sure that the farmer had done nothing, that
the youngster was nervous. The pilot reprimanded the soldier, but of course that did not save the farmer somewhere
back in the paddies.

Almost immediately after this burst of fire we landed. The
Vietnamese scrambled out into water that came up to their
shoulders. I decided it would come to my waist, jumped out
and felt it seep over my shoulders too, which meant a soggy
ham sandwich for lunch and the end of my Minox camera.
But there is one good thing about landing in a deep rich
paddy: the shock is so abrupt and complete that for the rest
of the day you won't bother trying to stay comfortable or
clean or dry.

The land spreads out flat and open, but the villages are
usually built about thirty yards inside treelines. These are the
Asian equivalent of Normandy hedgerows; they offer excellent protection, and camouflage is one of the military arts
that the Vietcong practice to perfection. When they arrive in
a hamlet for the night, they will immediately prepare perfect
defensive positions along the treeline. ("You can never tell
our Air Force that," one Vietnamese colonel said. "The Air
Force always wants to bomb the hamlet. You tell them, 'Bomb
the treeline, the VC are always in the treeline,' and they pay
no attention at all. The French were the same way; they always bombed the hamlet too.")

We started moving in small groups toward the treeline about a hundred yards away. This is the most dangerous part of an assault in the Delta, for you are out in the open and the treeline is an enemy haven. As you approach the edge of the woods, it looks like a set designed by a camouflage expert. Indeed, it may very well have been, as "The Fall of an Empire," a marvelous documentary made by CBS, can attest. Some Russian footage in this film about the Indochina war shows a bridge and two French fighter bombers flying lazily above it. Nothing moves: there is obviously nothing but a little shrubbery beside the bridge. Then the planes pass on, and suddenly half the bridge seems to come alive; a battalion of Vietminh has been hiding right in front of the camera. This is a particularly chilling shot from a chilling film.

Moving in a rice paddy is a bit like trying to run in one of your own dreams—slowly, your feet stuck, feeling exposed and all alone. I found myself curiously winded, my throat was absolutely dry and I felt terribly tall, easily the best target in the paddy. Captain Good and another American, Captain Gary Werner, a PIO (public information officer), were split up farther down the line. It is not a good idea for Americans to bunch up, for they make too good a target; similarly, it is always wise to stay away from the radio man in such situations, for the Vietcong will often fire their first burst at him, hoping to get an ARVN officer.

As we approached the treeline, we began to hear firing off to our right. In combat all firing—at least at first—sounds close. I ducked down in the paddy again, and then looked around; all I could see was one of the cheerful little Asians who had felt the hair on my arm. In the helicopter he had seemed like just another faceless Vietnamese, his life as casually and momentarily entwined with mine as a cab driver's might be; now, suddenly, he was a sergeant responsible for my life or death, and for the lives of the other ten men in the squad.

In that first moment of panic, followed by embarrassment and shame about the panic, I made the discovery that eventually comes to some Americans in Vietnam—that this really was a Vietnamese war. For though the Americans were al-

ways talking about it being a Vietnamese war, in many ways
it was not. Americans arrived in Saigon to find other Americans; they went to an American PX and American movies;
they rode in buses with other Americans, and flew with other
Americans in the field in American helicopters; often they
slept in American quarters with fellow Americans, eating,
more often than not, at American messes. This was the pattern for all but the small percentage of American soldiers
assigned to battalions or in a combat-related role, and up to
now it had been true for me. Now, all at once, the world
reversed itself: certain Vietnamese were responsible for my
life, and other Vietnamese had orders to kill me. I had spent
more than three weeks in Vietnam and had to come to this
paddy to learn where the war began.

We advanced, and reached the hamlet without encounter-
ing direct enemy fire. Once inside, we heard firing in the
background. There was no resistance in our hamlet and we
spread out quickly, ready to serve as a blocking force in case
other units drove the Vietcong toward us. There were only a
few women in the village, and several children—in Vietnam
the children were everywhere—and one goateed old man
looking like a Confucian sage or Ho Chi Minh. There were
no young men in the village; there never were, I was told. At
the first sound of the helicopters and battle they always fled
because they were automatically suspected of being Communists and at the very least would be taken back to My Tho.
The war shuttled back and forth for the young men; they hid
from the Communists too, but this was harder because the
enemy was always there, slipping in at night before there was
time to hide. Later I learned that during the morning three
young men had been caught in a field as a helicopter landed
and had made the mistake of running. One was immediately
brought down by automatic-weapons fire; the other two
stopped in their tracks. They were not, it turned out, Vietcong at all. They were simply two poor peasants from the
village, one an unemployed man with four children, the other
a widower so poor he could not even afford to marry again.

Now in the village one woman told the Vietnamese captain
that there had been no Vietcong in the area. The captain,

nine years in his rank—paradoxically, an indication that he
was probably a very good officer; those who were promoted
quickly were the political ones—did not believe her. There
was too much tension, he said, and he asked her a few more
questions about the village and its income, and when the
Vietcong were last seen. Where were all the young men? All
the young men, the woman said, had decided to go to the
next village because they feared the Vietcong were coming.
By now the captain was convinced that the woman was lying
and that she was probably the wife of a guerrilla; he told one
of his staff officers to guard her so that she could not com-
municate with the other women, and went quietly to another
hut. There he began to chip away at another woman's story,
and soon he found holes in both accounts.

The interpreter was impressed by the captain. "He is very
good at it," he told me later. "He starts talking about the
crops and about his own problems—what his wife is demanding from him, the difficulty of living in the big city of My
Tho, how he would like to come back to the country because
there is nothing in the city like a buffalo ride. For the first
five minutes he never mentions the war. In the end, they
always talk."

The second woman did talk. A platoon of guerrillas had
been in the village a day before, she said. They had been
very confident and had held a party for the villagers; there
had been much excitement over it. They said that they had
just scored a major victory, having killed forty of the American imperialists (this was apparently a reference to the ambush of the Catholic volunteer company, in which forty
Vietnamese had been killed). Then the Vietcong had exhib-
ited some of the arms they had captured, and the villagers
saw that they were American weapons.

One of the Vietcong had started serving tea, and another
had given a sermon in the form of a fable. In it there were
poor people who had no land and wanted to be free, but they
had no guns; there were rich foreigners who had guns, but
who were against the people; the foreigners gave these guns
to bad people who were their puppets, and they paid the puppets; but the puppets would not fight, and so the foreigners

themselves had to fight. But the poor people were brave and captured the guns, and now the weapons would be used against the foreigners and the puppets, and many of them would die because of it.

As he left the hut the captain cursed the woman who had talked, loudly and in rough Vietnamese; this was to guard her against reprisals, the interpreter said, since she had been good to us and there would be no troops there that night to protect her.

"It sounds like a pretty effective party the Vietcong threw," I said. We spoke in French; like many Vietnamese he felt he could speak more freely to the reporters in that language.

"Yes," he said, "the parties are very good. We do not give parties like that."

I asked what would happen to the first woman the captain had interrogated.

"What can we do?" he said. "She is one of them. She is a bad one. But taking her away will do no good; it will just make the others angrier. It is too late to work on her, and if we take her away, her children will definitely go over to the enemy. Do they teach about this at Fort Bragg?" he asked bitterly.

Those moments gave me a quick sense of what the war was about, but like many lessons it was obscured at the time. The sounds of battle were near and very real, and they were what I had come to hear, not an argument with an old lady whose teeth were stained with betel-nut juice. I was wishing we would move on to the battle—or at least near enough to see it, without being too close for danger. There was action less than half a mile away, and Captain Good was obviously anxious to move the battalion in that direction. But there were no orders, and he and the Vietnamese captain were both irritable. The Vietnamese were punctilious about sticking to plans instead of following their instincts.

Already by eleven o'clock the sun was punishing, and I brought the brim of my jungle hat down over my eyes. We cut a few coconuts and sipped the milk. There was never any fear of going thirsty in the Delta; the water was impure, but coconuts made life and the war a bit more bearable. We sat and watched the T-28's air-strike the nearby village. Later we found out that a Vietnamese Ranger company had been brutally ambushed at this village. They had landed in helicopters about a hundred yards from the treeline, where a unit of the 514th was perfectly camouflaged. Normally the unit would have opened up on the helicopters as they came in, but this time, with an impressive display of battle discipline, it held fire until the Rangers were about thirty yards from the treeline, their feet glued to the mucky bottom.

It was a swift little slaughter. Before they could even return a shot the Rangers suffered heavy casualties; a platoon was virtually wiped out in an instant. Even after recovery they had little option but to keep their heads down behind the dike walls and fire back as best they could. The only thing that allowed them to move at all was an almost perfect air strike by the T-28's, but this did not come until they had been under deadly fire for two hours. Finally Captain Jim Torrence, the American adviser with the company, sensed that the Vietcong were slowly slipping out, keeping their exodus covered with automatic weapons. By noon they had left, and the Rangers moved into the treeline. There were no bodies—not even any expended cartridges. The enemy was always cool, never leaving their dead behind; in part this was a matter of pride and in honor of their dead, but its purpose was also to shake the morale of the Government forces, to give them no satisfaction as to how much had been accomplished, so that there would always be doubt about any possible victories. Thirty Rangers had been killed and a few more wounded; virtually the entire platoon of an elite unit had been wiped out, an unusually high casualty rate for a Government-initiated action.

But almost obscured by the immediate sorrow and bitterness of this reversal was the fact that the guerrillas had changed their tactics: one small element of an enemy battalion had stood and fought. This was to prove of immense significance in the months to follow, for it marked the end of the post–build-up honeymoon in the Delta; it meant that the enemy had adjusted to the new heliborne tactics. But of course at the moment no one realized this; in our battalion we were only irritated by the failure to get in on the fight. For the rest of the day we played the game—which is to say, we chased the Vietcong unit. Overhead two light spotter planes kept circling in hopes of detecting the now-elusive guerrillas, or at least of drawing fire. But the Vietcong, knowing that a superior force was after them, were not anxious to make contact with the Government now.

We had a quick lunch in the village. One of the Vietnamese officers shared his food with me; there was little, but in the Delta sun one loses his appetite. The interpreter said that the captain had checked his company commanders and platoon leaders to make sure that the troops were behaving properly, and that they had paid for everything they had taken in the village. The conduct of ARVN troops in villages had become one of the major conflicts between the Government and the population. Too often the troops had stolen chickens or molested the people; in contrast, the well-disciplined guerrillas would work beside the villagers in the field, and they did not steal from them. It was generally agreed that the presence of American advisers had helped to keep the troops in line; however, Neil Sheehan had recently accompanied a special psychological-warfare team known as the Political Action Group, whose main purpose was to convert the population, and they had gone through a village, he recalled, handing out Government leaflets and stealing ducks.

After lunch we started eastward, moving along a main canal. Now I learned the special agony of pursuit in the wet season. The Delta is nothing but an intricate series of narrow canals linked with larger ones. There are no bridges as we know them; there are simply rounded bamboo poles which stretch from one side to another. The Vietnamese, who are all agile, had no trouble in crossing, but for an American, particularly this American somewhat out of condition and unsure of himself, it wasn't so simple. Four times that day I fell into canals to the delight of my comrades, and I soon forgot about the armed enemy we were chasing. By the end of the day I had mastered the trick—momentum at any cost—and was able to cross without incident. The Vietnamese troops took my new success with good grace, although I could tell they felt deprived of the diversion I had been providing. Soaked though I was, I failed to match the record of my colleague, Mert Perry of *Time*, who is the all-time champion Delta wader. Mert is a very heavy-set, enormously likeable man who simply is not built for bamboo. "I fell off so many times one day that it was like a USO show," he told me later. "Each time we got to a canal the entire company would run up to watch me cross. One burst of a BAR would have wiped them all out."

That afternoon, as we walked endlessly in the sun, two things made a deep impression on me: the difficulty of chasing guerrillas in that terrain, and the agony of the war for the peasants. Even the land which wasn't swampy or boggy was lush and rich, and an entire company could have been hiding within ten yards of any spot we passed. The canals, too, provide cover, for the Vietcong carry reeds for straws, and can slip under water and breathe for hours, suffering only from the leeches. The whole countryside is a natural hiding place: rich land mixed with thick brush, deep canals, sugar-cane groves, mangrove swamps, coconut groves. Unless the population was willing to tell the troops where the Vietcong had hidden, the Government had a nearly impossible task—and at that time the population wasn't telling; at best, the peasants were on the fence. One could hardly blame them; they did not like or trust the Government, and they were not going to risk their lives to inform for a regime which could not protect them.

The four-hour hunt that afternoon reeked of futility even to a novice like myself. The troops and officers obviously knew it too; from noon on there was usually little contact in this war. In those days it was largely a matter of following a script: one company reached its objective, another marched to its target—maneuvers were only carried out to please the people back at the CP (command post) with their arrows and their maps. The hopelessness of all this lowered the morale of the troops. About the only time the pattern varied in those days was when the Vietcong decided to shift the tempo.

Sometimes, after staying one step ahead of the sheriff all afternoon, they would spring an ambush at twilight, just outside the Government base, hitting quickly when the ARVN were tired and lazy and dejected, and then slip off.

Once during that long afternoon there was a brief glimpse of the enemy, about five hundred yards away; there was a quick burst of fire, but almost immediately the guerrillas slipped into a cluster of trees. As usual, the enemy had set the pace and determined the time, the place and the odds. It would take a major Government initiative and offensive to change all of this, and so far it was not forthcoming.

The other thing that struck the novice observer was the way the war shuttled back and forth for the peasants: they endured the Government troops during the day, the Vietcong at night. In all my time in Vietnam I never grew accustomed to the resultant sights. That afternoon, as we walked through the village where most of the fighting had taken place, a weeping peasant came out and stood in front of the charred remains of his hut. In one hand he held a dead piglet, in the other a dead baby. His grief was silent; I could hear nothing. For a moment one of our lieutenants broke from the line, but the Vietnamese captain saw him and gestured him back. There was nothing to be done, nothing that could be said.

About a hundred yards away we came upon a dead peasant lying in the yard of his hut with a poncho spread over him. Two huts farther on, a desperately frightened old man of eighty was genuflecting in front of the American and Vietnamese officers and telling them that he had never heard of the Vietcong. How many times had this old man had to tell Government troops that he knew no Vietcong? How many times had he had to tell the Vietminh or Vietcong that he knew no Government troops? "The war," a young Vietnamese said to me bitterly later, "only lasts a lifetime."

The sun was at its hottest about three o'clock; then the weather broke and there was a feeling that the going would be downhill from then on. My uniform, which had been soaked and then dried in the sun over and over again, finally seemed permanently dry. By now the only sign that there had been any fighting were occasional dead catfish floating in the canals, killed earlier in the day by mortars or bombs. After crossing the main canal and joining up with another battalion which had been covering the far side, we sat down and took a break. Trooper after trooper came by with a live chicken strapped to his pack. The American officer attached to this unit followed, and we looked accusingly at him. He caught our glances and said defensively, "What the hell can you do? They go all day and they don't get anything in the way of chow, and they put up with all this"—he gestured around him—"I can't tell them no. They've got little enough pleasure as it is." He was right, of course, but our officers were wondering what the reaction was in the village from which the chickens had been stolen, as well as the effect on the morale of the troops in our battalion who had been denied chickens.

After the break we marched single file for three more miles, until we met the rest of the division. It had been a rough day and the troops were tired and hot; about thirty ARVN had been killed, two helicopters had been shot down and one American gunner killed. The latter would give the guerrillas a boost; it was relatively early in the days of the helicopters, and victories over these craft helped to prove to their own people and to the peasantry that they could stand up to what they called "the iron birds."

At large cost we had found and hurt the 514th—to what extent, no one was sure, but the estimates were of at least ten dead. The operation was over; it was just past six o'clock. "Time to turn the country over to the VC," one young American officer said sardonically. The American advisers were bitterly opposed to this kind of office-hours warfare. They wanted to harass the enemy continuously, not just by day, in order to exploit the superior weaponry and potentially superior mobility the Government had. Theoretically it was easy to agree; pursuit seemed logical and militarily valid. But I was tired and worn out, and I was also glad to be alive. I would have made a very proper ARVN officer.

We sat around, waiting for trucks, and some logistical genius brought over warm beer. The American officers asked

me what I thought, and I told them I was more interested in
what they thought. Well, they said, this was what the war was
like—hot and frustrating and unrewarding, days filled with
violations of even the most obvious kind of military common
sense, days spent hoping desperately for the break which
would make the enemy fight.

Back at the base I learned just how much of a tenderfoot
I was. My neck was red, but my feet were a dismal pasty
white; they looked like the feet of the dead. I had come to
My Tho with just one set of footgear, and I had to wear
soaking-wet boots for the next five days. From then on when
I went into the field I brought two pairs of boots, combat;
one pair of shoes, civilian; and one pair of shoes, shower.

That night Lieutenant Colonel Vann and some of the officers recapped the operation. They were concerned about the
fact that there had been such a good chance to knock out a
unit of the 514th, that the knockout hadn't been executed, and
that the psychological reaction of the peasants in the area
where the battle had taken place couldn't have been anything
but unfavorable.

There was much more to worry about, we learned later.
The operation I have described took place on October 6, and
until then the Seventh Division had been working well. But
unbeknownst to all of us, that day really marked the beginning of the end in the Delta. President Diem, concerned about
the loss of the Ranger platoon and what he considered to be
excessive losses in Government-initiated actions, called Colonel Cao to Saigon. That night the American advisers of the
two offending units were summoned to Cao's headquarters
and they patiently went over the action with Cao. Early the
next morning Cao set out for Saigon with a well-rehearsed
explanation. According to Cao's account (told to Vann, and
later confirmed to me by Vietnamese sources), he arrived at
the Palace before breakfast. All morning he watched people
file in and out of the President's office. Lunch came, but not
for him. Finally, late in the afternoon, he was summoned by
the President.

Cao never had a chance to give his carefully prepared briefing; instead, Diem began one of those monologues for which

he was becoming increasingly well known. Cao was reminded—as if this was necessary—that there was a good
chance he would soon be general. But certain problems had
arisen recently: he was taking far too many casualties, more
than any other field commander. He would have to be more
careful; he was listening too much to his American advisers.
Diem further issued a very simple warning: if Cao wanted a
promotion, he would have to be more prudent. This threat
came at a time when the Americans were working desperately
to make Cao more aggressive, but of course he obeyed Diem.

VII

I returned to My Tho five days later, this time as much to stay out of Saigon and its demeaning bickering between the Americans and Ngos, and between the American mission and the American reporters, as to get out a story. A trip in the field offered both a chance to find out about the enemy and the war and also an opportunity to be treated as a fellow citizen by one's contemporaries. The American officers in a place like My Tho were extremely well informed, honorably motivated, and intrigued by the problems of this war; in addition, once you had walked through the paddies with them you were treated as an equal. This contrasted sharply with the antagonism of American officials in Saigon at the time. No reporter should expect to be beloved, but the atmosphere in the capital was heavy with suspicion and intimations of recrimination.

In the field a reporter received the kind of answers he deserved, but he had to prove, first himself, then the sincerity of his interest and his ability to protect a source. If a reporter shared the American advisers' food and dangers, and let them know that he was aware of their problems and responsibilities, he would gain far more than their confidence. He would also acquire a tremendous head start over nonresident correspondents, for not only would he be more trusted, but he would also come to know the officers' point of view and be able to assess the changes in their individual outlook on the progress of the war. Captain X, on arrival an almost professional optimist, will be seen changing from optimism to almost automatic pessimism; Captain Y, considered the most analytical and detached of the officers, will start becoming truly alarmed over the developments. It is these individual changes that will give an indication of the broader changes.

My next trip was on a mission to Dinh Tuong Province. A friend in the operations room warned me, "Bring your suntan lotion. It won't be anything but a long hot walk tomorrow." The American officers were disturbed; for months, with some measure of success, they had organized a joint planning group which emphasized traditional staff techniques and the use of military intelligence. Before that time the tendency had been for helter-skelter dashes into the countryside, operations based more on whether the local province chief was a friend of the division commander than on whether any of the enemy were in the area. Such operations might not produce any dead Vietcong, but they might encourage recalcitrant villagers to pay their taxes to local officials.

Now tactics had reverted to the old methods again. "They've just thrown away six months of work," one of the operations officers said. The Government would be operating in terrain where it *might* find the enemy, but there were other areas where enemy companies could be almost definitely pinpointed. In addition, even if the enemy were sighted, "that battle plan is almost guaran-damn-teed to let them escape to the last."

Next day's operation was a farce: short marches, long stops, interspersed with shorter marches and even longer stops. I was with Captain Raymond Whittaker of Sumter, South Carolina, a Negro officer and a patient man. At the start he was as gentle as he could be about the day ahead, but he gave little impression of hope. We landed in open fields from helicopters and made the brief, tense walk to the first village. But we found there only a few women and a vast amount of Viet-

cong propaganda material. Whittaker listened for several
minutes while his Vietnamese counterpart translated the
propaganda sheets in detail. "It says the Vietcong are going
to win the war," Whittaker finally said laconically. Then some
of the men brought over an old woman who was questioned
briefly and who told us that one hundred Vietcong had been
in the village the night before. She pointed in the alleged
direction in which the alleged guerrillas had vanished. "It's
always one hundred VC, and they always went thataway,"
Whittaker said.

The troops sniffed through the village, picking up what
they could. The atmosphere was relaxed and seemed to have
nothing in common with the tension of my first mission a few
days before. The women even gave the soldiers some pineapples. This could have been dangerous. A few months earlier, troops had been treated well in another village and the
women had given them little cakes. Eight of the men had
eaten them and had become violently ill two hours later.
Thanks to helicopters they were quickly evacuated, their
stomachs pumped out and their lives saved. Colonel Pham
Van Dong, their commander, had thought this very funny.
"So when the population is very good to you and gives you
all the cakes, you must perhaps be a little more careful," he
said.

The village was our first "goose egg"—the term for any
mission which draws a blank, and referring to the zeros on
the map—and we moved on to our next objective. En route
the troops were bunched up, and a sense of sloppiness pervaded the outfit; there was no point man, no flanking unit,
no search along the line of march, nothing but a methodical
crunching ahead. I looked at the troops and then at Whittaker, but he gave me a distant I-don't-ask-about-the-skeletons-
in-your-closet-buddy-so-don't-ask-about-mine look, and turned
away. At about eleven-thirty, when we reached our second
objective—a village by the river—the troops immediately settled down for lunch. They set up no defensive perimeter, and
their single recoilless rifle was pointed toward the command
post. A Vietnamese friend of mine, a photographer, came
over and I asked him what the troops thought about this mis-

sion. "The troops told me I should have stayed home and saved myself the walk," he answered. "They say they have been here many times before and know all the old women by now, and that they will never find the Vietcong here. They say they have come here often enough to be fathers of the little children. But there are worse places to be, and now they will have lunch." The men were already setting up their portable cooking gear—one soldier making a charcoal fire while another cleaned a chicken and a third prepared rice.

My strongest memories of the ARVN soldier are, first, of his courage and ability to suffer pain without wincing, and second, of him eating. The troops cherished food greatly; it was one of their few pleasures, and they were willing to risk their lives for it. Horst Faas later told me of a particularly harrowing experience he endured in early 1963 in the swamplands of the Camau peninsula. There the Vietcong control the countryside and the population; they even tax the charcoal industry. The Vietnamese battalion to which Horst was attached had been operating in this enemy country for several days, and everyone was understandably nervous. On one patrol, which lasted for several hours, they would not even let Horst click his camera because it might alert the Vietcong. After several hours of silence, highly unusual for the Vietnamese, they reached a small village deserted by every living thing save a very healthy pig. For five days the troops had eaten nothing but dried shrimp, and so of course the pig was immediately captured. Then the patrol set off for its base through the same tortuous route it had just covered. They were all terrified of an ambush, and the same silence was observed on the way home—by everyone except the pig. The pig was gagged, but he managed to continue to grunt just as loudly. Someone suggested slitting the pig's throat, but the sergeant pointed out that the meat might be ruined by the hot sun by the time they reached the base. Next they blindfolded the animal, on the theory that it would think it was nighttime and would fall asleep. But this worked no better, and so all the way back through enemy territory they went, the pig grunting away the whole time, "everyone hating that animal,'' according to Horst, ''and looking forward to eating it, as no one has ever looked forward to eating pork.'' To everyone's relief and amazement they got back to the base safely, and there was much excitement about the feast to come. But suddenly the company commander arrived on the scene, and the troops stood at attention while the officer inspected them. Then he said, ''You have captured a Communist pig. Very good. You are to be congratulated,'' and took away the pig; that night the officers had a pork dinner. ''All armies are the same,'' said Horst.

''We will be here a long time today,'' the Vietnamese photographer said now. ''The men say that their captain does not like to fight. They say he is a political officer, but they do not mind because it means that not so many of them have to die. So they take it easy.'' Take it easy they did: from noon until three they took a siesta. It always staggered the Americans; again and again, combat operations came to an almost complete halt at midday. We used to hope that the Vietcong observed this tradition too.

It was hard to get any sense of war at moments like these in the field. These troops, sprawling casually in front of me, their weapons carelessly tossed aside, some sound asleep, could be as brave as any man could ask. But as soldiers they were only as good as their leadership, and too often their officers were sloppy and indifferent. The troops themselves were mostly peasants, not city boys from Saigon raised in an atmosphere of insidious comfort and affluence. Instead they had grown up knowing nothing but war; from the time they were born they knew that they would have to fight for one side or the other. In the Vietcong they would make no money, but would probably become deeply committed to its cause; by fighting for the Government they would at least draw some pay and could spend more time with their families.

They were not the best-paid warriors in the world; though they were the allies of the richest nation on earth, and fighting a war which deeply affected that affluent nation, they made less than Saigon's taxi drivers—perhaps fifteen dollars a month, plus a small allowance for their wives and children. They were inordinately cheerful about life; because they were Buddhists and because of their lack of knowledge of anything but war, they were fatalistic about life and death. If a soldier lost a friend he wept—not for his friend but for himself. They carried weapons made for men twice their size and never complained. They passively accepted fraudulent operations and corrupt officers. Their ability to bear suffering was beyond the comprehension of any Westerner; I saw many dying Vietnamese, but I never saw one cry.

The ARVN troops loved sentimental songs and sang them constantly in the field. One, a sort of Vietnamese "Lili Marlene," was a particular favorite. Madame Nhu eventually banned it because it was not sufficiently anti-Communist but that didn't stop them, and the American advisers and correspondents learned the words and sang along with them. This haunting ballad, called "Rainy Night on the Frontier," goes something like this in English:

> When the sky is turning rose
> And the jungle path is emptied of shadows
> And you change into your warm clothes,
> Remembering those in the far distance
> The young man at the front line is thinking of the one at
>   home
> Loving the color of the souvenir sent him at the battle
>   front,
> And his heart is full of love.
> But there are many winds and rains in his way.

All Vietnamese dote on children, and part of the reason why the soldiers liked the American officers who supervised their units was because the Americans fell in love with Vietnamese kids. In turn, the U.S. officers admired the incredible patience and bravery and willingness to endure that the ARVN troops possessed. One time I talked to an American lieutenant who had just returned from an operation. That day he had lost a squad leader who had served in the Vietnamese Army for eighteen years. "Can you imagine," he said, "eighteen years of this, eighteen years of going out every day on operations and coming back at night, and then finally buying the farm one day. Good God!'' The lieutenant was no more than twenty-four years old.

The Vietnamese soldiers were small by American standards, a little over five feet tall and weighing perhaps one hundred pounds, but they were wiry and looked like little wrestlers. They could walk for miles, and their feet were like iron. Because their pay was so small, they had become accustomed to life without money. Their wives near headquarters would sometimes take unexpended cartridges from their husbands and barter them in the market for food. It was a short-sighted way of surviving, of course, because the bullets inevitably ended up in the hands of the Vietcong, but the Vietnamese peasant has never been able to afford the luxury of thinking ahead.

That day I ate at the officers' mess and tasted *nuoc mam* for the first time. This staple in the Vietnamese diet is a sauce made out of the oils of rotting fish, and it is used on everything. The Vietnamese let fish rot, then press down on them with weights and squeeze out the oils of decay; what emerges is *nuoc mam*. There is a great competition among Vietnamese towns to see which can produce the best sauce. It smells just as bad as you would think it does, but surprisingly, it really does add to the taste of the food. Many Americans have grown to like its tangy flavor, and for the troops it is a main source of protein.

The Vietnamese captain, a round-faced little man who could have been twenty-one or forty-five and would look the same until one day he would suddenly look seventy-five, was delighted to have me eat with him: here was a new listener to his speech. He gave what you might call The Number One Anti-Communist Speech for Visiting Americans. Obviously he was experienced at it; if there was ever a discourse designed to tell the Americans what they wanted to hear—a Vietnamese art subsequently being practiced with considerable finesse by Nguyen Khanh—his discourse was it. The Communists were terrorists who controlled the people only by murdering them, but now the Government was protecting the people, who were rallying to the Government, and victory would follow victory. And so on; the lunch went on too, and it was followed by the siesta.

The speech had been long, the lunch had been longer, and the day was hot; eventually everyone fell asleep but Whittaker and myself. He asked me if I had seen any of those big victories which the captain had just described. I said that I hadn't, and Whittaker said neither had the captain.

At three o'clock the siesta ended and the American advisers, restless and irritable, got ready to move out. But all afternoon we stayed in that same little village while the Americans grew more and more tense and the Vietnamese became more and more serene. We drank tea, we ate coconuts—and we did not move. "What do the troops say?" I asked the photographer. He came back in a few minutes. "The troops say we will spend the night in the field. They are not surprised at what has happened; they say it could be worse—because it is not raining. One of them says this is better than the mountains because there are no coconuts and chickens there, and it is much warmer here. I think they are all very tired of this war."

We ate a second meal in that same village, which increased the tension. Finally, after dinner, we set off again. After cutting through some tree clumps we reached a nearby river; there we boarded landing craft and motored upstream about ten miles. Trucks were supposed to meet us at a small village, but they didn't arrive. As usual the troops were right; we spent the night in the field.

A few of us stayed in the house of the district chief. We slept on flat wooden beds, and fought the hard surface and the mosquitoes until dawn. In retrospect the worst thing about the whole operation was that we were more tired by our night of rest than we were by our day of chasing the enemy. When I returned the next morning to My Tho and talked to the other American officers, I discovered that other units in the operation had behaved in the same way.

* * *

Ten days later, from My Tho again, I went out with the Rangers and my friend Captain Jim Torrence. On this occasion armed helicopters escorted us into battle for the first time. Carrying four .30-caliber machine guns and sixteen rockets each, they gave us a vast sense of security. After we had landed we walked into what sounded like a furious battle. Firing seemed to be coming from everywhere; the Rangers were opening up with everything as we moved across the paddy. Suddenly, right in front of me, I saw an old farmer behind a water buffalo calmly working his field. A fierce battle appeared to be going on all around him; helicopters were still firing rockets overhead, troops were moving across the paddy directly toward him, and bullets were whizzing all around. But that farmer and buffalo kept plodding back and forth, never looking up, never acknowledging our presence. "That's some farmer," I said to Torrence.

Torrence seemed equally stoic in the face of all that fire. I was crouched over in the paddy, but Torrence was standing straight up, calmly surveying the field like a football coach watching practice. Why, Torrence is as brave as that damn farmer, I thought, he's the bravest captain I know; why can't I be that brave? Though we were totally exposed, Torrence only looked angry, and when I slipped over to talk to him I found out why. He didn't think there was any answering fire; he suspected that the Rangers had become jittery because of the fire from the armed helicopters, and that they were blasting away at nothing. I told him he was wrong; I could hear enemy fire. But Torrence was so sure (West Point men, I thought, were always so damn sure of themselves) that after a while I began to crouch a little less—until several soldiers brought back a wounded man, badly hit below the shoulder. "There," I told Torrence, "there's your theory shot to hell," and immediately returned to my coward's crouch. Torrence nodded calmly and said that he'd be willing to bet that the man had been hit from the rear by one of his own men. Two hours later we checked the medical report and found out that Torrence was right.

We found few VC that day, but we saw plenty of traces of them. We found fresh footprints in the mud, Vietcong handkerchiefs (with an embroidered Vietcong flag in the corner), guitars and songbooks; we even found three VC girls. We stumbled on the latter in a small hut at about ten in the morning. They were busy eating, and of course there were no men in sight. Lieutenant Doan Thi, the company commander, asked them their names; they had no names, they said. He asked where the Vietcong had gone; they had never heard of the Vietcong. At this Lieutenant Thi became very angry; the troops had found a great deal of Communist propaganda in the village, and he was convinced that some kind of rally had been interrupted by our strike. "These are VC girls," he said. "The VC can't get young people to come to meetings, so they use these young girls as entertainment." They didn't look like my kind of entertainment; perhaps I had been spoiled by the *Saigonnaises* with their long hair and their fancy native dress, the *ao dais*—or perhaps I lacked the revolutionary spirit. The girls looked thin and rough to me.

Lieutenant Thi called over one of his soldiers who came from that vicinity, and asked him to talk to the girls. After a few minutes the soldier said that their speech was slightly different from the peasants' who lived there, and that they did not seem to know much about the area. "The Vietcong bring along girls like these because it is good for the morale of the troops and because it helps them in recruiting," Lieutenant Thi said. He pointed at the girls. "They would be willing to kill you," he said to me. "They are convinced that you are going to rape them."

After leaving the village we came upon a couple of crude signs, the kind which were popping up increasingly in Vietnam: *If the Americans stay here, we the Vietcong become very angry,* Lieutenant Thi translated the first; the second, at the beginning of a wide expanse of paddy fields, said in English: *Please to let the Americans go first.*

We walked on. Lieutenant Thi said that Torrence and I had to go first because it would mean loss of face if we did not, but that he would walk ahead with us. He was in a particularly good mood; did I know Francois Sully, the *Newsweek* journalist, he asked. I said that I did. Well, Sully was quite a good correspondent, he said; he had been out with him

several times. What did I think of Sully? But before I could
answer he asked what I thought of his country, and before I
could answer *that*, he told me that he had been to America.
He liked Fort Benning. Marvelous PX—bigger than any store
in Hong Kong. Had he been to Hong Kong? No, but he was
sure. Unfortunately, the food was too heavy in America. "You
Americans eat greasy food," he said accusingly. Still, he was
very fond of the United States; he had driven from one end
of the country to the other, and it was very pretty.

"What about the Vietcong?" I asked.

"Well, the Vietcong are not so stupid, are they?" he said.
But then, enjoying his role of interviewing an American reporter, he wanted to know my opinion of Vietnamese girls,
and thereafter our conversation deteriorated.

Later, as we walked along, I asked Thi what he would do
if there was no war. He said he would sleep late, and then
perhaps he would be a painter. He thought it would be nice
to be an artist and paint pictures of pretty girls.

We never saw the enemy that day. When we returned to
the base we learned that a handful of guerrillas had been
captured by Ken Good's unit, but that four of his ARVN had
been killed. It had been a typical day in the war.

That night we went back to My Tho; we were all soaking wet
and tired and a little disappointed. We sat in the bar in the
officers' mess at My Tho talking about the war as if it were
our own small private property. One of the officers did an
imitation of the U.S. civilian's attitude about "that war in
Vietnam—wherever Vietnam is, anyway." I told the group
about a letter that Mal Browne, the AP reporter, had received
from a firm in Greeneville, Tennessee, addressed to him in
"Saigon, French Indonesia." Malcolm had had a bad day
and he banged out an angry reply noting that American lives
were being lost every day in Vietnam, and that perhaps if
American citizens took the trouble to interest themselves in
this area of the world, the war might end some day. Later
Mal showed a copy of the letter to me and asked if I thought
there had been any point in sending it. I said that it was a

hell of a letter, but it was too bad he had spelled Greeneville "Greenville."

A helicopter pilot told us that he had been home on leave recently and that he was on his way back the day after a helicopter had been shot down in Vietnam. At the airport terminal, a prosperous-looking businessman saw his uniform and asked him what he did. The officer replied that he was a helicopter pilot, and the businessman asked where he was stationed. The pilot said, "Saigon." "Well," said the businessman, "that's good. You can thank your lucky star you're not out in that Vietnam."

There was an atmosphere of camaraderie in the bar that night, for we were all participants in this private little war in Vietnam. We were all obsessed by it, and awed by the vast ignorance, even indifference, about it in the United States. We felt that the showdown of a generation was going on here, and though my paper cared, and some readers cared, not very many other people seemed to care. To us it seemed an unqualified war. It had the elements of danger and sense of loss of other wars, as well as some qualities peculiarly its own; as one veteran of World War II and Korea said, "The trouble with this war is that there's too much time to think about it."

There were times when we participants felt especially forsaken—like at the pathetic, brief services for the military dead that were held at the Tan Son Nhut airport in Saigon when the body was about to be shipped home. There would be just a few American friends on hand, and perhaps some Vietnamese; a chaplain would read a few words, often drowned out by the noise at the airport. Somehow such ceremonies made our grief seem solitary; in those days it was a very lonely war.

The American field advisers and many of the reporters had a good deal in common; for instance, I was twenty-eight when I arrived in Vietnam, and like many of the officers I was a volunteer. It was basically a captain's war; captains were usually battalion advisers, the best and most important assignment in Vietnam. They envied me my freedom to move around and sample the fighting in other areas, and the fact that I would not automatically be transferred after a year; had they not had wives and families many would have volunteered for another tour of duty. Like myself they had changed from a state of almost total ignorance about Vietnam to almost total immersion in it; now this war and this place were all they cared about. Most of us were six or seven or eight when the Japanese bombed Pearl Harbor; some of the enlisted men were not even born then. Thus, we were ten or eleven or twelve when the war ended, and three years older still during the Berlin airlift. When the North Koreans crossed the Thirty-eighth Parallel we were in high school, and we were finishing college when that war ended. In our lifetime the enemy had become clearly identifiable, and many of the officers and reporters felt strongly and instinctively that Vietnam was the place to draw the line.

Our generation of Americans had been raised in relatively prosperous years in America. Too young during the Depression and World War II, we had little sense of deprivation and catastrophe, unlike the Europeans of our age. I remember the relationship in the Congo between Georgi Fediachin, the Tass man, and Ungeheuer of Reuters, a German. They loathed each other, but they were fascinated by World War II and the common past they shared, and when they were drinking they would seek each other out and tell each other that they were the only ones who really understood war, that in their countries, it had taken the lives of one in four people. But when the American officers—having grown up in a prosperous and powerful nation—first arrived in Vietnam, they had a remarkable confidence in what they could accomplish. They felt, for instance, that the white men before them had failed because they were colonialists; *they* were not colonialists, and this, they were sure, would immediately be apparent to the Vietnamese.

But of course the Americans were doomed to disappointment; in the postcolonial years it was almost impossible for a Western country even to equal the lesser accomplishments of the old colonial power under the law of the governor general. So, from the high hopes many of the Americans would sink into a kind of cynicism as the Asian reality set in; then, if they were good men—and many of them were extraordinarily good—they would concentrate on their specific jobs and accept the difficult realities of trying to do the best possible day's work under extremely complicated conditions.

These officers were sympathetic to the world around them: they liked and respected the Vietnamese, and by the end of their tour many of them could speak the language well and were proud of their knowledge and understanding of the country. On the whole they were a remarkable group; of course they had all been to college or West Point, and with the Army's help many of them were working toward additional degrees. Far more than most of their contemporaries, they had a sense of America's responsibilities and problems, and they were committed to one of the most pressing problems of our time. In general they were more alert, better motivated and more sophisticated than the average American of their generation, they adjusted easily to their surroundings and they never lost their sense of humor.

One of my dispatches reflecting the light-heartedness of which Americans are capable even in times of stress was filed on April 5, 1963, from Bac Lieu, the seat of the Twenty-first Division in the lower Delta:

BAC LIEU—This is no ordinary Vietnamese town in the Mekong Delta. One can tell that the moment he lands at the dusty airstrip and sees the sign: 'Bac Lieu International Airport. Elevation: dry season, two feet above water; wet season, two feet below water. Check with customs.' The Americans clearly have come to Bac Lieu.

Two months ago the Vietnamese Twenty-first Division and its American advisory group transferred headquarters here. As a result the prices of haircuts and cyclo rides have risen, all the ambitious young people in town are studying English, and large numbers of passing Vietnamese school children have the privilege of watching large numbers of GI's shave outdoors.

Bac Lieu has a splendid assortment of the problems that are the stuff of many war stories. Hot water comes from the oldest heating system in the world—the sun. The best time to take a shower is at 5 P.M., the worst at 7 A.M.

The officers have newly thatched huts, and now, as the dry season is ending, the huts are being propped up a foot as protection against the rising water. The betting among the enlisted men, however, is that with the rainy-season props, officers and all will sink below water level.

The Bac Lieu social whirl is by any standard a bit limited. The Americans have thus started their own clubs. There are quite a few, but the first one you hear of is the Greek God Club.

The Greek God Club was started because one officer, Captain Allison Henson, an all-Army wrestling champion, brought his bar bells to Bac Lieu. Other officers decided that they too could develop muscles, and that this would be worthwhile, as it would make it easier to lift heavy radios in the Delta sun.

One of the anti-Greeks, Major James Butler of New York City, said that the club's membership had nothing to do with radios. It stemmed, he said, from the glory that fell to two of the Greeks. Captain Richard Jones of San Francisco was photographed by both the *National Geographic* and *Newsweek*, and Captain Jeff Tuten of Miami appeared in a full-page picture in *Life*.

"The young guys coming in are pretty savvy," Major Butler said. "They know there'll be other photographers and cameramen coming through here, and they know these photographers aren't going to send back pictures of fat, placid GI's. So they're all lifting weights."

Major Butler, the club's severest critic, formed a rival club called Athletics Anonymous. "The idea is that if you get a terrible, uncontrollable urge to participate in sports," he said, "then you call some other member and he comes over and talks you out of it."

Several days ago Major Butler, taking a midnight stroll, stumbled on a bar bell and broke his toe. The glee among the Greeks was uncontrolled. "The Gods were angry at Butler," said Captain Tuten. Now over the officers' club bar is a special homemade plaque with a purple heart on it, awarded to Major Butler, "wounded by the Greek God Club."

Members of both of these clubs are working together

initiating the new officers into another club well known in Vietnam. This is the Blackfoot Club. Admission is easy: all you have to do is walk all day in the wet rice paddies; Vietnam does the rest. By the end of your first day, your feet are a horrible sight; they have a terrible texture from the long immersion, and an even more horrifying tint from the black dye in the boots and the color of the paddy muck. Though the dye runs easily from the boots, it finds a permanent home on one's feet, particularly around the toes. Here it stays and stays.

Many of the Blackfeet are now finishing up their one-year tour, and are beginning to struggle with the major problems of readjustment to the United States. One of the major problems will be diet. Captain Tuten, for instance, has been living with a Vietnamese battalion for most of his tour and has paid only nine hundred piasters a month (about fifteen dollars) for all his meals. Tuten says he is resigned to going without such delicacies as curdled duck's blood and boiled dog, and he is even prepared to pay more for his food. But what about table manners? "I'll have to be careful about throwing chicken bones over my shoulder—they don't do that in Florida," he says. He is also worried about getting a supply of *nuoc mam*—the foul-smelling, sharp-tasting sauce made of the oil of decaying fish, which the Vietnamese use on every dish. The only solution, he says, is to carry several bottles back with his gear, and hope his luggage is handled gently.

VIII

We never saw much of the enemy. We saw his handiwork—the ravaged outposts, the defenders with their heads blown off, their women lying dead beside them—but more often than not the guerrillas only showed themselves when they had superior strength. The first lesson that an American adviser in Vietnam learned was that the enemy was good; if he stayed on a little longer, he learned that this was wrong: the enemy was *very* good. He learned that the Vietcong concentrated on only a few things and that they did them well; that they made few mistakes; and that—in sharp contrast to the Government forces—they rarely made the same error twice. The American officers also learned that the enemy had a reason—political, psychological or military—for almost everything he did. Even when he appeared to be doing nothing, we learned belatedly that this did not mean he was inactive, only that he was content to *appear* inactive.

If they paid attention, Americans also learned that the enemy was absolutely sincere; he was willing to pay the price for the difficult task he had set for himself, and he had a far better sense of these difficulties than the authorities in Saigon. If he was underrated in Saigon, this was certainly not the case in the field; there it was widely known that we were fighting his war on his terms.

The Vietcong had no illusions about the type of war in which they were engaged. It was a war of revolution, and they knew the weaknesses of the Government as well as their own strengths. The American military thought of them as men carrying weapons, but the fact was that they were most effective at night indoctrinating the peasants— when they carried no weapons and wore no uniforms. The misery of the people was their ally, and they played on it. Where Americans often parroted slogans about improving the world of the Vietnamese peasant, the Vietcong, who had risen from this misery themselves, knew that lip service was not enough. To them the war was entirely political; its military aspects were simply a means to permit them to practice their political techniques. They made every grievance theirs: long-standing historical antagonisms, whether against Asians or Caucasians, became *their* grievances, as were economic inequities, the division of land, the arbitrary system of tax collection—even the ravages of disease.

As the Vietcong achieved military success through their political techniques, the Government and the Americans responded with increased weaponry and more troops. But this did not mitigate the grievances; indeed, the increased number of troops often meant more bombings, more deaths and more suffering. The strategic hamlet program was an ill-fated attempt to correct this imbalance, but it strangled in Vietnamese mismanagement and also because, for all their talk of "winning the people," the American mission never understood the war as the enemy did.

The Asian Communists had developed their guerrilla style by fighting Chiang Kai-shek, and a previous generation of Vietnamese had refined it in the war against the French. Guerrilla warfare is virtually an art form, and the Vietcong were more than craftsmen at their trade; they were artists. So knowledgeable and successful were they that when American officers prepared for their tour in Vietnam, they read not the writings of the French or American tacticians, but the writings of the enemy. The United States was there because the

Vietcong had proven stronger than our allies; we were fighting a war among his people and on his soil, where he had
been successful for twenty years.

The Vietcong, of course, were not the Vietminh; it was
not that simple. For one thing, the American role was not
comparable to the French; we were, after all, fighting to get
out, whereas the French had fought to stay on. Yet the heritage and the legacy and the enemy's impetus were very much
the same. To much of the peasantry the Vietcong was the
same as the Vietminh; it dressed the same way, it used exactly the same tactics and techniques, and it operated in
exactly the same manner.

The Vietcong never used the word Communism. Once Paul
Fay, Undersecretary of the Navy, came to Saigon and delivered a rip-roaring speech on how to teach the peasantry about
the evils of Communism. A CIA friend of mine who heard
the speech said, "God, wouldn't that be lovely! These people
have never heard of Communism, but if we went around
preaching against it, they might decide that it's a pretty good
thing and want some of it."

Just as the Vietcong resembled the Vietminh in the peasants' eyes, the Government troops too often acted like the
soldiers in the same uniforms who had fought during the days
of the French: patrolling the hamlets during the day, grabbing
village chickens for lunch and disappearing after 6 P.M., so
that just in case some villager was inclined to help the Government, he would have no protection at night when the Vietcong arrived.

Inevitably the Government forces played into the enemy's
hands. The Vietcong would prophesy that the Government
troops would come, that they would be led by Americans,
that this would mean bombings from planes piloted by Americans and that as a result villagers would die. Sooner or later
there would be a battle, there would be strafings of the village
and there would be troops with American advisers. Then at
night the Vietcong cadre in the area would arrive in the village and dispense medical aid, and of course they would gain
more recruits.

The guerrillas had prepared for this kind of fighting long

in advance. At the end of the Indochina war they had carefully set to work developing cadres, gathering ammunition and preparing weapon-storage points, digging secret, cave-like hideaways and tunnels, and training cadres to take over the schools. They had had another advantage: in the embryo years of the new nation they were the dissenters. It was the Government's job to deliver; their role was only to sit by and criticize. In underdeveloped countries a new government starting out with a tiny number of trained people must somehow develop a competent administrative staff. It cannot meet—at least no new government has—the vast expectations of a newly independent people: glittering hopes in education; in the standard of living; in reforms, agriculture and health.

Such new governments are inevitably clumsy. The Diem government was no worse than most, but in South Vietnam the problems were greater than in most other newly independent states. The French had left behind a civil-service system fraught with corruption; Diem was a poor administrator; what little talent there was in the country was quickly siphoned off to the military—where, if it was really outstanding, it was ignored. Too often the only contact the villagers had with their government was corrupt local officials who showed up often enough to collect taxes, but not often enough to provide services.

In contrast, the Vietcong did not have to provide; they merely promised to. They would divvy up the land holdings of absentee landlords; this cost them nothing and won them the peasants' allegiance. Suspecting that the Government would take their land back, the peasants would simply not inform on the Vietcong, and often they and their families were active agents. The fact that when victory had been won the Vietcong intended to collectivize the land, as they had in the North, was something else; there was no need to bring that up now.

In addition, the Vietcong had years of experience behind them. As one American intelligence officer told me, "The trouble with this war is that everywhere in the countryside the enemy has some political commissar who's been fighting revolutionary warfare on the winning side for twenty years, with all the training and professionalism that entails, and up against him we've got someone who, if he's trained at all, was trained by the Americans or the French, and who has been on the losing side.'' Because competent officials who were a threat to the Vietcong were killed, there was a tendency toward fence-straddling on the part of local officials. While sending in enthusiastic progress reports to the capital, they tried not to see what the enemy was doing; in effect, they had come to a gentlemen's agreement with the Vietcong and were thus providing a vacuum in which the guerrillas could work.

The Vietcong started indoctrinating their people when they were very young—the younger the better. They offered them adventure and excitement, and they advertised themselves as the enemies of oppression, as the heralders of a better world— but they always based their appeal on the most fundamental issues. If land was the grievance in one community, their pitch was based on land reform; if bad local government was the source of unhappiness, the Vietcong would execute the offending village official while the peasants watched. To a young boy growing up in the total deprivation of an Asian back-land, only dimly aware of the inequity between his life and that of other, wealthier Asians, the enemy's call was persuasive—particularly when, say, a member of the Vietcong ran the local school.

Soon the youngsters would be involved as bearers for troops or as messengers, earning advancement only on merit and being fully committed every step of the way. There was a thoroughness in the enemy's political indoctrination which was completely missing on the Government side. Before a youth was permitted to hold a Vietcong rifle he would first undergo long political and psychological training. He *believed*. His, he was sure, was a righteous cause: he was liberating his people; the Government was cruel and owned by the Americans; his war was to liberate his countrymen from the Americans—just as his father had liberated half of the country from the French. Also, it was part of the Vietcong's mystique that they were the poor robbing the rich, so for this reason they often went to great lengths to capture weapons when they could more easily have smuggled them into the country; it gave them a sense of pride and self-reliance.

Only when the enemy was convinced of a young man's political commitment and complete indoctrination was he allowed to begin his miliatry training. Here again there was an insistence on excellence. A weapon was priceless and significant; when it came into his hands for the first time a ceremony was part of the promotion. On that day the recruit became a man.

This, then, was the enemy's raw material: tough, indoctrinated men, willing and ready to die; men of great physical endurance who had known few softening distractions in a lifetime of hardships. The leadership was equally good. The battalion commanders were usually men who had fought in the Indochina war; though they were mostly from South Vietnam and usually from the specific area in which they would serve, they had been given additional training in the North. The best of a good army, they had been fighting for years and had risen on ability alone—and they knew that they would lose their jobs if they made mistakes.

The Vietcong also had a sense of military cunning that few Americans took into account. During these twenty years they had fought constantly against an enemy which had superior equipment and air power. By necessity they had learned to be careful and shrewd, and how best to exploit their limited resources. In order to survive they had to be wily; to be careless, sloppy or indifferent meant sure death. They could never rely on an air strike or on armored personnel carriers to bail them out of trouble; rather, there would be air strikes to wipe them out and APC's to crush them. They had to be elusive. "Their commanders," an American captain once told me, "have a sixth sense about their flanks. It is almost impossible to surround them."

If the Government troops failed to train, so much the better; the Vietcong trained regularly. They studied the techniques of U.S. helicopter pilots, and before a major attack they built mock models of the Government emplacements on which to practice the assault. Within Vietcong units were groups specially trained for each phase of an attack: troops for the first wave, troops for the demolition of key points of the defense, troops for gathering up weapons, troops for covering the escape.

In this war the ambush was a vital ingredient; it involved relatively little man power and it often inflicted heavy casualties. Always there were preordained escape routes. In addition to killing Government troops and capturing weapons, the enemy achieved a psychological advantage through the ambush: it scared Government troops, made them less anxious to leave their bases and slowly helped to dry up Government access to the countryside, thereby allowing the Vietcong to move around that much more freely. Frequently an attack was made only to set up an ambush; thus, the attack might be a minor part of the operation, the major objective being to ambush the Government relief columns. For this reason there was little enthusiasm on the part of Government troops to come to the aid of their less fortunate colleagues under attack.

By nature the Vietnamese are afraid of the night and of the jungle. Very early in a young man's career the Vietcong broke his fear of the darkness; the guerrillas were taught that the night was their friend, the enemy of the white man and his airplanes. To operate in the dark became a way of life with the Vietcong: they lived, taught, traveled and fought at night. The same was true with the jungle; by force of necessity the Vietcong came to know and use the tropical forests, as their countrymen under the Government flag would never do.

The Vietcong's military commanders were completely under the control of their political commissars. Every decision was based first on political needs, only secondarily on military ones. ''If we give them a licking in a certain area,'' said one American officer, ''we can almost bet that within ten days or so they'll knock off a good-sized outpost in the same neighborhood—just to show the flag and let the peasants know that they're still in business.''

The first time you met a member of the Vietcong there was

a sharp sense of disappointment. He was not, it turned out, very different; he was simply another Vietnamese. When you saw him he was usually either kneeling and firing at you, or he had just been captured—or, more often than not, he was dead: the bodies were always lined up, their feet in an orderly row. The guerrilla wore little, perhaps a simple peasant pajama suit, perhaps only shorts. He was slim and wiry, and his face would remind you of your interpreter or of that taxi driver who drove you to My Tho. Only the haircut was different, very thin along the sides, and very long on top and in front. It was a bad haircut, and like the frailness of the uniform and the thin wallet with perhaps only a few pictures of some peasant woman, it made the enemy human. But one's sympathy did not last long; this was the same face that had been seen by the outnumbered defenders of some small outpost before it was overrun.

There were not many operations in which the Vietcong were caught; few prisoners were taken in this war. One of the few exceptions to this that I ever observed took place in April 1963, when I accompanied the new armed-helicopter units in the upper Camau peninsula on what were known as Eagle flights. An Eagle flight was risky business; it meant that a small number of elite troops circled above the paddies in the choppers, looking for likely targets. When an objective was sighted the helicopters dropped out of the sky, virtually on top of a hamlet, and the troops made a quick search, probing and scouting. If the enemy was there, other regular units, waiting in the rear with other helicopters, would be thrown in quickly. But dropping swiftly out of the sky and exploring the unknown with a handful of troops was sometimes terrifying; the helicopters have the visibility of a press box, but you were watching a war instead of a football game. When you plunged earthward, little men sometimes rushed to different positions, kneeled and started firing at the press box while your own tracers sought them out.

On that day in April the 21st Recon Company, a particularly good outfit composed largely of troops who had fought with the Vietminh during the Indochina war, was with us. We were scouting a Vietcong battalion, moving along a line of villages which we thought the battalion had been using as its main line of communication in that region. But this was the upper Camau, almost completely enemy territory,where one could find a Vietcong squad in virtually every village.

It is perhaps deceptive to use a word like "battalion" here; when such a unit attacked a given point it might number three hundred men, but immediately afterward it would break up into small groups slipping into neighboring villages and awaiting the signal for the next operation. A single large force would make too good a target for the Government; besides, by splitting up, more men could indoctrinate more peasants, and no single village would have to take on the task of feeding three hundred extra mouths.

At about eight-thirty in the morning we saw some movement in a village below, followed by a few light crackles around us. It was ground fire; the bait had been taken. We came in low over the village and saw some men scurrying to positions. Three of the helicopters, including our own, dropped their troop load while the others circled and strafed some of the positions. We were making our advance on the treeline under fire when we saw a man in a black suit desperately running across the open field. It was the dry season and the fields were covered with sun-caked mud. Suddenly a helicopter descended almost on top of the man; he stopped and held up his hands. The Vietnamese commander ran over to him. There was no weapon on this Vietcong; neither was there any of the bowing or scraping that local guerrillas posing as farmers sometimes employed.

The captured man was angry and defiant, and at first a little scared as well—until he saw me and spat at me. The commander slapped his face very hard and said something in Vietnamese. Later I was told that the captain had said to the prisoner, "The Americans are very kind. They do not kill, and they are always telling us not to kill you, but I am not so kind and I will kill you. You will see." The interpreter thought this was very funny. "You know, the enemy takes these young boys and they tell them how fierce you Ameri-

cans are, and so they are all convinced that the Americans
will eat their hearts for breakfast as soon as they are captured.
The captain is right; you have no real taste for war.'' The
Vietnamese commander interrogated the captured guerrilla
and told us that he was well indoctrinated. ''They are taught
well to hate,'' he said a little apologetically.

It is true that the Vietcong were better at hating than our
Vietnamese, though at times Government troops could be very
cruel. Once, south of Bac Lieu, Vietnamese Marines had
fought a particularly bitter battle but had captured a number
of Vietcong prisoners. According to a Vietnamese friend of
mine who was there, the enemy were very cocky and started
shouting anti-American slogans and Vietnamese curses at
their captors. The Marines, who had lost an officer that day
and were in no mood to be called lackeys of the Americans,
simply lined up the seventeen guerrillas and shot them down
in cold blood. ''They had to believe their own propaganda,''
my friend said.

The captain said that the guerrilla was probably from an
elite battalion operating in the area. ''I think maybe he was
a squad leader.'' Then the officer turned and spoke briefly
and intensely to the guerrilla. He was telling the prisoner that
they would kill him unless he talked—and perhaps they would
kill him by throwing him out of the helicopter. ''The captain
is very smart,'' said the interpreter. ''It will be the guerrilla's
first helicopter ride and he will be very scared.'' They tied
up the guerrilla and placed him in the helicopter (later we
were to find out that he had indeed been frightened but did
not crack), and the captain and I walked back across the open
field to the village. We could hear a good deal of firing, and
as always I hunched over as much as I could, but the Vietnamese officer strolled casually. He carried a small swagger
stick, and he looked as if he were a large landowner inspecting his plantation. I was impressed.

By the time we reached the village the troops had rounded
up two more guerrillas. They did not even pretend to be farmers; they had not surrendered until they began to take fire not
only from the ground, but from some of the nine other helicopters in the area. The captain was convinced that there

were other Vietcong somewhere in the village, that there had been at least five or six of the enemy stationed there. But he also suspected that the others had excellent hiding places and that we would not find them. "They are probably dug in under this village somewhere," he said. He checked his watch. Time was important because the helicopters had been aloft for along while. He told his men that they had five more minutes to search the village, then turned to the prisoners and started to talk to them. One, about nineteen years old, gave him a look of defiance and turned away, but the other, who might have been twenty-five, gave the captain a curious look. "Maybe," the captain said later, "he is a little more tired of the war and the propaganda. We shall see. The other will not talk." He was right; the next morning the elder one confessed that they were members of a battalion which had hit two outposts in the Camau the week before and had come here to rest. This guerrilla was tired; he had been fighting too long—for seven years—and he wanted to leave the Army.

At the appointed minute the troops were back. They had found an American carbine, and the captain was surprised because it was more than he had expected. The weapon had been found in a false thatch in a roof. The captain was pleased. "Good troops," he told me. "When they search they want to find something, and when they fight they want to kill."

Then the helicopters returned and we all jumped in and prepared for the next assault.

The next two villages produced only some crude grenades made by an old farmer. "The local guerrilla," said the Vietnamese captain. These were the lowest of the three types of Vietcong: they farmed in the day and fought at night, and they had the worst weapons. When I first came to Vietnam their arms were all homemade; by the time I left they were using French equipment and even some American M-1's. But even in April 1963, in a village where there were no other weapons, a homemade grenade or a rusty rifle had great power.

The local guerrillas were a vital part of the Vietcong apparatus. They gave the village a sense of Communist continuity, they could provide intelligence on Government activities and serve as a local security force for a traveling commissar, or they could guide the professional Vietcong troops. This last was particularly important to the success and mobility of the guerrillas; everywhere they went they had trained, local guides to steer them through seemingly impenetrable areas. Because of these local men the enemy's troops could often move twenty-five miles in five hours—which meant that a raiding force attacking at night was almost impossible to find by daylight. These local guerrillas were also part of the propaganda network, for in a village they might be the only ones with a radio. (Sometimes it was only the shell of a radio, but the local man would pretend he could hear news and would give out information of Vietcong victories.)

We flew back to the base to refuel, and then returned to the area. Shortly before noon we hit pay dirt. Out of one village came a flock of Vietcong, running across the paddies, and there was intense fire from the treeline. While five of our ships emptied their troops, the rest of the choppers strafed the area. Soon the guerrillas broke from their positions and ran for a nearby canal, where they might find hiding places. We came hurtling down on them at a hundred miles an hour, just a few feet off the ground. We were still drawing fire, but it was more sporadic now.

We bore down on one fleeing Vietcong. The paddy's surface was rough and his run was staggered, like that of a good but drunken broken-field runner against imaginary tacklers. We came closer and closer; inside the helicopter I could almost hear him gasping for breath, and as we bore down I could see the heaving of his body. It was like watching a film of one of your own nightmares, but in this case we were the pursuers rather than the pursued. The copilot fired his machine guns but missed, and the man kept going. Then there was a flash of orange and a blast of heat inside the ship, and the helicopter heaved from the recoil of its rockets. When they exploded the man fell. He lay still as we went over him, but when we turned he scrambled to his feet, still making for the canal, now only about fifty yards away. While we circled and swept toward him again he was straining for the bank, like a runner nearing the finish line. We had one last shot at him. Our copilot fired one last burst of the machine gun as the guerrilla made a desperate surge. The bullets cut him down as he reached the canal, and his body skidded on the hard bank as he collapsed.

We turned and circled again. All over the paddies helicopters were rounding up Vietcong soldiers. We landed near the village which other members of the Recon company were searching. The troops were gentler with the population than most ARVN soldiers I had seen; in front of one hut a medic was giving aid to a wounded guerrilla.

"I have never taken this many prisoners before," the Vietnamese captain said. There were sixteen of them. He turned to one of his men. "Show the American the poor little farmer," he said. They brought in a wiry young man. "This one says he is a farmer," the officer said. He pushed the young man in front of me and flipped the prisoner's palms over. "He has very soft hands for a farmer," the captain said. "He has the hands of a bar girl in Saigon. He is not a very good soldier yet. In a few months, though, he might have been very good."

The prisoner was beginning to tremble. The conversation in a foreign language obviously frightened him, and I was sure that this was why the captain was using English. I asked the captain what kind of enemy we had surprised. "Territorial," he said. This was the middle rank of Vietcong guerrillas; we called them provincial guerrillas. They operated in groups of up to one hundred and were often attached to the hard-core units to beef up their strength for a major attack; they would also hit smaller outposts.

"The leadership was not very good," the captain said. "If it had been a hard-core unit, there would have been more fighting and more dying. I think we surprised them."

Before we took off again, I walked over to the canal. The little soldier's body had actually crossed the finish line; his shoulder was over the bank, his blood was still running into the canal and there was a look of agony on his face.

The helicopter pilots and the Vietnamese captain decided that they had enough fuel for one more strike. The pilots were in very good humor, pleased with the day's bag. As we skimmed over the countryside once more, they boasted of how they had made the Air Force look sick again. There was a running battle between the helicopter pilots, who were Army officers, and the Air Force over the respective merits of the helicopter and the fighter plane. In particular, the feeling was very strong between Major Ivan Slavich, commander of the armed helicopter company, and Major Bill Burgin, who was the Air Force liaison man in the Twenty-first Division. Burgin called himself "the only law south of the Mekong River," and was distinguished by his violent hatred of both the Vietcong and helicopter pilots.

"Hey," said Slavich now, "go back to Bac Lieu and ask your friend Burgin if he's got a T-28 that can land in a paddy, capture some Communists and then take off again."

We hit one more village and encountered no resistance. But as I was walking toward the treeline I suddenly heard shouts and cries all around me. I was terrified, for I was unarmed and about fifty yards from the nearest soldier. Suddenly from deep bomb shelters all around me more than twenty women and children came up; they were wailing and pointing at me. Clearly, they were scared. Judging from its defensive preparations, this was a Vietcong village, and for years these people had heard propaganda about vicious Americans like me. As far as I was concerned they were dangerous too, and we stood looking at each other in mutual fear.

I yelled out to Major James Butler, asking him what to do. Butler suggested that I try to give a good impression of Americans. "Protect our image," he said. Later he congratulated me on being the first *New York Times* correspondent ever to capture a bunch of Vietcong women. I gladly turned them over to the Vietnamese captain.

The troops were remarkably restrained in what was obviously a Vietcong village. At times the quick change in Vietnamese behavior was amazing. One moment they could be absolutely ruthless; the next, they might be talking to a prisoner as if he were an old friend. The enemy was different, however; I was told by those who had been captured by them during the Indochina war that they were not so tolerant. This was hardly surprising; much emphasis was placed in their indoctrination on teaching them to hate. They were the have-nots fighting the haves, and even after capture their feelings rarely changed.

We flew back to Bac Lieu. It had been a good day. There had been few Government losses, and there was a chance that from all those prisoners we might learn something important. Everyone was tired and relaxed and happy. If nothing else, the day seemed to prove the value of the Eagle flights. Only Mert Perry of *Time*, who had also come along to observe the new strategy, seemed a bit depressed. It had been a good day, he agreed, and in one way the Government had done very well. But after all, he pointed out, it was a pretty limited business, and in the long run it might backfire. There was no follow-up; no one would be in those villages tonight working with the people. These peasants had seen helicopters and they knew that Americans flew the helicopters; they had seen killing and they had seen their men disappear. The conclusions that the villagers would draw were obvious—particularly if the Vietcong were there to help them. Every man taken today, Mert said, probably had a brother or a son or a brother-in-law who would take his place after today.

We listened to Perry in silence, for we knew that he was right. The Government had scored a quick victory, but in Vietnam, victories were not always what they seemed. It was an endless, relentless war to which ordinary military rules did not apply. We went to bed that night a little less confident, knowing that although for the moment the enemy was paying a higher price, he was still out there somewhere in the darkness, living closer to the peasants and ready to seize the initiative once more.

IX

I had left the Congo for a brief visit to New York City when Bernie Kalb, then with the *Times*, asked me if I had fallen in love with any city or country in Africa. I allowed as how I hadn't. Bernie was horror-stricken; every foreign correspondent, he insisted, should fall in love with at least one city. I tried to explain to him about the Congo, but my talk fell on deaf ears. Then I went to Saigon and found out what Bernie meant. I fell in love not only with my job, but with the people and their country.

It was a bittersweet assignment. At first glance the war was very far from Saigon, but just below the surface the scars of twenty years of war were deep and painful. One's reaction depended on whether he wanted to dig down and get the whole story, or whether he was content to remain on the surface and keep his illusions. A reporter could take a girl out for a magnificent French meal, knowing—or not knowing, depending on his curiosity—that she had one brother in the Vietnamese Army, and perhaps another brother in North Vietnam's. Early the next morning he could take a steaming hot shower in the Caravelle Hotel—designed for tourists who never arrived—climb into his fatigues, ride a jeep to Tan Son Nhut, eat a tense breakfast with helicopter pilots and then fly into combat with them.

In sum, Vietnam was a reporter's dream. It had everything: a war, a highly dramatic and emotional story, great food, a beautiful setting and lovely women. It was also everything that Africa was not. Whenever a colleague finished a brief tour in the Congo, we would go to the airport *en masse* and watch wistfully as the one Pan Am flight a week took off for Western capitals. In Saigon, where we were constantly being threatened with expulsion by the Government, we spent a lot of time worrying about the depressing prospect that someone else might get our assignment.

A few days after my arrival in Saigon, Horst Faas took me to La Cigale, which was to become our favorite night club. The ban on dancing had drained the city's night life of some of its flavor, but the Cigale remained a first-class place, for it served good food and had the best singers in town. To be a good singer in Saigon carried great prestige; the performer would travel from club to club each evening, entertaining at four or five a night, and only a first-rate restaurant was able to schedule the best singers at the best hours.

The Cigale was also special because it was a great center for intrigue. Dr. Tran Kim Tuyen, the former director of the secret police and an on-again, off-again plotter of coups, used it as a meeting place; so did CIA agents. I suspect that half the waiters worked for Colonel Le Quang Tung, a key man in Nhu's police apparatus. The club was run by a very independent Corsican who had a great flair for décor and a tough head, which he often used to keep trouble to a minimum by butting boisterous soldiers.

That first night we sat in the Cigale and listened to Miss Yen Hung, who looked like a Vietnamese Joan Baez and who sang French songs with the anguish of an Edith Piaf. Yen Hung was one of the most attractive women I have ever seen; she had a long, haunting face and hair that fell down to her waist. Horst had had several drinks and was in a very sentimental mood: Yen Hung was singing songs of the *Légionnaires*, and Horst had just come from Algeria, where he had seen the demise of the OAS and of French rule. Suddenly he beat on the table, drunk and owlishly serious. "We can't let this country go over to the Communists," he said sadly.

* * *

In Vietnam the French left behind them a tortured political
legacy, but in their appreciation of the amenities they were
the best of colonizers. Nowhere was this more evident than
in Saigon, with its wide, tree-lined streets, its three-hour siesta and its excellent cuisine. We correspondents would sit
on the Rue Catinat—renamed Duong Tu Do (meaning Freedom Street) but called by that name about as often as Sixth
Avenue is called Avenue of the Americas—and watch the corrupt life of Saigon unfold. The Catinat is a handsome thoroughfare, lined with trees and American dollars; it abounds
with pickpockets, moneychangers, whores; instant dentists
who pull teeth for ten cents; stores that sell satin jackets prepared especially for Americans and proclaiming in English
that the owner will go to heaven because he is now spending
his time in hell; portable kitchens selling Chinese soup for a
nickel; the Paris Bar, the Capitol Bar and many other Amer-
ican-style bars—and, of course, the women.

Saigon was a great city for girl watching, particularly on
Sunday—there was, after all, no giant paper to read that day—
when all the Vietnamese girls (except perhaps the ones from
the very best families, who would be ashamed to walk there,
just as they would be ashamed to go out with an American)
promenaded down the Catinat. The younger ones wore what
were considered Western clothes, or at least Western prom-
enading clothes: tight Capri pants and Western blouses. More
mature women, however, swirled by in their *ao dais*, the
traditional, close-fitting sheath which is at once graceful, sedate and very sexy. The costume was most becoming, because the Vietnamese women were thinner and more graceful
than the Chinese, with slimmer hips, and the *ao dais* made
them seem a little taller. I thought they walked with consum-
mate grace, though I was challenged on this once by the very
attractive wife of a visiting publishing executive from New
York. She had asked me what I liked about Vietnamese
women, and I mentioned, among other things, their walk.
This promptly launched her into a tirade about how poorly
they walked, how clumsy they were, and what little style they

had. "All right," I said in desperation, "but they fooled me."

In point of fact, the *Saigonnaises* were like women everywhere else in the world; for one thing, they always wanted to get married. I had lunch with Miss Yen Hung one day, and she let it be known that she did not like Americans. When I asked her what was wrong with them, she said, "All the Americans want to hear me sing, but none of them wants to marry me, because I am Vietnamese." She followed this with a swift, accusing look. I could think of nothing to say other than that she should understand that Americans like music very much.

Madame Nhu had banned dancing, but much as she would have liked to, she could not ban the obvious affection between the Americans and Vietnamese girls. She had an ally in General Harkins, who once issued the following order: "I do not think that intense public farewells between American servicemen and their Vietnamese girl friends are fitting or appropriate, and particularly not so in the eyes of the Vietnamese people when these farewells occur in such places as the waiting room or lobby of the airport."

Not much attention was paid to the general's opinions in this case—one reason being that there *was* an intensity about the Vietnamese women, from the little bar girls, who were ordered to wear white uniforms but managed to look brazen anyway, to the First Lady herself.

I remember one girl who worked behind the bar at the officers' club for helicopter pilots at Soc Trang. She was a tough little thing, and her knowledge of English—and, one suspects, of her own tongue—was limited to the crudest and most basic expressions. She was a delight to the pilots, who would tease her after a long day of flying among the paddies, for she would hiss back at them like an angry cat. Yet one day, when a helicopter was shot down and two of the pilots were killed, she asked for permission to go to Saigon for the sad little service. At the airport, while a chaplain's words were drowned out by the noise of other helicopters going into combat, she broke down and wept hysterically. Supported by a huge American on either side—two giants holding a little rag doll—she was a picture of grief that still haunts me.

Sadness was everywhere in Saigon, but the Vietnamese, who know grief better than most people, did not inflict it on Americans; they accepted it fatalistically as part of their life. I knew a girl at the American embassy who had always impressed me as a particularly light-hearted spirit. But one night over dinner she told me about herself. Like many Vietnamese who worked for the Americans, she was from the North; she had come down with her grandfather ten years before in the wave of refugees. The family had been worried about him; her job was to stay with him, comfort him and remind him that he had a family. Her parents, her one brother and her five sisters were still in the North; she had not seen them in nine years. Her brother might be in the North Vietnamese Army; she said this quite matter-of-factly. She did not hear often from her parents; it was very hard for them to get mail, and she didn't write often because there might be reprisals if they received letters from her. Her father had been a lawyer and had owned much property; now he was a clerk for the state. She did not think her parents were very happy with the government in the North, but when she did receive letters from them, they never mentioned politics.

I asked her whether she would like to see her family again. Of course, she said, but she doubted that this would happen. "You do not hope for things like that. You are an American—what do you think the chances are?" Implicit was the Vietnamese belief that Americans knew many of the answers and simply were not telling.

Later we went for a drink at the Dai Kim Do, a famous dance palace during the days of the French; now it was a vast and virtually empty symbol of the changing mores of sin. As soon as we got there I realized I had made a mistake; listening to the singers there was like hearing an audition in an empty basketball auditorium.

"No dancing now," I said.

"Yes," she said, "it is very sad not to twist." On the

surface she seemed as disturbed over this as over the loss of her family.

For the young men in Vietnam, the outlook was even bleaker. They grew up knowing that unless they had rich parents who could keep them out of the Army, or send them to Paris to lead the frivolous life of a professional exile, or perhaps buy them a position as a staff officer in Saigon, their young manhood would be spent among the country's rice paddies in long years of service and with no promise of an end to the war.

Friendships between Americans and Vietnamese were forged only slowly. The Government was suspicious of Vietnamese who were too close to Westerners, and too many Vietnamese had been damaged by indiscreet and naïve Americans who learned too late the consequences of loose talk. Moreover, if a Vietnamese made one American friend, it was likely that he soon would have many more and hence would become known as an American's Vietnamese—in which case he would be watched both by the Government and the American mission. In this environment it was remarkable that any Vietnamese at all were willing to take the risk of becoming our friends. Of course, we had the advantage of being called liars, cheats and Communist dupes by the Government; since the population did not believe a single thing the Government said, anyone regularly criticized by it was considered something of a hero.

Vietnamese-American friendships were cautious relationships. We were wary about using the telephone and about being seen in public. There were a few close friends with whom we could associate publicly, but most of these were Vietnamese who were on the American payroll and consequently already marked men in the Government's eyes. We also had some very good friends in the military. Often we would be the guests of a commander in the field, but in Saigon an officer who talked with American reporters was immediately suspect.

Therefore our closest Vietnamese friends were apt to be newspapermen like ourselves: Pham Xuan An of Reuters, Nguyen Ngoc Rao of UPI, Vo Huynh of NBC and Ha Thuc

Can of CBS. They were all remarkable men. For the American reporter working in Vietnam in those days, life was tense and sometimes dangerous, but this was nothing compared to the danger that these young men faced. After all, we owned American passports and could only be expelled, but the penalties were likely to be much higher for a Vietnamese. Their situation was fascinating because they, who had never seen an uncensored newspaper, were working for free Western newspapers; in most cases they had never been out of Vietnam, and they had usually learned English on their own, in their spare time. Yet despite these handicaps, they all had an intuitive sense of what a reporter's job was.

During the Buddhist crisis, when the Government was arresting any Vietnamese in sight, Sheehan and I had a terrible time trying to keep Rao of UPI away from the front line of the demonstrations. We argued that these demonstrations were too dangerous for him and that we couldn't risk having him arrested, but he insisted that as a reporter he belonged there. Rao, who was a Catholic and a refugee from the North, had very good sources among the Buddhists. They were all proud men; they were the only free members of a closed society, and they were perhaps even more offended than we were when anyone tried to feed them phony stories.

Before the coup we were rarely invited into Vietnamese homes; only the highest officials felt secure about entertaining Americans. Originally Horst and I had stayed at the Caravelle Hotel, the newest and most intrigue-filled hotel in Saigon. But we had been living in hotels for over two years, and even without the constant rifling of my papers, stealing of his negatives and tapping of our phone, we would have wanted to move; the attention from various Vietnamese security networks simply hastened the decision. As long as a reporter stays in a hotel in a country like Vietnam he is essentially an itinerant; he writes his story, retires to the bar where he meets other correspondents, and then goes out with them for dinner. But once we had our own place, we began to have a life of our own. In December 1962 we rented a huge villa from a German embassy official who was going on home leave for six months. We were able to invite people for dinner, visiting officers in from the field could stay with us, and our Vietnamese friends could drop by for drinks. We no longer felt like resident tourists.

We inherited the German's household of servants, including the head man; known only as The Chef, he did not cook, but he was in charge of those who did. The Bep—this is the Vietnamese word for kitchen—was the real cook, and he was in a constant rage because after standing the whole day over the stove, he would hear guests congratulating The Chef on a beautiful dinner.

The Chef had been the major-domo for a French general, always wore a tie, and had some reservations about serving two reporters who never wore jackets or ties. The fact that we sometimes came home and announced that ten people were coming for dinner—or even worse, asked him to prepare a *Vietnamese* dinner for four—did not help our relationship. The Chef adopted a policy of nonrecognition toward us for the first three weeks (in part because his salary was still being paid by the absent German), and we were only able to make the grade eventually because of an impromptu visit one day by a friend of ours from My Tho, Major Sandy Faust. Sandy was a good-looking officer who drove his own jeep, just as the French had; The Chef, who did not understand American insignia, was convinced that Sandy was a colonel and took to him immediately. He decided that if we had such friends there might be hope for us. From then on, the atmosphere in the house changed, and Horst and I were treated with a modicum of respect.

The Chef also liked another friend of ours named Chuck Walsh, a Special Forces sergeant belonging to the team of Captain George Gaspard stationed along the Laotian border. Walsh wore a beret and a mustache and could speak some French, and this impressed The Chef; the only thing that bothered him was Walsh's lack of rank. Finally The Chef rationalized this by deciding that Walsh must be an intelligence man; when he asked the sergeant, Walsh nodded slyly, and The Chef, delighted at having penetrated a spy's disguise, took him to his bosom and treated him far better than Horst or me.

Many of the officers we knew in the field had no base or friends in Saigon, so they always came to our house. Gradually the villa became something of a hotel: once I went off for five days to the Delta and returned to find that the officers of an entire helicopter company had thrown a party there, that a general had attended (which meant that our prestige with The Chef has risen another notch), that the streets had been blocked off and that police had guarded the house, and that the cop on the local beat had become very respectful.

Our huge villa with endless space had everything we could possibly want save hot water. But one day some of our friends in the military quietly showed up, installed a hot-water heater in the bathroom and disappeared. We took the hot-water heater with us on the German's return, for it had become a treasured possession.

The Chef viewed his new masters as a mixed blessing. His work was more profitable, since most of the visitors, feeling guilty about having stayed for free, tipped him generously. But life was also more unpredictable. He woke me up at three o'clock one night and led me into the living room. An incredible sight greeted us: in that vast room an American Special Forces man and a pedicab driver were chasing each other around and over the furniture. Apparently the pedicab driver felt that there had been a lack of generosity in the tip given him for having introduced the American to one of Saigon's finest. While the girl cowered in the corner, The Chef shouted—whether in reference to the incident or to the girl I have no idea—*"pas jolie, pas jolie."*

Gradually, however, The Bep became the star of the house. He was a magnificent cook, and he was pleased to serve so many hungry young men. He took great delight in buying fresh food at the market; by way of proving to us that we were getting the best available, he was apt to barge in while Horst and I were having breakfast, open a paper bag and set six live crabs loose on the floor. We were always duly impressed. He prepared his own menus, would confer with us each morning about them and the number of guests, and would then set off for the market.

The pecking order among the servants changed noticeably

during our stay, for after a while when we liked a meal we would summon The Bep from the kitchen to congratulate him. Under the glare of publicity he prospered. He bought himself a tie, and often hovered near the door after meals to be introduced to the guests. As he reaped more praise the meals improved even further. When our six months were up and the German returned, we stole The Bep from him and moved to a house on Phan Thanh Gian Street. Here The Bep assumed the title of Bep *and* Chef.

We did not always eat at home. Saigon is one of the great cities in the world for a gourmet—particularly if you like sea food or the French and Chinese cuisine. Regularly we would go to Cholon, the Chinese enclave of Saigon—in particular to a restaurant called The Diamond, which specialized in cracked crab. We would order vast quantities of the shellfish, which was sautéed in lemon and so hot that we always burned our fingers; throwing the empty shells aside, we barely talked to each other in the scramble for choice pieces.

In our quest for new and exciting places we always traveled by cab; we were all willing to fly in helicopters and go on night patrols in the field, but we were not brave enough to drive in Saigon traffic. The traffic regulations were very simple: they were designed to bring together as many cars as possible at one crossing at the same time. There was no such thing as right of way; to yield was to lose face. The main means of transport was thousands of tiny little Renault taxicabs, their doors fastened by wire clothes hangers, their motors sounding like rusty Chinese burp guns, their fan belts resembling makeshift rubber bands. They were always running out of gas, particularly when you were late for an appointment; then, while you sat there in a rage the driver would smile, take a small can out of the glove compartment, pour gas into the tank, kick the car several times, smile again and drive on.

The taxis added a touch of suspense to life, for you were never sure where you would end up. On getting instructions the driver would nod excitedly and indicate that he knew exactly where his passenger wanted to go. The Westerner, often preoccupied or tired, would settle back—to realize five minutes later that he was speeding in exactly the opposite direction. An Army friend of mine was trying to return to his base late one night, got into a cab and fell asleep, only to wake up twenty minutes later to find that the cab had taken him miles out of his way, to the other side of town. My friend stopped the taxi, threw the driver out of the cab, drove back to the base and left the car outside the gate.

Still, our social life was somewhat limited. We were not invited to the homes of the high American officials except for special national holidays, and most American cocktail parties always seemed to end in some acrimonious debate. On one occasion the wife of a major general came over to me, announced that she had majored in psychology in college, and asked me if I was married. I said I was not. That, she announced triumphantly, was the trouble with my reporting; bachelors had no patience, they expected too much and had no sense of balance. I told her that she was probably right, and that it was a shame Diem was single too.

Public entertainment was also somewhat limited. There was the Cigale, but I and Ha Thuc Can, one of my close friends, liked to go to another place called the Duc Quynh. It was an odd place to find in Vietnam—or any other country, for that matter. A cross between Harvard Square and the Mysterious Orient, it had a dank, cavelike atmosphere, and its walls were covered with signs saying "I love you" in many languages. Its clientele consisted of the usual assortment of Vietnamese intelligence agents and secret policemen, and its floor show specialized in young Vietnamese singers fresh from the country, trying out for the big time. Duc Quynh, the proprietor who had named the club after himself, did not pay them very much, and I always suspected that he took the same kind of interest in their careers that an enterprising Hollywood director does in the starlets on the lot. Duc was a short little man, and he was something of a Vietnamese Ed Sullivan. He had a portable microphone, and as he walked around the club he would often break into song. His favorite was "Joshua Fit de Battle of Jericho," which with his accent sounded very much like "Za Za feet de ball of Cheracoal."

The nice thing about Duc's place was the informality. The singers would come over and talk, and we always had a pleasant time. Young Vietnamese girls trying to break into show business are exactly like their American counterparts; there is the same self-conscious walk, the same frantic clasp on the pocketbook. The singers would come over to our table because my friend Can was a prominent figure: he owned a white sports car and was a well-known "cowboy" (a cowboy is the Vietnamese version of a playboy). He was also a television cameraman, and though none of the girls had ever seen television, the aura was potent. One of the singers was particularly nice to me for a while, and I was highly flattered until I learned her reasons: she wanted me as a reference at the American embassy so that she could marry a Special Forces sergeant who had been transferred to Okinawa.

All in all it was a good life. From time to time, particularly later, as we were criticized by *Time* and some tourist colleagues, and as the Government began to use force against us, we received solicitous letters from friends. But the sympathy was unnecessary; those of us who were lucky enough to be reporters in Vietnam considered ourselves the privileged few.

X

In the spring and summer of 1962 the arrival of the American helicopters had given the faltering cause in Vietnam a booster shot. It had not altered the nature of the war or the enemy's techniques, but they were caught off guard by the new equipment and the increased fire power of the Government troops. From May to September it appeared that the Government might regain the military initiative in the upper Mekong Delta region. Though the Vietcong were still showing considerable superiority in political and psychological warfare, they would have been in military trouble if the new weapons and human resources had been used properly.

It was a time of considerable optimism in Saigon but of considerable uneasiness among the Americans in the field, who for the first time were observing operations daily. At this time the strength of the main units of the Vietcong was relatively limited: about two hundred men each and very few automatic weapons. Theoretically they should hardly have been a match for the big, well-armed, well-equipped Government units.

But this was also a time of vital mistakes on the part of the Government, which were ignored by the American high command and which were to affect the future of the Delta and of the entire war. One of the most tantalizing questions of the American experience in Vietnam is to speculate what would have happened if the Americans had chosen to force a showdown with Diem over the situation in the Delta at this point in the game, when the war was, by international standards, a relatively small problem. The Cuban missile crisis and other, more dramatic events than the Vietnamese were occupying the front pages. Washington had other matters to cope with; officials there were not eager to hear about problems in Vietnam. As a result, the conflict there was a crisis seeking recognition.

In the rich and populous northern half of the Delta, the last major operation of the Seventh Division for many months was the one I observed on October 6, 1962, when the Vietcong's 514th Battalion changed its tactics: they stood and fought instead of fleeing, and decimated the Ranger company. Three days later a Civil Guard (provincial militia) battalion was operating in a nearby region when one of its companies suddenly came face to face with a reinforced Vietcong company. This was not an ambush; the units apparently stumbled on each other, and there was only time to draw. The fire fight was short and vicious. When it was over, eighteen of the Civil Guard were dead, but there were also eighteen guerrilla corpses. The American captain attached to the unit was pleased with the way the Civil Guard had reacted; his men had given as well as they had taken.

Still, the fact remained that within one week two Government units in a single division area had suffered quite heavy casualties. As mentioned earlier, Colonel Huynh Van Cao, the division commander, was summoned to President Diem to render a personal explanation. From that day, prudence became the byword of the Seventh Division. Almost all Vietnamese commanders were prudent, but some more than others. Diem had had a good listener. Cao was the most political-minded and most ambitious of all division commanders, and he was the least respected by his Vietnamese colleagues. Like Diem, he was a Catholic from central Vietnam—indeed, also from Hué, site of the Ngo ancestral home. His religion and his birthplace made him a member of that elite group trusted for military command in the Saigon area. The personal loyalty to Diem that he had demonstrated in the past had gained him a key position ahead of many Vietnamese considered far more capable and more experienced.

The Seventh was strategically located: only about forty miles from the capital on a main road, this division could help to depose—or to rescue—the chief of state in a matter of hours. Cao had earned this trust by coming to the aid of the beleaguered Diem during the 1960 paratrooper coup. In part this was because of genuine respect for the President; in part it was opportunism. Cao had hitched himself to Diem, and clearly he realized that he would rise or fall with him.

Cao was a vain man, the author of a thinly veiled, laudatory novel about himself entitled *He Grows Under Fire*. He admired Napoleon greatly, and his headquarters had attempted to duplicate Napoleon's map room. (This caused a certain amount of trouble, since in order to be an exact replica the only door into the room had to open smack in the middle of Long An Province on the war map. Cao was finally persuaded to move Napoleon's door somewhere else.)

Cao was apt to speak of victories in first person singular ("I kill fifty Vietcong today") and to exaggerate the enemy's casualty figures outrageously. Reporters finally devised the "Cao Formula": one took his figures, subtracted the announced Government casualties in the same action, then divided by three for a figure approaching reality. He was forever announcing that he had killed high-ranking Vietcong officials during battles; it was estimated that he had "killed" eight Communist zone chiefs the previous year. He also felt that he was the only officer who truly understood guerrilla warfare, and as a result believed that he could plot Vietcong movements four or five days in advance. He was invariably wrong, but the idea fascinated him.

Like many high-ranking Vietnamese officers, Cao was extremely skillful in handling visiting American officials. When General David Shoup, commandant of the Marine Corps, arrived in My Tho on a brief visit, he was greeted by the Seventh Division band playing the "Marine Hymn," and by a huge sign reading: "The United States Marine Corps: From the Halls of Montezuma to the Banks of the Mekong River."

Shoup was duly impressed. Before the arrival of Brigadier General Jerry Kelleher, chief of operations for Military Assistance Command, Vietnam, Cao grabbed Lieutenant Colonel John Vann, his U.S. adviser, and asked him what Kelleher's particular interest was. "Night patrolling and night fighting," Vann answered. When Kelleher arrived, Cao devoted a large part of his briefing to the importance of night fighting, emphasizing that his division needed to do more. "Then why don't you?" demanded Kelleher, leaving Cao speechless.

Like too many other politically appointed Vietnamese officers, Cao, who was a member of Nhu's Can Lao Party, had heard few shots fired in anger. He seldom visited the battlefield while fighting was going on, and he had almost no idea of how his troops reacted under fire. He was fond of saying that his men were the best trained in the world; they were, in fact, poorly trained and they needed instruction desperately. He rarely saw the province chiefs in his area, and he scheduled operations on the basis of whether a chief was being cooperative politically.

Cao was also an intriguer. At one point he told Colonel Frank Clay, a son of General Lucius Clay who was acting as adviser attached to his command, that a coup d'état was taking place in Saigon. Clay immediately notified his headquarters, which notified the Palace. Soon Diem called Cao and chewed him out for playing games. This was probably Cao's way of testing Clay to see how he would react.

Cao was extremely bright, but impressionable, so his American advisers attempted to create an aura of aggressiveness about him. They set out to convince his countrymen, other Americans and Cao himself that he was aggressive—in the hope that he would begin to act that way. New reporters were told about Cao's legendary aggressiveness. I bit the first time, and Cao was shown the resultant stories to prove to him that offensive action against the enemy was good publicity for him. At first this policy had some success, and it permitted his American advisers to plan operations that might otherwise have been considered too risky.

But in the long run, trying to sell American military tactics in what was not a buyer's market did not pay off, for well-intentioned Americans were bucking the Vietnamese system, and above all else Cao was a product of that system. His American advisers had no real leverage other than personal persuasion. Colonel Clay had threatened to withhold helicopters from Cao if he were not more aggressive, but it was an empty threat; the Vietnamese were well aware of how desperate the Americans were for more offensive operations. A Vietnamese commander could simply freeze out an American adviser who stuck to his principles, and before long the American would be replaced. Nowhere was this tactic more damaging than in the Delta. At this crucial time, in this single most important area of the country, Cao typified the system whose components were Diem's controls and suspicions, a hesitancy to risk casualties and use initiative, a failure to reward skill and courage.

The irony was that had it been to Cao's political advantage to be an aggressive commander, he would have followed American advice. But there was a basic disagreement about tactics between the Americans and the Ngo family, and Vietnamese like Cao and American advisers like Colonel Vann were victims of it. At this time most of the military emphasis and resources of the country were given to the central coastal region because the Ngo family trusted its people and none others. If the American military had had their way, the Delta would have received priority. Although 80 percent of the war was in the Delta during this period, only two of the nation's nine divisions were stationed there.

As mentioned earlier, the Americans in the field were uneasy about the progress of the war and felt that there was undue optimism about it. Lieutenant Colonel Vann, for instance, was particularly bothered about an operation on July 20, 1962, which had been called, both officially and in newspaper accounts, the greatest victory to date of the war. In this the first large helicopter operation at night, Government troops had landed smack on top of a Vietcong battalion near the Cambodian border. The Government troops fought well and inflicted heavy casualties on one company of the guerrillas; one hundred and forty-one Vietcong were killed almost immediately, whereas the Government losses were less than thirty.

However, nearly two hundred members of the enemy managed to escape. Vann, who had landed with the initial assault, called for a helicopter and pursued them. He radioed headquarters and advised Colonel Cao to have the reserve battalion that was waiting back at the command post dropped to the west in order to block the guerrillas attempting to escape in Cambodia. If the tactic had been executed properly, the disorganized, panicky enemy battalion would probably have been wiped out. Instead, as Vann watched in exasperation, the enemy moved off safely. When he finally returned to headquarters, Vann learned that some of the reserve force's helicopters had been used to fly the captured Vietcong weapons to the command post for display, that Vietnamese VIP's had been flown down from Saigon and that a huge victory party was already under way. When he pulled Cao away from the party and tried to find out what had happened, the Vietnamese explained that the reserve battalion was under a different command and that his regimental commander had not wanted to share his victory with another outfit.

Once again Government forces had let the Vietcong off the hook. To the American officers, this great victory was a very limited one. A battalion which might have been destroyed was still intact; in two weeks it would be back in action, harassing or wiping out small outposts, its members indoctrinating peasants, and very effectively and quietly challenging the Government for the control of a large area.

But there was worse to come. After the Diem-Cao meeting the entire momentum of the Seventh Division came to a halt. The joint planning staff, which the Americans had worked patiently on for a year and a half to set up, became a sham; Cao started to plan operations entirely on his own. Any attempt by the Americans to teach the Vietnamese the importance of military intelligence became futile. Despite improved intelligence about the whereabouts of the Vietcong, thousands of men were launched in operations aimed at areas free of the enemy. Escape routes were deliberately left in the planning of every operation lest the Vietcong be forced to hold their ground and fight, thus inflicting more casualties on Government troops. Assaults on treelines were preceded by prolonged artillery barrages in order to alert the guerrillas. Cao's prudence was almost phenomenal; in fourteen division operations, from the time of his October meeting with Diem to December 22, 1962, when he was duly rewarded for his loyalty and obedience, only four of Cao's regular troops were killed. During this same period hundreds of Civil Guard and Self-Defense Corps (village, or local, militia) troops were lost while defending static positions.

The *Times'* "News of the Week in Review" section stated on October 20:

> In the continual attempt to judge how well the war is going and how the increased American aid has affected it, there sometimes seems to be a tendency to describe results before they have been attained, and a parallel tendency to discredit pessimistic reporting. After all, it is said, how can anyone really judge how a war like this is going? Similarly, there might be a tendency to select what evidence you want to show that it is indeed going well. Thus, in recent months a stream of VIP's has breathed the official line of cautious optimism until it seems that each man, buoyed by the optimism of the last, is a bit more optimistic than his predecessor. It should be reported that there is considerably less optimism out in the field than in Washington or Saigon, and that the closer one gets to the actual contact level of the war, the farther one gets from official optimism.

The story then listed some of the mistakes which were being repeated regularly in Vietnam, and noted that the Americans

> were bothered by the lack of a sense of urgency in the fight against a quick and elusive enemy. There is some feeling on the part of Americans in the field that despite all the talk of counterguerrilla tactics, the real battle has yet to be joined. "Sometimes I think this war is being officially reported to look good on short-range progress

reports," one high American officer said. "Some basic
things just aren't being corrected and I don't know if we're
in a position to correct them." . . . Much of the optimism
still seems unwarranted. This is a war fought in the presence of a largely uncommitted, somewhat unfriendly peasantry by a government which has yet to demonstrate much
appeal to large elements of its own population. The enemy
is lean and hungry, experienced in this type of warfare,
endlessly self-critical, and above all an enemy who has
shown he is willing to pay the price for what he wants.
For that is the crucial question: Will the price be paid?
Despite all the American aid, this is not yet an American
war, and it remains for the Saigon government to show it
will pay the price . . .

Although none of us fully realized it then, this was the
decisive time in the Delta. A guerrilla war is seen first-hand
by the local population; for this reason, not only must a successful force in such a war prove that it has political benefits
to offer the peasantry, but it must also prove that it can protect
them. In such a military and political situation there is sometimes a crucial moment of truth, which is often unperceived
by fairly knowledgeable observers: the moment when the local population senses which side is winning. During those
months in the fall of 1962, I and others, although realizing
that the war was not going well, did not fully comprehend—
because the lack of Government momentum did not affect us
as directly as it did the peasants—just how badly things were
going. We talked in terms of stalemates, but I have since
become convinced that there is no such thing in a guerrilla
war. One side has the momentum and the other doesn't—it
is just that simple—and the first people to be aware of this
momentum are the peasants.

Moreover, guerrillas almost always try to attain their
objectives—both military and political—with as little fuss as
possible in order not to warn their opponent. In the Delta the
Vietcong had had all the momentum in the early part of the
war. In those days the Government forces were unprepared
to challenge the Vietcong, and the peasants sensed immediately that the guerrillas would probably be victorious in the

end. Then came the American build-up and the infusion of aid, which gave the Government forces a new vitality and mobility. For a time in the spring and summer of 1962, when the Government was challenging the Vietcong control of the upper Delta, the peasants moved back on the fence and our intelligence began to improve.

But in the fall of 1962 the slowdown came; the Government failed to utilize its mechanized equipment and other resources, and it squandered its momentum. Government battalions were not hunting and chasing and punishing the enemy; the Vietcong were allowed to lead more leisurely lives, and Government troops were not straying from the district capitals. Once again the first to realize the implications of this change of tempo were not the American intelligence officers in Saigon, or even in My Tho, nor the reporters, nor the optimistic officials in the Pentagon; it was the peasants living in the areas being fought over who knew that outposts were being overrun, knew that the guerrillas were moving about freely, knew which side was more willing to fight. The Vietnamese peasants are extremely realistic people, and they have a keen sense of the directions of the winds.

The sense of frustration of the American advisers during this period was acute. They were irritable and unhappy, and they were anxious that Cao get his star so that they could get on with the war. Their intelligence reported that the Vietcong was becoming stronger every day.

In My Tho in early February 1963, a young captain came over to me and said, "Do you want to see what this war is really like?"

I remember this incident quite well, though I wrote nothing about it at the time. It was not the kind of story I was eager to write. I was an American, and I was looking for operations and victories and captured weapons, not for small outposts which had been silently overrun and which would never be heard from again.

We flew in a helicopter to a small Self-Defense Corps post about forty miles away, which had been overrun that morning just before dawn. There we found the bodies of twenty of the SDC, almost all of them shot through the back of the head, which meant that many of them had been asleep at the time. This kind of incident was to become a familiar one in Vietnam; at the time its significance escaped me, but if I could have read the handwriting on the wall, I would have reported it.

The widows of the troops, frightened and bewildered, were wailing and asking for help. What little security they had enjoyed in life had just disappeared. They were surrounded by swarms of suddenly fatherless little children—the more isolated the hamlet, it seems, the greater the number of children. The American captain walked among the dead, making a point of showing me those corpses which had been badly mutilated by the enemy. We had an interpreter with us, and he talked to the women. "They want some troops to come here," the interpreter said. The captain told him to tell the women that he would try. "How can you promise anything in this goddamn country," he said bitterly. Then he asked the interpreter to tell the women that he was sorry about what had happened. He seemed embarrassed about saying this.

There was an old man among the remaining villagers, and through the interpreter the captain began to question him.

Were any of the SDC missing?

Two were missing.

How long had the fight for the post lasted?

There had been no fight.

Did the men from this post ever go out and patrol?

The old man said he was sorry, but he did not know about any patrols. (On the way back to My Tho, the captain said cynically, "They go out at night, walk down the path, take a leak, and then call it a night patrol.")

Did he know how many Vietcong there had been and what unit it had been?

At this the old man simply turned away. One could not blame him; the Vietcong were very strong in that area.

Later the captain said, "This happens every night. Half the time they get it in the head. Sometimes it's treachery, a plant inside, but not always. Those boys weren't out of that

outpost once in the last two months—you could tell by looking around. Why should they go out? What can they find?
What the hell do they protect?'' The captain had been in
Vietnam for only five months, but it was long enough for him
to be angry at the way the war was being fought. He told me
that the outpost had lost fifteen weapons, including a BAR—
enough arms for a platoon. ''They hit places like this every
night,'' he said.

In early December of 1962 we had learned that Cao would
get his star; he was to command the Fourth Corps, which
was responsible for the entire Delta. The announcement of
this and other promotions was one of those sleeper stories;
vitally important to American interests but virtually unno-
ticed in the United States—reports like this rarely make even
the back pages. The news media and the American public are
far more interested in stories about battles and casualties.

Cao's appointment showed once again how little influence
the Americans had in Vietnam. Indeed, American interven-
tion on behalf of a Vietnamese officer was likely to hurt him.
The three officers generally regarded by our military mission
as outstanding were at this same time all shunted into insig-
nificant positions. Duong Van Minh was given the title of
military adviser to the President; General Tran Van Don lost
command of the troops in the First Corps and became Army
commander—which meant that as a kind of official greeter he
had to go out to the airport and meet all visiting Americans.
Colonel Pham Van Dong, who was considered by many Americans the outstanding field commander in the country, was made
an inspector of the strategic hamlet program. The demotion of
Colonel Dong from deputy corps commander in the Delta was
a particularly hard blow to the Americans. They had been so
impressed by his leadership that they had urged Diem to make
him a general. Diem, however, did not trust Dong, and many
people—including Dong himself—believed that the American
recommendation had hurt his chances.

Curiously, troop command, which was sought by so many
competent Vietnamese officers, went to one man who was

unhappy in the role. In the Seventh Division, Cao was replaced by his former chief of staff, Colonel Bui Dinh Dam.
Colonel Dam was a nice little man and a good staff officer,
but the last thing he wanted was direct responsibility. He was
terrified of battle, of airplanes and of Cao. In his subsequent
days as division commander he was so frightened at the prospect of losses, particularly helicopter losses, that he almost
never employed the aircraft except when absolutely necessary
to ferry him back and forth from My Tho to the command
post. During these rare rides he would always sit alone, nervously fingering his rosary. He was not an imposing figure.

Cao had pushed Dam's appointment, since in effect it would
keep the division under his control, by telling Diem that Dam
was as loyal as Cao himself. It was indeed an intriguing way
of choosing an important officer for a key role in the war.
Yet, Dam's faults notwithstanding, there was a general sigh
of relief among the American advisers as the year 1962 ended
and the new shifts were made. The Americans felt that they
could exert more influence on Dam than they could on Cao.

Just how large the improvement was they found out very
soon. Late in December very reliable intelligence had reported the location of a Vietcong company in western Dinh
Tuong Province, just south of a village called Babeo. This
was in the same vicinity where the Rangers had been mauled
on October 6. It was a singularly tough area. Located on the
edge of the Plain of Reeds, about fifteen miles northwest of
My Tho, there was little access to it. "You can get into a
fight any time you want to up there," one American adviser
said. Its villages were lined with foxholes, and beneath some
of the huts were bomb shelters. Now, on December 28, heavy
enemy concentration was reported in Babeo. Colonel Vann,
working with Colonel Dam and hopeful of exerting influence
as soon as possible on his counterpart, urged the Vietnamese
officer to strike immediately, preferably on January 1, 1963.

Dam, who was extremely considerate of the people around
him, did not feel that American helicopter pilots should have
to get up at 4 A.M. after celebrating New Year's Eve. He had
a point, and the operation was set for January 2. The target
area was just north of a small village called Ap Bac. This

was to become a notorious name in Vietnam, and the event was to be scrutinized, debated, reviewed, investigated. The Americans in Saigon were, in fact, to do everything but learn from it.

When reading about Ap Bac it is important to remember the context in which the battle took place. The mercurial elusiveness of the Vietcong had become more and more exasperating and frustrating to the American advisers. Over and over again one heard the same sentence (which was to change as the Vietcong became stronger): *If we could only make them stand and fight.* The U.S. military were desperately eager for a traditional set-piece battle into which they could throw the Government's vastly superior material resources. At that time a Vietcong battalion averaged a little over two hundred men, equipped with a few automatic weapons. Only eight months later the same battalion was apt to average between four hundred and five hundred men, with—thanks to Government generosity—perhaps eight to ten machine guns, a large number of BAR's and several recoilless rifles.

Ap Bac was to be as close to a golden opportunity as there ever was in Vietnam; instead, it was a battle which demonstrated on a grand and dramatic scale all the tiny failings of the system, all the false techniques, evasions and frauds which had marked the war in Vietnam. It was also typical of the atmosphere existing at that time in Vietnam: having suffered a stunning defeat, the American military headquarters referred to it as a victory. Also, headquarters officers became angry not with the system which produced the defeat, nor with the Vietnamese commanders who were responsible for it, but with the American advisers who observed and criticized it and with the American reporters who wrote about it.

After the battle, when a Vietcong after-action report fell into Vietnamese hands, it was learned that the enemy had had a strong notion that an attack was imminent. Ironically, the guerrillas had been encamped at a point about two miles west of Ap Bac; fearing that an attack was coming there, they had moved eastward to the village itself—right into the pocket of the Government attack.

The Vietcong after-action report also revealed a hitherto

unsuspected guerrilla capacity to monitor the Government radio; the enemy knew when each Government unit crossed the line of departure, when and where the reserve was placed, what orders were given—and those which were not obeyed. There was even some glee expressed in the Communist report about the delay and difficulty in getting the ARVN troops to attack.

In the beginning our luck in the Ap Bac operation seemed very good. The Government force was three-pronged: a battalion of the Eleventh Regiment was to be landed to the north by three helicopter lifts; in the meanwhile, two task forces of Civil Guard troops, each of battalion size, would move up by foot from the south. In addition, a company of armored amphibious personnel carriers would assault from the west. This combat vehicle, commonly called a 113, is the closest thing to a tank in the Delta; if properly employed it can be an awesome weapon in this kind of war. It moves well through wet rice paddies, and it can deliver sustained fire against an entrenched enemy. Moreover, in those days the Communists had little in the way of antitank weapons.

If a reserve force were needed, it would be landed by helicopter in one of the many paddies to the west. The east was deliberately left unguarded because it consisted of relatively open rice land; if the Vietcong tried to flee across that barren terrain, they would make an excellent target for aircraft and artillery.

The planned assault of the three attacking forces looked something like an open claw. Inside this claw was the Vietcong's 514th Battalion, reinforced, according to our intelligence, by local guerrillas with at least three machine guns and a dozen or more BAR's. In the area there was also a vast and thorough network of foxholes. Most of the enemy were regular troops, disciplined and extremely accurate with their limited firepower. Since automatic weapons were highly prized by the Communists, the men handling the BAR's and machine guns were superbly trained. "When you recapture a BAR from them," an American captain told me, "it's a sign that you've wiped out an entire heavy-weapons squad. You usually get three or four bodies as well.''

The Vietcong had moved into the Ap Bac treeline because their battalion commander was wary of a heliborne force. Such evasion was typical of guerrilla tactics; they fought only when they had superior forces, and even then only when *they* could pick the time, terrain and circumstance of battle. When the Eleventh Regiment battalion landed to the north on the first of its three helicopter lifts, there was no shooting; only the third lift drew fire. The Vietcong did not want to tip off their position or join battle until necessary, for, unlike the Government force, they could not reinforce their troops, and they were only equipped for a one-day battle. Then, probing to the south, the guerrillas ran into Task Force A; gliding off to avoid an encounter, they moved slightly to the west, where they ran into Task Force B. At each point of contact, brief but fierce fire fights took place. After the second of these, the Vietcong moved back reluctantly to the treeline at Ap Bac and dug in. At last the standing battle the Americans wanted was about to take place. Analyzing his decision in the after-action report, the Vietcong commander wrote: ''It is better to stand and die than run and be slaughtered.''

Now Colonels Dam and Vann decided to land the reserve force to the west side of the village treeline. It was here that some of the most publicized aspects of Ap Bac took place, more dramatic than some of the weightier implications of the battle, for nearly all the helicopters ferrying in the reserve troops were hit. One managed to unload its troops but was so badly damaged that it could not take off again; a second, returning to the landing zone to help the first, also suffered direct hits and was unable to take off. A third helicopter then returned, drew heavy automatic-weapons fire, crashed and burned. All told, five American helicopters went down in the combat area, three of them when they returned for their downed companions. (Eventually this reopened an old debate on helicopter tactics. Some Americans—Vann among them— claimed that under such circumstances we were throwing good money after bad; others, like Brigadier General Joe Stilwell, Jr., chief of the support group and an officer particularly sensitive to the pilots' morale, felt that it was important for them to know that their own people would back them up.)

What else was happening made a dismal scene as well. All the flaws and lack of training came back to haunt the Government troops as the Vietcong stood and fought. The reserve troops that the now-crippled helicopters had ferried in suffered heavy casualties as they spilled out of the aircraft. Those who survived were almost immediately pinned down in paddies by heavy fire from the treeline, for the enemy, well armed and well camouflaged, had a clear field of fire.

The two task forces were only half a mile to the south, and the company of 113's, the perfect combat vehicle for this situation, was a little more than a mile to the west. But on this day they were useless. With the Americans desperately asking for help, Colonel Dam ordered the 113's to the site of the downed helicopters. Unfortunately, the commander of the mechanized unit was Captain Ly Tong Ba, a key Diem appointee. He was a complex officer; most Americans felt contempt for him, but others were quite impressed. He was a Southerner and an aristocrat, intelligent, quick, at times appallingly arrogant, something of a spoiled child. If he did, in fact, have some good days, this was not one of them; at this moment he refused to move his APC's. American officers trying to spur him on drew only curt remarks; he was a Vietnamese and they were Americans, and they could not tell him what to do. Overhead, Colonel Vann, circling in a light spotter plane, radioed Ba's unit that Dam had ordered it to advance. But Ba refused to move; he would not even send out a reconnoitering party to choose the best place to cross the canal—something that should have been done long before.

Finally Captain James Scanlon, an American adviser with the unit that had been pleading with Ba to attack, scouted a path for the unit himself and found a route from the crossing site to the treeline about a mile away. But even when Ba finally agreed to move, it took the armored unit four hours to reach the site of the battle. (After it was all over, Vann clocked the unit while it returned over the same stretch, and found that the carriers covered the same distance in fifteen minutes.)

When the 113's finally arrived at the open fields west of Ap Bac, they turned in a singularly futile performance. Despite the fact that these carriers were mounted with .50-caliber machine guns, recoilless rifles and light machine guns, they did not put a dent in the enemy's fire power. At times they cowered behind the downed helicopters; their gunners were firing without raising their heads, and often their tracers streamed off vainly into the sky. Ba fired the .50 in the command carrier for a few minutes, then relinquished it to a sergeant; within minutes the man was killed, and thereafter Ba had even less desire to fight than before.

In the meanwhile, Scanlon and an American sergeant named Bowers, who had landed with the reserve and had been pinned down with the helicopters, had to carry the wounded into the 113's by themselves. Following this, Scanlon, whose bravery was typical of that shown by many Americans that day, slipped behind the wall of the rice paddy where the troops were crouching. He found them thoroughly disorganized, holding their weapons over their heads and firing blindly. When he tried to rally them to attack a machine-gun post, the Vietnamese turned away from him. Scanlon found a young Vietnamese lieutenant who spoke English—or rather, as Scanlon was to recall later, who knew English "except when I asked him to attack." Although Scanlon then made the same request in Vietnamese, the officer pretended not to understand.

The armored personnel carriers, which had been designed by the United States for just such a situation, proved utterly inadequate. They failed because an ally did not use them properly, and because the officer commanding them felt no obligation to listen to the advice of his ally or to the commands of his superior. The carriers made a few sporadic stabs at the treeline but never a unified assault. Consequently, they suffered six casualties, though they never came close to the enemy, because the Vietcong were able to concentrate their fire on single vehicles.

To the south the situation was even worse. There, in a command post several miles from the battle zone, the province chief, Major Lam Quang Tho, a political appointee in

command of the province's troops, refused to allow his units
to budge. Theoretically, in a situation like this a division
commander had authority over a province chief, but in reality
it was purely a matter of who had more influence at the Palace. The Ngos were delighted to play division commanders
and province chiefs off against one another; the conflict would
keep both parties vacillating and insecure. As a result, province chiefs were in effect independent commanders.

Certainly, that day Major Tho was strikingly independent.
On his own he turned the two task forces into blocking forces;
in case someone just happened to chase the Vietcong out of
the treeline, forcing them toward the south, Major Tho would
be there waiting. Yet Tho had the best tactical position that
day, for both task forces were only a short distance from Ap
Bac and would have been able to slip up on the enemy's flank.
Unlike the reserve force to the west, which was bearing the
full brunt of the Vietcong fire power and which would have
had to attack across an open field, the units to the south would
have been protected by the treeline itself as they advanced.

Three times that day, according to both Vann and Dam,
the latter ordered Tho to attack to the north with his task
forces. Each time Tho refused. Four times a young lieutenant
commanding Task Force B asked for permission to attack;
each time it was denied. (It was incidents such as this which
kept alive a spark of hope among reporters that under some
circumstances the war could go better.) Like Captain Ba, Major Tho was never court-martialed or even investigated for his
disobedience at Ap Bac.

By midafternoon, when it became increasingly apparent
that the regular units would not attack, let alone overrun the
Vietcong, the commanders and advisers decided to ask for
the reinforcement of an air-borne battalion from Saigon. But
here again the American advisers ran into the Vietnamese system, and this resulted in the third fatal mistake at Ap Bac. The
decision to call on the airborne battalion was made at 2:30 P.M.,
which meant that it would probably arrive just before dark.
The Americans believed that in the meantime there would
be little change in the battle lines, and therefore their idea—
with Colonel Dam's concurrence—was to use the air-borne

battalion to try and block the one open side, the east, in order to bottle up the Vietcong for the night. While the terrain there was too open for the Vietcong to move safely during the day, the canal system would permit them to get away under cover of darkness; it was a foregone conclusion that they would try to slip away at night. But Vann and Colonel Daniel Boone Porter, the corps adviser, hoped that if the air-borne battalion plugged the gap, and if flares were dropped all night long and the area was bombarded with artillery, they could contain the Vietcong until the next morning.

This was hardly a foolproof method; nevertheless, the enemy had taken a heavy pounding all day from Government fighter bombers and armed helicopters, they probably had a fair amount of wounded and they might not be as mobile as usual. General Cao, however, who was now the corps commander and who was at the command post with Porter, disagreed with this plan. He decided to drop the air-borne to the west, behind the reserve force. The Americans protested vigorously; as Vann said later in discussing this decision, "They chose to reinforce defeat rather than to try for victory." Cao was adamant; obviously he had suffered more casualties than he wanted (the final figure was sixty-one dead and one hundred wounded) and he was determined to break off the fight.

Thereafter, to all intents and purposes, the battle was over. Ironically, the air-borne battalion landed at dusk, as estimated, and in the resultant confusion a fire fight costing several lives took place between them and the reserve force.

A bitter parody of Ap Bac, written by one of the helicopter pilots to the tune of "On Top of Old Smoky," went:

> The paratroops landed
> A magnificent sight
> There was hand-to-hand combat
> But no VC's in sight.

Several days later, when Cao's decision came under increasing scrutiny, he attempted to blame Dam for the decision, claiming that Dam was in command and that he, Cao, had only *suggested* the landing to the west. In the presence

of General Le Van Ty, the Vietnamese Army commanding
general, Vann defended Dam and said that he had been over-
ruled by Cao. Cao's behavior was hardly a surprise; when I
showed up at the command post a few days later, he made a
special point of saying to me, ''This is the first operation of
the Seventh Division since I left it. It is now under a new
commander.'' That same night the inevitable happened: the
Vietcong escaped. They policed up their brass and left only
three bodies behind. Their battlefield discipline had been excellent. Madame Nhu, who had been told that the battle was
a victory and that the only problem had been caused by an
American colonel flying around in a small plane contradict-
ing American advice, never forgave me for quoting our advisers on how well the Vietcong had fought.

In Saigon the reporters heard about Ap Bac in the middle of
the afternoon. Peter Arnett, Mert Perry and I started checking around. At first all we could learn was that three helicopters were down and that a heavy fire fight was going on.
Finally, at 6 P.M., we were able to put together a fragmentary
story. But none of us was satisfied, so we went out to Tan
Son Nhut air base to talk to the tired, tense and bitter helicopter pilots as they came in.

Later, General Harkins and the public information officers
seemed surprised at the extent of our knowledge about the
battle; how they expected to keep such a disaster secret when
it had taken place within fifty miles of Saigon is puzzling.
However, it was typical of the American command in Saigon
that though we filed stories about Ap Bac for three days, none
of the military or State Department information officers ever
bothered to go down there; the reporters went every day.

That evening we got a very good story from the pilots
about the helicopters' part in the battle, and returned to Saigon to file. We showed far less initiative, however, than Neil
Sheehan of UPI and Nick Turner of Reuters, who had hired
a car immediately and driven down to My Tho that afternoon.
There Sheehan pieced together a much fuller and more basic
account of what had happened, and of the failure to attack.

Ironically, Arnett's and my stories received much wider use—
because they were concerned mainly with what interested
Americans the most, the downed helicopters—than Sheehan's
piece, which was about more disturbing and significant aspects of the battle.

On January 3 we flew down to the command post at Tan
Hiep airstrip, where I asked Vann what had happened. "A
miserable damn performance," he said, "just like it always
is." The Americans' bitterness was compounded by the frustration of watching a perfect opportunity squandered, by the
loss of three Americans, including Ken Good, and by the
death of so many Vietnamese. It was still early in the morning, and no Government troops had set foot inside Ap Bac;
yet the advisers knew instinctively, like a good fisherman
whose line has gone slack, that the Vietcong were gone.

Arnett and I went to Ap Bac in a helicopter. We circled
the area for several minutes. The parachutes lay like tiny
handkerchiefs in the paddies, the dead still sprawled there,
and the tracks of the armored personnel carriers told the story
more clearly than any after-action report. Below us, Sheehan
and Turner, who had arrived before we did, were walking
through the village with Brigadier General (now Major General) Robert York.

"What happened?" Sheehan asked York.

"What the hell's it look like happened, boy," York answered. "They got away—that's what happened."

There was almost no hope of any pursuit. On the field to
the west of Ap Bac, Captain Scanlon was again having trouble with the Vietnamese—this time to get them to load their
dead into a helicopter. Most of the loading was being done
by Americans, and only when Scanlon threatened one soldier
bodily did the men come out of their trance. Sheehan helped
them. "I saw all those bodies covered with blankets, with
their little feet sticking out, and I did something I hadn't done
in years," he told me. "I crossed myself."

Moments later, while General York and Sheehan and
Turner were waiting in the open paddies to hitch a ride back
in the helicopters, the final bitter touch of the nightmare occurred: from a distant CP, Major Tho began to fire artillery

into the village. There was no forward observer, of course, and by the time the barrage ended, five Government soldiers had been killed and fourteen wounded. Sheehan and York hit the marshy ground as shells landed within fifty yards of them.

When Arnett and I flew back to the CP we found a brass-plated, white-helmeted honor guard paying tribute to General Cao, who had not bothered to visit the battlefield. General Harkins was also there, about to leave for Saigon, and we asked him what was happening. "We've got them in a trap," he said, "and we're going to spring it in half an hour." We looked at him, completely bewildered. The enemy was long gone, the Government troops were so completely disorganized that they would not even carry out their own dead, a province chief was shelling his own men—and a trap was about to be sprung? As on so many other occasions in Vietnam, we never knew whether Harkins believed what he was saying, or whether he felt that it should be said.

The battle of Ap Bac was followed by a second battle—a press battle. Two days later Admiral Harry Felt, Harkins' superior officer, arrived in Saigon on an inspection trip obviously precipitated by Ap Bac. At the airport Sheehan asked Felt if he had any comment. The admiral replied, "I'd like to say that I don't believe what I've been reading in the papers. As I understand it, it was a Vietnamese victory—not a defeat, as the papers say." He turned to Harkins, who said, "Yes, that's right. It was a Vietnamese victory. It certainly was." As they turned away Harkins apparently identified Sheehan, for Felt turned around and said, "So you're Sheehan. I didn't know who you were. You ought to talk to some of the people who've got the facts."

Sheehan, who can hardly be described as a shy young Irishman, answered, "You're right, Admiral, and that's why I went down there every day."

However, Ap Bac had created a sharp reaction in the States, where a combination of public disinterest and official optimism had left most people unprepared for bad news. Suddenly the fact that three Americans had been killed and five helicopters downed aroused the interest of the American public in the failures that were taking place. "People keep writing me," Ambassador Nolting said several days later, "asking, 'Fritz, what's going on out there all of a sudden? I thought we were doing so well.' "

On the second day after the battle, a group of Vietcong troops in the vicinity of Ap Bac were actually flushed out. When Government officers refused to provide a promised blocking force, Vann finally rounded up every available American, including clerk typists, water purification men and cooks, and formed his own blockade to help capture some of the enemy. Ironically, because I was covering this incident I missed a conference which was symbolic of the whole dispute between the American press and its government. Roger Hilsman, then Assistant Secretary of State for Far Eastern Affairs, was in Saigon and had expressed the desire to meet reporters informally. During the discussion some of the reporters, particularly Charley Mohr, tried to explain why the Government was failing in its mission, and of Nhu's basic hostility to the United States. Hilsman implied that the reporters were naïve, that the important thing was not to be liked, but to be tough and get things done. It was an acrimonious session.

Our reporting about Ap Bac brought us immediate criticism from the mission. Every army, the line went, had its defeats; why build up Ap Bac? But time after time we had watched the ARVN turning in sloppy performances, regularly disregarding both American advice and common sense. We had filed stories on these skirmishes but had found it extremely difficult to present the true picture to our readers; a typical piece would end with a little note saying, "The Vietcong got away," which hardly did justice to the situation. To us and to the American military advisers involved, Ap Bac epitomized all the deficiencies of the system: lack of aggressiveness, hesitancy about taking casualties, lack of battlefield leadership, a nonexistent chain of command. The failures at Ap Bac had been repeated on a smaller scale every day for the past year, and if not corrected quickly, they boded even greater trouble for the future.

We were also under fire for two press mistakes made during the confusion of battle: an early AP story, quickly corrected, stating that eight helicopters instead of five had been downed; and Sheehan's story, gleaned from a bitter field adviser, that Ken Good had died while trying to rally troops. Good had actually been killed by a stray sniper bullet, though he had been in the fore, pushing the attack heroically all day. Our substantive account of Ap Bac and its failures was entirely accurate; if anything, reporters had not elaborated fully on the incompetence displayed.

On January 6, I wrote a piece reflecting the feeling of most field advisers:

> Apparently the only people not surprised are the American advisers in the field, who have long felt that the progress of the war was not so good as the high brass was claiming, and who felt that conditions in the field made a defeat like this virtually inevitable. Americans hope that one product of the defeat will be an improved and more fruitful relationship between American advisers and Vietnamese counterparts . . . What is more, these American advisers, not just in this area, but throughout the Mekong Delta, feel that what happened at Ap Bac goes far deeper than one battle and is tied directly to the question of whether the Vietnamese are really interested in having American advisers and listening to them . . . These advisers feel that too much of the burden of the relationship has been placed on the Americans "to get along . . ."

Many advisers felt that Ap Bac gave the American high command tangible evidence of what they had been reporting for months, and there was much hope that something positive would finally happen. One captain even told a reporter that he was sure Harkins would make a strong case with the Government over the failure of Ap Bac. The adviser was so emphatic about this that the correspondent went to see John Mecklin, the head public affairs officer, to ask whether it was true that Harkins planned to make a formal protest to Diem.

Of course there was no protest, formal or informal. The set policy, or at least the interpretation of it by the high American officials there, was to get along with the regime and to convince the American people that the war was going well. A fuss over Ap Bac, which had such basic implications for the military, political and diplomatic status quo in Vietnam, would almost surely incite Diem, and this, given the nature of the Government, was sure to be useless. Moreover, it would be hard to maintain the picture of a successful war at home if disputes between American and Vietnamese officials were reported. Thus, the reaction of the American mission to Ap Bac was just as important as the battle itself, for eventually the mission focused not on what had gone wrong and why, but on the men who had talked and written about it.

But the American officials' blindness went even further. In the curious Vietnamese lexicon, Ap Bac became a victory. This theme, sounded first at the airport by Admiral Felt, was reiterated two days later at a joint press conference held by Harkins and Felt. The admiral—a shrewd, tough officer—spent the early part of the press conference talking about how well things were going. When someone asked him about the defeat at Ap Bac, Felt repeated what he had said at the airport to Sheehan, and turned the session over to poor Harkins. The general, who had been doodling on a pad, suddenly looked up and said, "Yes, I consider it a victory. We took the objective." We were all stunned at these new rules for guerrilla war—evidently the objective now was terrain, not the enemy. Harkins did not mention that "the objective" had been taken twenty-seven hours late, long after the enemy had departed.

After the press conference the PIO's handed out a brief statement by Harkins; the powers that be were going to have their say and we were not going to be able to question them on it. The statement defended the bravery of Vietnamese troops. "I am very concerned," the statement said, "over recent allegations critical of the valor and courage of the Vietnamese soldier. I believe that anyone who criticizes the fighting qualities of the armed forces of the Republic of Vietnam is doing a disservice to the thousands of gallant and courageous men who are fighting so well in defense of their country."

That night I filed a story quoting Harkins' statement, noting that he was knocking over a straw man; it was not the courage of the individual soldier that was being questioned, but the way he was led and the basis of the advisory relationship. Most Americans felt the Vietnamese was about as good a soldier as his leaders wanted him to be. The story added: "Americans who deal with President Diem claim that Diem knows there will be casualties and is willing to allow for this. If this is true, say the field advisers, then the word has not yet reached the Vietnamese in the field."

This story and all the others inspired by Ap Bac infuriated the embassy, and Ambassador Nolting ordered Mecklin to draft a white paper on the role of the press. The resultant statement said that the American interest in Saigon was being hurt by sensational reporting. The journalists, it said, were young, immature, not used to working in such a complicated and sensitive atmosphere, and tended "to seek black-and-white answers where they do not exist."

Mecklin, who was soon to change his view as the Government continued to abuse the population, and who was to become a real friend of the reporters and to take considerable personal risks in helping them to cover the story of Vietnam, wrote two drafts of the white paper. The first was not strong enough to satisfy Nolting, and Mecklin was ordered to make it tougher (he later noted that leaving his name on it was the silliest thing he had ever done). It was typical of the atmosphere in Saigon at this time that the division between the heads of the mission and their subordinates was so sharp that though this was a classified paper, an American immediately turned it over to us reporters. We said nothing about it, but we were the wiser for reading it.

Regardless, the point of the white paper was clear: the problem was not one of night fighting and of outposts; it was one of public relations. Several months later, in a letter to the *Washington Post*, my brother, commenting on Joseph Alsop's views, referred to this attitude as the "old but naïve theory that if one . . . writes nice things about the high school team perhaps it will finally win some games."

In an attempt to counter the bad publicity about Ap Bac, Nolting ordered the release of a four-month-old captured Vietcong document. This stated that the Vietcong had underestimated American intentions in Vietnam and that the Communist timetable had been slowed down. But I and my colleagues felt that in general this document was a much more accurate and perceptive description of the war and the forces at play in it than any American statement we had ever read. It predicted that the Americans would become bogged down in a frustrating, unrewarding war; it described prophetically the built-in contradictions of the American-Diem relationship; and it noted that though the Government had a vast military superiority at the time, the Vietcong retained "absolute political superiority." We were all a bit chilled by its acute analysis. None of us wrote the stories that I believe the mission anticipated; for example, Mal Browne borrowed the American mission's favorite phrase at the time and noted that the Vietcong appeared "cautiously optimistic."

While American officials turned on the reporters—thereby abdicating hope for any new leverage with Diem by telling him in effect that it was all right for him to do whatever he pleased—the rewriting of history was taking place. General Cao was telling Americans, particularly ones with new faces, that seven Russian advisers had been seen in Ap Bac. In Saigon the Government-controlled papers were already attacking Vann, who, they said, had given contradictory orders to Vietnamese troops from a plane above Ap Bac. According to this version, the troops had done the proper thing in all the confusion by staying where they were, thus showing considerable bravery. Sheehan, whose reporting on Ap Bac had shown particular enterprise and initiative, was also singled out. One paper ran a photo of him in uniform, with a banner headline exclaiming: "The American Adviser Sheehan; What Does He Really Want?" There was no story—just the headline and the photo—but henceforth Sheehan was known among us as The-American-Adviser-Sheehan, and was repeatedly badgered by the question, "What do you *really* want?"

General Ty, the commander of the ARVN forces and a nice but powerless man, showed up in My Tho a week later to find out what had happened at Ap Bac. Cao and Dam were there, and Vann was summoned to listen while Cao exonerated himself at great length, blaming Dam for the failure.

Finally General Ty turned to Vann and asked if he agreed with what he had just heard. For the first time Vann criticized Cao to his face in the presence of a third person. But by trying to save Dam from being the scapegoat, Vann made an enemy; he and Cao were never to have any mutual confidence again.

Next, General Ty asked, "Colonel Vann, why do our soldiers perform so poorly in battle?"

Vann took a deep breath, and then pointed out that though there were five Vietnamese field-grade officers in the room, he, the single American, was the only one who knew how the troops performed because he was the only one who had ever observed them on the battlefield, who had ever seen what went wrong, and who knew why plans frequently did not work. He noted that despite Cao's claim that his troops were the best trained in the world, they could not even set up a simple field of fire.

General Ty, who as an orphan had been adopted by French troops, and who had served with them in the field as a master sergeant and knew a good deal about men and combat, simply nodded. A few minutes later he excused everyone but Cao, and then gave the general a tongue-lashing. Every time his voice could be heard through the door, Dam shuddered.

There were others who did not believe that Ap Bac was a victory for the Government. In the Vietcong after-action report—which was much more detailed and accurate than the Government's—they analyzed the Government errors, pointing out that the battle was a major psychological setback for the ARVN, and that the effect it would have on the population would benefit the guerrillas enormously.

Then, in order to gain a further psychological edge, the Vietcong commander took his troops back into Ap Bac a week later, flew the Vietcong flag from several rooftops, and sent Cao a letter daring him to come back and fight. The Americans pleaded with the Vietnamese for an operation. The photos taken by a reconnaissance plane were studied, plans for an operation were drawn up, and in Saigon two Marine battalions were placed on alert for several days. But there was no operation. Cao refused to engage the enemy; he wanted no more part of the 514th Battalion.

Three months later Cao finally returned to Ap Bac, this time with five thousand men—one of the largest operations in Vietnamese military history—carefully telegraphing his moves so that there would be no major contact. In a preliminary scouting expedition the night before the operation, a Civil Guard company ran into a battalion of Vietcong, probably in an ambush. A Government regimental commander immediately ordered two companies of his regulars to close with the guerrillas. They were moving toward the trapped company when Dam, now even more conservative under pressure from his corps commander, told them to break contact. The next day the huge operation went forward and the troops found no sign of the Vietcong. In the meantime the Civil Guard company had been decimated.

XI

For Lieutenant Colonel John Vann, the battle of Ap Bac and the subsequent Vietnamese and American reaction to it were a bitter disappointment. Many Americans considered him one of the two or three best advisers in the country. In September 1962, when General Maxwell Taylor had come to Vietnam on one of his frequent trips, he had lunched with four advisers of different rank who were generally considered outstanding; Vann had represented the division advisers.

Vann was a man of curious contrasts. Thirty-seven years old, one of the young lieutenant colonels in the Army, he was clearly on his way to becoming a full colonel, with a very good chance of eventual promotion to general. (His recognizable superiority is the reason that some of the high people in the Pentagon wish that Vann had never happened, for his case documented and symbolized so many embarrassments that might otherwise have been swept under the rug.) He was clearly about to take off in his career—one of those men who reaches his mid-thirties and suddenly begins to pull away from his contemporaries.

Yet most Army officers of this type tend to be sophisticated and polished, usually with a West Point background, often from second- or third-generation Army families—in contrast to some of their colleagues who excel as combat officers, but

who find other aspects of the Army a bit baffling. Vann, however, could hardly have been more different from the traditional gentleman-soldier. There was little polish to him: he
was a poor boy from Virginia, who always reminded me of
a good old Appalachian South redneck—and it was literally
true that on operations his neck and arms always turned an
angry red.

Vann had risen by sheer drive, vitality and curiosity. After
one year of college he had enlisted at the age of eighteen,
and became a B-29 navigator at the end of World War II. In
1950 and 1951 he commanded the first air-borne Ranger company to be sent to Korea, specializing in actions behind enemy lines and against North Korean guerrillas who were
trying to harass UN forces behind our lines. After Korea the
Army sent him to Rutgers to teach the ROTC units there; he
learned as well as taught, going to night school and receiving
his B.S. degree. Then he was assigned to the University of
Syracuse (the Army is very good about encouraging its people to pick up extra degrees), where he got an M.A. in business administration and all the credits necessary for a Ph.D.
in public administration. (He has written one thesis, which is
all he lacks for the degree, but is not satisfied with it.) He
also attended the Army's Command and General Staff College.

Vann is a blunt, essentially conservative, at times almost
reactionary man. One of the ironies of Vietnam was that at a
time when the Pentagon and other elements unhappy with our
reporting were claiming privately that the foreign correspondents in the country were a bunch of liberals who opposed
Diem on ideological grounds, much of our information came
from men like Vann.

Vann had volunteered for duty in Vietnam. Once there, he
had shaken a desk job; then, knowing that he was to replace
Colonel Frank Clay in the Seventh Division, he had gone on
as many helicopter missions in the Delta as possible while
preparing to take over; by the time he left Vietnam he had
participated in more than two hundred helicopter assault land-
ings. As a result, he knew as much or more about his area
of Vietnam than any other adviser—or indeed than any Viet-

namese officer—that I ever met. He also *walked* through one operation every week, and even ordered his Air Force liaison officer, Major Herb Prevost, to walk with the field soldiers regularly. Hence, Prevost became that rarity in Vietnam: an Air Force man who knew something about the effect of his weapons and about the political complexities of the war.

Once a week Vann also visited the three regiments and seven provincial capitals within his bailiwick, driving to some, going by light plane to others. His Vietnamese counterparts, Cao and Dam, who hated traveling by light plane and frequently became airsick, were delighted to have him take over these inspection tours. He frequently stayed in these local headquarters as a guest of the province chief; invariably the chief would send a girl up to the room—an attempt, Vann suspected, to get something on him and thus give the chief some leverage if there should ever be any conflict.

Vann endlessly interrogated the missionaries and priests in his area, and any time a reporter saw him, he was likely to be questioned closely about what he had seen in other parts of Vietnam.

Vann also tried to set an example by his personal courage, and his walking in the field on major operations had a considerable effect on the Vietnamese troops, who had never seen any of their own officers above the rank of captain in the field. But the walks had another purpose: they were a futile attempt to shame Vietnamese officers into walking in the paddies too. What Vann, and many others like him who tried similar tactics, failed to realize was the power of the mandarin legacy: the whole point of being a major or colonel was that you *didn't* have to go into the field, and therefore the distinction and class separation of such officers from their juniors was much sharper than in a Western army, and the prerogatives of a high rank were more fondly cherished.

What the Americans were attempting to do, by setting examples like this, epitomized our entire problem in Vietnam. They were trying to persuade an inflexible military ally, who had very little social or political sense about its own people, to do what the Americans knew must be done, but this would force the Vietnamese officers to give up the very things that really mattered to them and that motivated them in the first place. How could anyone make the Vietnamese officers see, almost overnight, that the purpose of promotion was not primarily to separate them from the misery whence they came, but to get them to inspire or lead others?

Vann also insisted on driving his own jeep unescorted after dark in an attempt to change the Vietnamese belief that the night belonged to the Vietcong. Moreover, he ordered all his advisers to go out on at least one night operation or patrol each week; this well-intentioned directive failed, simply because many of the advisers could not persuade any troops to go with them. Eventually, at Cao's request, the colonel rescinded the order.

If Vann had any shortcoming, it was one typical of the best of the American advisers in Vietnam: the belief that the adviser's enthusiasm, dedication and effort could, through diplomatic guidance of his Vietnamese counterpart, successfully buck the system. This naïveté was the result of favorable encounters with other systems, and an overly optimistic view that in time of war common sense will prevail and allies will be inclined to agree on basic goals. This hope was doomed in Vietnam; the system was stronger than the men bucking it, particularly in the pressure of the fighting in the Delta. Tantalizingly, there was always just enough of a glimmer of success, or a transitory victory or just plain luck, to make the advisers keep trying.

We reporters admired Vann greatly, not because he gave us scoops—there are no scoops in a rice paddy—but because he cared so desperately about Vietnam, because he knew so much about his area, and because whenever we were with him we had a sense that a very real war was being fought— and not fought on a peacetime footing with peacetime hours and peacetime arrogance toward an Asian enemy. The remarkable thing about Vann, and a few others of his caliber who were fully aware of the shortcomings of the war, was that they still believed that under certain circumstances the war could be pursued successfully. This was the best kind of optimism; it was not the automatic we-are-winning push-button chant of Saigon, but a careful analysis of all the prob-

lems on both sides, and a hope that there were still time and
human resources enough to change the tide.

In part, the reporters believed this too; though we were
frequently criticized for being too pessimistic, I believe that
a more valid criticism would have been that we were too
optimistic. This is debatable, of course, but I think that anyone watching so much bravery squandered during those
months could not have helped wondering what would happen
if that talent were properly employed.

In the days before Ap Bac, Vann was something of a ce-
lebrity and reporters were quickly channeled to his area by
the PIO's. Later, after the atmosphere began to sour in the
Delta, visiting reporters and officials were sent to the montagnard region, inhabited by primitive mountain people,
where they were often initiated into a tribe, watched a buffalo
being slaughtered, drank rice wine (or pretended to drink the
raw liquid), received a genuine montagnard tribal bracelet,
and were told, with varying degrees of accuracy, that the war
was going well in that region.

The first time I ever met Vann he shook hands, told me
that I was lucky because there would be an operation the next
day that I could go out on, and then said, "Well, Halberstam,
the first thing you'll learn is that these people may be the
world's greatest lovers, but they're not the world's greatest
fighters." He paused, and then added, "But they're good
people, and they can win a war if someone shows them how."

Over a period of time Vann and a few officers like him
taught most of the foreign correspondents the essentials of
guerrilla war: why the outposts were a detriment ("They
know where we are, but we never know where they are");
the danger of using the wrong weapon ("This is a political
war and it calls for discrimination in killing. The best weapon
for killing would be a knife, but I'm afraid we can't do it that
way. The worst is an airplane. The next worst is artillery.
Barring a knife, the best is a rifle—you know who you're
killing"); the dangers of the American material commitment
("By giving them too much gear—airplanes and helicopters—
we may be helping them to pick up bad habits instead of
teaching them to spend more time in the swamps than the

enemy''); the importance of the weapons exchange (''I don't think the Vietcong have any problems of recruiting; I think for varying reasons they can get all the people they want. Their problem right now is getting weapons; that's the only thing limiting the size of their units and the nature of their attacks, so unless we stop arming them we'll be in a very serious situation'').

There was nothing ideological in Vann's make-up; he was simply a man of consuming curiosity and drive. He ran all the time, and he forced the young American officers around him to run just as hard, whether it was in the field or playing volleyball at the old seminary, where the Seventh Division advisers were housed. It was hard for him to compromise; he once told me that the trouble with compromise was that often it meant taking a position between something that was right and something that was wrong, with the result that you ended up with something that was neither right nor wrong. In war, Vann said, that's not good enough. It was this sense of commitment, and this unwillingness to compromise and blend in with the system—the American system, which was fast becoming a parallel of the Vietnamese—that finally brought Vann to a showdown with his superiors.

In February 1963, in the midst of the dry season, the Seventh Division was still virtually inactive. It had refused to fight at Ap Bac, and now it was refusing countless other opportunities to engage the enemy at a time of year that favored the hunter rather than the guerrilla. Our intelligence had improved, and knowledge of the enemy's whereabouts vastly exceeded the Government's willingness to act on it. For weeks the officers in the advisory group waited and fumed about the sham operations that the division was launching. Finally, in the first week of February, Vann sent a long and detailed message to American headquarters. In it he noted that there were now ten points where the Vietcong were known to be located in company strength or more; about thirty-five areas where they were known to be located in platoon strength or more; and that despite this intelligence the Vietnamese refused to act. It was a very strong and fully documented indictment.

When it reached Saigon, the message created a major controversy. President Diem was already angry with Vann because of the press coverage of Ap Bac and had urged General Harkins to remove him. Consequently, Harkins was less than enchanted with Vann; in addition, he held Vann partly responsible for the press coverage of Ap Bac. The general felt that somehow Vann should have been able to manage the outflow of news better. He was so angered by Vann's latest message that he called a meeting and designated a staff officer to investigate the report. If there were any mistakes in it, he wanted Vann relieved.

The officer spent eight hours checking the intelligence reports at My Tho. On his return to Saigon another staff meeting was held, and the officer announced that the only thing wrong with Vann's paper was that all of it was true. Harkins still wanted to relieve Vann, claiming that his relationship with Colonel Dam must be unsatisfactory. After the meeting, however, several other generals on the staff persuaded Harkins that if Vann were relieved it might seriously damage the morale of the advisory group, and that when the reporters found out about Vann's dismissal it might create a major scandal. (As a matter of fact, Vann never told any of the reporters about this; I only learned of it weeks later from another staff officer who was still angry about the incident.)

Thus began the quiet struggle between the field advisers and Harkins. Gradually others became involved, but throughout this showdown Harkins was aided immensely by the traditional pressure an army places on its younger officers not to contradict a superior.

The task before General Paul Donal Harkins could hardly have been more difficult; he was a diplomat without leverage, a commander without true command authority. (For example, on Thanksgiving Day in 1962, after the largest helicopter operation of its kind had turned into a major flop—fifty-six aircraft had been used in an assault which resulted in the death of seventeen water buffaloes—Sheehan had written that the operation had taken place with the cooperation of MACV under the command of General Paul Harkins. Lieutenant Colonel Jim Smith, the PIO at the time, called Sheehan to complain about the use of Harkins' name. "Uncle Paul doesn't want his name used. We're only here as advisers," he said. Sheehan answered, "Tell Uncle Paul that he's in charge of the American Military Command here, that he's the man who released those helicopters, that those are American helicopters flown by American pilots and that his name goes in my stories.") Although Harkins was a general, his job was not so much to command fellow soldiers, but to get along with Diem and Nhu, extraordinarily difficult and suspicious allies with most unmilitary minds.

Harkins is a West Point man who served with distinction as a staff officer to General George Patton during World War II. He had been chosen for this post in Vietnam by General Maxwell Taylor, who had written the victory plan for Vietnam. Harkins was also known in Army circles as a good diplomat, a man who could be counted on to get along with a difficult man like Diem. His boiling point was relatively high and he was not likely to pound the table, speak indiscreetly to reporters or veer from the policy line. His appointment was, in fact, a substantive *part* of the policy; the hard line against Diem had been abandoned and the soft line, the tactic of smothering Diem with kindness and keeping our own people in line, was put into effect with Harkins' appointment.

The private instructions that Harkins received from Taylor are a matter of conjecture, but almost certainly they must have included the suggestion that Harkins turn his cheek to a great deal of Vietnamese mendacity. Thus, when Vann challenged the direction of the war in his area—the Seventh Division—he was raising doubts about the effectiveness of our whole policy and questioning the role of the man who had been specifically chosen because he would go along with the policy. If the Kennedy Administration, knowing that it was a tenuous policy at best, had selected as its instrument someone more likely to draw a line, there is a chance that the story of Vietnam might have been slightly different—but of course this is pure conjecture.

Even today when Washington admits to the great discrepancy between its prolonged optimism and the obviously serious existing situation, it talks in the most superficial terms about increases in terrorism and post-coup command changes, rather than facing squarely the substantive factors that, step by step, determined the pattern and rhythm of defeat.

Harkins had other problems. He had spent a lifetime in conventional-war situations and had no particular preparation for a complex and delicate political war, where the most important voices often spoke in the softest whispers. He was probably more willing to settle for the straight "kill" statistics characteristic of traditional military situations than for the circumstances which produced those statistics. One's impression was always that MACV's figures reflected what MACV wanted to hear. There was no differentiation, for instance, between Government forces killed on offensive operations and those killed in static, defensive points, though this would have been one of the truest indicators of how successfully the war was being conducted. An estimated 70 percent of the total casualties—and this remained a constant, according to American advisers—were inflicted at static points, thus proving that the attempt to mobilize the Government forces had failed.

Another factor was against Harkins: his age. He was born in 1904 and was in his late fifties during his years in Vietnam. The problems that existed in Vietnam in those days—the legacy of a colonial war, racial tension, poverty, anti-Western feeling—were alien to the experience of a military man whose formative years had been spent in far less complex situations than those created by nationalism emerging from vast colonial empires. (In this connection, I believe that part of the truly remarkable admiration for President Kennedy in much of the underdeveloped world came from the feeling of these peoples that because he was young, he *understood*.) In contrast, Lodge, though virtually the same age as Harkins, had been in politics all his life and immediately sensed the turbulence of the situation on his arrival.

The middle-aged Western military man, regardless of his nationality, has been trained in military orthodoxy and has little feel for a war practiced by guerrillas; in such a situation he clings to whatever traditional evaluations he can—such as statistics. In reality, however, statistics mean next to nothing in this kind of war and inevitably give an erroneous impression by favoring the side with the most equipment. (I remember a sharp argument between Sheehan and an American senior officer. The latter cited the high rate of Vietcong casualties and claimed that this proved that the war was being won. Sheehan insisted, however—and most guerrilla war authorities support him—that this was simply a sign that the war was being lost and that the Government was losing control of the war and the population. In a successful insurgency, he insisted, when you are doing well the casualties do not rise; they drop, and the war simply goes away.)

Consciously or subconsciously, the Army staff system tends to reflect the thinking of the senior officer. If the commander wants to see an aspect of a war a certain way, the staff will find facts to confirm their superior's thesis. "I am an optimist, and I am not going to allow my staff to be pessimistic," Harkins was quoted by *Time* in a cover story in May 1962. I remember with chilling clarity an interview I had with Harkins about the outpost problem in October 1963. Colonel Basil Lee Baker, at that time the chief PIO, was present, and he spent much of the interview interjecting bits of what he considered positive news about some place in the mountains where "hundreds of montagnards had come in," or about another place where there had been "lots of Vietcong killed, and even our own people think it's pretty good." I was convinced that he was talking not to me but to Harkins, and I had a terrible feeling that the scene resembled those taking place at Gia Long Palace, where Diem had surrounded himself with carefully chosen assistants and where bad news was softened, strained, diluted and rewritten.

For such reasons MACV headquarters decided not to listen to Vann's warnings in those crucial months early in 1963. Whether by then the situation was already beyond recall is difficult to tell; the impression of some Americans then was that there was still time. But Westerners have always underestimated the Vietcong, and it may be that even early in 1963 the guerrillas' capability was already far greater than was imagined and that they were simply not exploiting their full capacity.

Ignoring Vann's warnings meant two things: first, that the situation in the Delta would deteriorate even more rapidly as the Vietcong was permitted to move virtually unchallenged; second, that the split within the American ranks would grow sharper as more people realized that Vann was right. Some of these people included Ralph Harwood, head of the strategic hamlet program in the Delta; Vann's eventual successor, Colonel Larry Brady; and Lieutenant Colonel Elzie Hickerson, the military representative on a joint civilian-military investigative team in the Delta, who received sharp criticism from Major General Richard Stilwell, Harkins' young deputy chief of staff, because of Hickerson's pessimistic view of the Delta hamlet program. Finally, in September 1963, Rufus Phillips, who was in charge of the strategic hamlet program for the whole country, went to Washington to warn officials there of the critical situation in the Delta and of the rotten state of the hamlet program, thereby setting off a bitter reaction at MACV.

Throughout all this MACV insisted that the war was going well—though by mid-1963 it qualified this by stating that the war was being won more slowly in the Delta than in other parts of the country. By the fall of 1963 the line had been revised again: the war was still being won in the Delta, but—in the words of one of the PIO's—"the guerrillas had been pushed down south by successful operations in northern areas."

Shortly after Vann filed his report, pointing out the ARVN's failure to follow intelligence in the Delta, MACV and Harkins were to receive one more thoroughly documented warning. Once more it was from an impeccable source: Colonel Daniel Boone Porter, Vann's immediate superior and the corps adviser who was responsible for the entire Delta. Porter is a mild, professorial sort; there was always a briefcase under his arm, and he looks as if he was on his way to give a lecture on the use of the English language. But people who knew him said that he had been a fire-eater in the past; moreover, he was reputed to know as much about basic small-unit infantry tactics as any man in the Army. He was a dedicated, hard-working soldier, and those who knew him, Vietnamese and American alike, swore by him. Charged with the responsibility for the entire Delta, Porter had seen the vast disparity between Vietnamese potential and accomplishment; similarly, the optimism of his superiors conflicted with the danger signs he saw in the field.

In February 1963, Colonel Porter submitted his final report before going home. Friends who read advance copies warned him that it was unusually strong and suggested that perhaps he sweeten it by noting some of the progressive steps taken: the increased number of operations, better communications, better care of equipment, and so on. Porter declined; he had already noted some of the improvements in an earlier report, he was deeply concerned over current trends and he was going to write what he felt.

Before writing his report Porter consulted his two immediate subordinates: Vann in the Seventh Division and Lieutenant Colonel Fred Ladd in the Twenty-first. Though the report included ideas of both Vann and Ladd (who was as pessimistic as Vann, but whose division commander was more aggressive), it was, according to one officer who saw it, fully "Porterized" in its final form. Officers who read it considered it the most acute study of the situation ever made by an American. It analyzed the character of the enemy, the character of the Vietnamese peasants and the character of the Government officials.

According to one officer, Porter's final recommendation particularly angered Saigon. He suggested that responsible high American officers confront top Vietnamese officials and that they discuss their mutual problems. It should be done tactfully, the report said, but it must be done. "We would tell them our problems and they would tell us theirs. It was also quite detailed on the failings of some of their senior officers. I think what angered the American command was that it would be a terrible thing if the Vietnamese knew we felt like this—and of course we did feel like this, and of course they knew it," one staff officer said who read Porter's report.

Harkins was so upset by the report that he ordered all copies of it collected. At a meeting of senior advisers, according to one officer who attended, the general said that Colonel Porter's report would be "sanitized," and that if there was anything of interest in it afterward, it would be made available to them. The report was never seen again. This was highly unusual; most senior officers' reports were immediately made available in Saigon for other officers to read.

Unfortunately for us reporters, Porter was extremely close-mouthed about this whole affair; none of us learned of the incident until long after he had left Vietnam.

At about this time Harkins received still another report on the Delta, this time from a general on his staff. A friend of mine who saw it after it left MACV headquarters said that all along the margins of it were notes in Harkins' handwriting which said simply, "Vann," "Porter," "Vann again."

Meanwhile, in April 1963, an angry Vann was on his way home from Vietnam, his tour completed. Unlike most Americans who were unhappy with our role in Vietnam, he was not just a dissenter, but a dissenter armed. A business statistician by education, Vann had spent long hours documenting the failures and errors of the war in terms of meaningful statistics. He could point out that during his tour in the Delta the number of small outposts had not only not decreased, but that despite their vulnerability and the fact that they sharply reduced mobility, there were actually more outposts than on his arrival. He could prove that as everyone had suspected, the province chief's political relationship with Diem had a direct bearing on the number of troops he received. Long An, for instance, a heavily populated province immediately south of Saigon, in which the majority of the Vietcong incidents in Vann's zone had taken place, had fewer troops than Kien Phong, a thinly populated province in the Plain of Reeds, which had less than 10 percent as many incidents. As a result, by the end of October 1963 the Vietcong were virtually in complete rural control of Long An.

Vann could also offer unique documentation of the charge

that Government commanders were unwilling to risk casualties with their ARVN troops; in his year as senior adviser
fewer than fifty of over fourteen hundred friendly troops killed
were of the ARVN, the best-equipped and best-armed soldiers the Government had. This did not show, as Saigon liked
to think, that these troops were fighting well; it simply proved
that they were doing very little fighting at all. The casualties
were being suffered by the Civil Guard and the Self-Defense
Corps, and they were being inflicted in defensive positions at
night.

After spending a month with his family, Vann showed up
for duty in the Pentagon in mid-May 1963. There he found
that no one seemed to be interested in Vietnam or in his
opinions on it, though he had just returned from perhaps the
most critical and certainly the most controversial area in this
country's only war. Although men of division-adviser rank
were normally de-briefed in Washington, the three ranking
Delta experts, Colonels Porter, Ladd and Vann, were not
asked to give their views. When Vann began a search for the
de-briefing officer, he was told that it was "Saigon's wish"
that he not be interrogated.

So at first the Colonel gave informal talks to a few friends,
but as word spread he slowly found himself in increasing
demand among higher officers. Finally General Barksdale
Hamlett, the Deputy Chief of Staff of the Army, heard Vann's
briefing, and at the general's request the item was placed on
the agenda of the Joint Chiefs of Staff for July 8. Vann was
advised by some of the generals who had already heard him
talk that he must be more moderate, and that in particular he
must be careful not to be critical of General Harkins, the
personal choice of Maxwell Taylor, the Chairman of the Joint
Chiefs of Staff.

By a curious coincidence the Chiefs had just heard another
briefing on Vietnam by McNamara's special adviser on guerrilla warfare, Marine Major General Victor Krulak. Krulak
was to play an important role in Vietnamese affairs as a special investigator, and according to him the war was going
well. At this point Krulak had just returned from a brief trip
to Vietnam and had written an extensive report, which was

extremely sanguine about the strategic hamlet program. According to one member of Harkins' staff, the report had been prepared with the close collaboration of the MACV; in any case, Krulak was simply telling the Pentagon what it wanted to hear. Vann's feelings were well known, and when his appearance before the Joint Chiefs was scheduled, Krulak's office began to telephone Vann's superiors for a copy of his report. Vann was warned by several high officers to stall and not to let the report be seen by others until the last possible minute. His briefing was set for 2 P.M. on a Monday; at about 9:45 A.M. on the morning of the briefing he sent a copy of the report to Krulak's office.

Vann arrived very early for the briefing and waited outside the office of General Earle Wheeler, the Army Chief of Staff, in case there were any late developments or questions for him to answer. According to his wife, "He was as shined and polished as a man can get—John was really prepared that morning. There wasn't a wrinkle near him."

What follows is Vann's report of the incident, but it has since been confirmed by a member of Wheeler's staff.

At 10:45 A.M. there was a telephone call to one of Wheeler's aides in the waiting room outside the general's office. The conversation went like this:

"*Who* wants the item removed from the agenda?" asked the aide.

After a silence the aide said, "Is it the Secretary of Defense or the Chairman's office?"

There was more talk at the other end. "Is that an order or a request?" Wheeler's aide asked. Then, after listening to the reply, the aide said, "Let me get this right. The Chairman *requests* that the item be removed." He then added that he would check with General Wheeler and call back. Hanging up the phone, he turned to Vann and said, "Looks like you don't brief today, buddy."

In a few minutes the aide returned, dialed a number on the phone and said, "The Chief agrees to remove the item from the agenda."

And so the Joint Chiefs did not have to hear Vann's briefing, nor did anyone else during the brief period that he remained in the Army while waiting for his papers to be processed. On applying for retirement he was immediately placed under the strictest orders not to talk to anyone about Vietnam. After hearing the news in Saigon I cabled our Washington bureau and suggested that Rick Smith, the *Times* man covering the State Department, meet Vann and try to get the expert knowledge I knew was impossible to secure in Washington. Smith tried his damndest, and then cabled back that nothing "can persuade your friend Vann to unclam."

For whatever reasons—perhaps because he was not a general, perhaps because he lacked expert advice in how to handle and exploit a protest of this sort, perhaps because it was not an election year, or perhaps because no one was that concerned over the state of the war in Vietnam in those days—Vann's retirement caused little stir at the time. There were a few stories and interviews—one in the *Times*, an excellent story in the New York *Journal-American* and a good interview in *U.S. News and World Report*—but they were sparse, so the Pentagon was really never forced to explain why Vann had left the Army.

Colonel John Vann retired from the Army so that he could speak out on Vietnam. He took a job with an aircraft company in Denver—at a considerable increase in pay—and spent his spare time and weekends speaking publicly to all kinds of audiences about where we had gone wrong in Vietnam. Even today it is obvious that he misses the Army with all his heart. "You know you miss it, John," his wife said at the airport in Denver when I visited them in the spring of 1964. "You know you've never really been happy since you left."

Vann had done, however, what no other American official has done in defense of his convictions about our role in Vietnam: he thought that the lies and failures were serious enough for him to retire from a service that he loved. In temperament he is not the kind of man who protests or who rebels against the system—but he had become personally involved. He had tried desperately to warn his own country of what was happening in Vietnam, and he had failed. Everything that he had predicted would happen in the Delta had happened—and happened even more quickly than he had imagined.

When I left Vann in Denver last March, I remembered another airport scene—in Saigon, when Vann was going home, another frustrated and disappointed American whose tour had ended. A group of correspondents had accompanied some other officers and pilots to the airport to say goodbye to him, and in recognition of his remarkable courage and integrity, as well as for many happy hours together in the field, we reporters presented him with a silver cigarette case, signed by us and inscribed, "Good soldier, good friend." As Vann was about to board the plane, I told him that we had always been worried about writing about him and about his area of the Delta for fear of making life more difficult for him with his superiors. He looked at me with a very small, tight smile and replied, "You never hurt me any more than I wanted to be hurt."

XII

By April, what Colonel Vann had predicted was already happening. The ARVN had shown that they were afraid of contact with the main Vietcong units, and the unchallenged enemy were becoming bolder and bolder. Better armed than before, they were picking fights with Government troops, something they had avoided six months earlier. It was a never-ending cycle: the more cautious the ARVN became, the more the Vietcong were able to move freely; the greater the guerrillas' freedom, the easier it was for them to slip up on large Government outposts and capture weapons; the better armed they became, the more the population was impressed and the Government forces intimidated—thus, a full circle.

Under these circumstances other faults came more into focus. Local officials and commanders became dependent on lying their way out of situations. For instance, because Diem did not want the ARVN to risk casualties and because Colonel Dam had reported that the war was going well, it became impossible for Dam to meet the enemy challenge. To do so would have required taking casualties, and then Diem would have demanded to know why there need be casualties in an area which, according to Dam, the Government had long controlled. Thus, potentially good men became prisoners of their past mistakes, and in the early months of 1963 the Vietcong took over the Delta countryside virtually unchallenged.

One of the best examples of what was happening—or not happening—in the Delta came a few weeks after Vann had left the country, when the Vietcong struck a major outpost of Camau called Bien Nghi, in An Xuyen Province. The post was outside the artillery range of Camau, in an area where the peasants were completely dominated by the Vietcong. The Americans had argued against the post because it was outside artillery range, could serve no positive political purpose, gathered no intelligence and was extremely difficult to keep supplied. But Diem had personally ordered the building of the post; as he saw it, he was flaunting his flag deep in enemy territory, and it became a point of pride to him.

Bien Nghi was well staffed, with one hundred and fifty-five troops: one hundred and eleven ARVN and forty-four SDC. On the night of April 21 the Vietcong attacked. The defenders fought back, but it was, as the Americans had feared, a hopeless situation. The enemy, using a striking force of nearly six hundred men, had heavy mortars, recoilless rifles and other captured heavy weapons. They overran the post and slaughtered the defenders, shipping some of the dead bodies down the canal on a barge, for interested peasants to see. They burned the ARVN commanding officer at the stake next to a portrait of President Diem, and they razed everything except a sign which announced that this was the Government post of Bien Nghi. They also took away with them eighty-one M-1 rifles, an estimated sixty carbines, ten BAR's, and several machine guns and mortars—virtually enough to arm a brand-new battalion.

This was a particularly stupid, senseless, brutal and bloody defeat. But what happened the next day was even worse. The Government reaction was very slow; no one was in a hurry to get into a fight with the Vietcong on its own stamping grounds. The American advisers were aware that the reinforcements purposely delayed, to ensure that the Vietcong would be gone when they arrived at the post. General Cao, who was in charge of the operation, had a massive force at his disposal; his command post south of Bien Nghi had a lovely map filled with arrows. Not surprisingly, however, no contact had been made during the long morning.

Shortly after noon a squadron of helicopters was flying back from Bien Nghi to the CP when an entire treeline seemed to open up with fire. Later someone asked one of the pilots if the VC had .30- or .50-caliber machine guns. "They had nothing but five-hundred-calibers down there," he answered. The helicopters reconnoitered and quickly flew back to the command post; one of the pilots told General Cao what had happened and where, and that he estimated there might be two companies in the treeline.

"No," said General Cao, "I do not think they are there. I think they will go here"—pointing to his operation—"in order to celebrate their victory. They will have a party here and then we will attack. I know the Vietcong."

Dumbfounded, the helicopter pilot looked at Colonel John (Poopy) Connor, who had replaced Colonel Porter and who had apparently decided to go along with Cao in almost all situations. When Colonel Connor shrugged his shoulders the pilot could do nothing but walk out.

Later that afternoon another American lieutenant colonel tried to make Cao move his troops.

"Ah, but you don't understand guerrilla warfare," Cao told him.

"General Cao," the American said, "you better hope that you and I are always on the same side in this war, or I'll teach you which one of us understands guerrilla warfare."

Later the helicopter pilot who had talked to Cao, and who was a close friend of mine, confided to me that as he flew home that night "for the first time I became absolutely sure that we are going to lose the war out here."

At the briefing in Saigon that night the PIO's gave the correspondents a report—unconfirmed of course—that a Vietnamese air strike had killed a hundred Vietcong in the wake of the Bien Nghi battle. "Cao's down there," said Mert Perry at this news, and even the briefing officer laughed.

Day after day there were smaller, less dramatic incidents like this. "I can show you the plans for every operation for the last three months, and you'll see that there is a deliberate escape hatch in every one," an operations officer in the Seventh Division told me in July.

Even Government victories were badly tarnished. On July 21 we were told of a great Government victory in the Cho Gao area, northeast of My Tho, where a large force had clashed with the 514th Battalion. According to the original reports, three hundred guerrillas had been killed, and so the next day the PIO's, very eager to have us down there, laid on a press junket via helicopters. It turned out that in a prolonged battle fifty-eight, not three hundred, guerrillas had been killed and that twelve weapons had been captured. Eighteen Government regulars had been killed, fourteen of them in a single company which had made a very difficult infantry assault across an open rice paddy.

It was clear that despite Cao's claim of wiping out the 514th, it was still very much in operation. Nevertheless, there was an official ceremony celebrating the victory, in which Colonel Dam rose and gave a humiliating little speech about what a great commander Cao was, and how this victory was all his. (Of course neither of them had been on the battlefield.) Then Cao spoke: it was not his victory at all, but that of President Ngo Dinh Diem, who had personally ordered him to destroy the 514th Battalion.

The battlefield told a somewhat different story—despite Madison Avenue Cao's attempt to dress up the scene for the television cameramen by having his men prop the dead bodies of the Vietcong in empty foxholes. The fact that only a dozen guerrilla weapons had been captured meant that most of the enemy had managed to escape. Indeed, American intelligence later confirmed that the 514th was at normal operative strength several days later. In addition we learned that only one unit had made an assault and that apparently the 113's had failed to overrun the treeline.

We also noticed at the time that some of the American divison advisers were not taking part in the festivities. Later, after the coup, when the advisers talked more freely, we were told that once more the battle plan had been drawn up with a deliberate escape hatch for the Vietcong, that the 113's did not assault, and that Cao himself had been terrified through-

out the operation and had refused to commit units that might
have blocked the enemy's escape. In fact, we were told, Cao
had been so jittery that early in the day the artillery fire had
gotten on his nerves; he had ordered it stopped, and refused
to rescind this command throughout the day. Another rare
chance to annihilate a hard-core enemy unit had deliberately
been turned down. "We didn't wipe them out," an American
adviser said later, "we just scratched at them."

Three weeks later there was another loudly proclaimed victory at a place called Go Cong—a victory that had many of
the same elements as Cho Gao. On this occasion a Vietcong
battalion had struck a district post, then moved down the
main road and set an ambush for the relief column. However,
the Vietnamese roared up the highway in 113's and caught the
vast Vietcong force in an open field. Usually the Vietcong
were more careful, by preparing an exit route along treelines,
but this time they were too cocky and the 113's had a field
day rolling over their positions. But in the middle of the battle, with the Vietcong being routed in confusion, Colonel
Dam told the armored unit to break contact with the enemy.
As usual the Americans protested, but Dam was adamant; he
had inflicted heavy casualties on the enemy, had suffered few
himself and was not going to press his luck. Turning to the
chief American adviser of the armored unit, Dam said, "Call
your ambassador and your reporters and bring them here."

As the adviser later said, "All they cared about was the
ball score."

In Saigon, Go Cong was nevertheless hailed as a considerable Government victory. After all, the friendly troops had
reacted quickly and well. But a friend of mine, a non-
American who was an expert on guerrilla warfare, took me
aside and told me why he felt it was hardly a victory, why in
fact it was a sign of imminent disaster. The action had taken
place very near a district capital outside of My Tho, he noted,
and at least five hundred Vietcong had participated. Yet this
large a force had been able to gather near a major center in
a heavily populated area, without one single peasant warning
the Government. Therefore, my friend said, it was not a victory, but rather a grim lesson in making it clear which side

controlled the population and could move freely in the countryside. The war, he said, was closer to being over than anyone realized.

In those days, anyone who expressed doubts about Vietnam's future was immediately inundated with facts about the strategic hamlet program, which was an attempt on the part of the Government and the United States to create fortified villages where a number of social and educational services would be provided to the peasants. It was the key, the American command said, "to winning the people," and it would counteract all the failures of the war. If the critic expressed worry about the peasants' feelings toward the regime, he was assured that under the strategic hamlet program injustices were rare, that the basic needs of the people were being met and that this was "democracy from the bottom up." If one mentioned the military failures in the Delta, he would be told that the program was making all the difference in that area, that it was way ahead of schedule. Progress was there, the American official would say; it might not be readily discernible, but it was there.

Yet common sense evoked suspicion: the idea that the hamlet program, a difficult and complicated undertaking, would succeed so easily where so many other contrivances had failed; that a government unable to handle its people and with a reputation for appointing police-state hacks to key positions would suddenly appoint talented, vigorous and honest men to administer the program; that an administration which had such a quixotic attitude about the priorities of the war could handle a vast and complicated program like this and make it work—all this was difficult to believe.

The hamlet program was what Homer Bigart referred to as "another American gimmick," one more attempt to change what was unalterable under the Diem regime: that the Vietcong were more effective with the peasants, were more dedicated and had better leadership. Vast amounts of American resources went into the program; so committed were we to it that there was general agreement in those days that if the effort failed, it would be clear that our side had nothing to offer the peasants and that the Government was bankrupt at the rural level.

Though a similar program had been tried unsuccessfully before, under the French—the people had been herded into *agrovilles*—in theory the strategic hamlet program was as good an answer to the problems of Vietnam as anyone could think of in those days. It was not a cure-all—though in the bankruptcy of the American-Diem relationship it was treated as such—but a complicated, chancy idea, and if the executors of the program were smart, tough and lucky, it might provide part of the medicine needed for a very sick country.

The hamlet program was designed to help the peasant to help himself and to separate him from the guerrilla. It assumed that the peasant wanted to help himself—unfortunately this was not always the case—and that his sympathies were with the Government side, all things being equal. The program was designed to provide the peasant with both the arms and the desire to defend himself, by giving him services which he had lacked in the past and whose absence had made him susceptible to Vietcong propaganda. The program was an idea as much as an entity, and when it fell apart completely in mid-1963, it was not from lack of weapons.

The hamlet program was better suited for the central coastal region and for the highlands than for the Delta. In the coastal and plateau regions the peasants lived in small, clustered villages which lent themselves to the type of defense proposed; there was little need for relocation; withholding food from the enemy was more feasible because of the limited resources of such regions; and communal use of the land was traditional because of the limited amount of rice acreage. Also, the Government had put its major effort into these regions because the Ngos were more interested in them.

The Delta was quite a different story; yet the difference was never recognized in high American councils. It took only the most superficial knowledge to realize that the programs which worked farther north were unsuitable in the Delta. For one thing, the Delta guerrilla found it easy to live off the land. Even more important was the fact that the population of the Delta was not clustered into convenient little groups; it was spread out aimlessly and endlessly over this rich soil. Therefore, all too often this meant relocating people from an area which they loved and had held for many generations, to a region for which they cared not at all—in order to fight an enemy they did not really consider their enemy. By and large the population of the Delta had been on the fence, but the very act of relocation turned thousands of peasants against the Government.

Even so, under certain circumstances the hamlet program might have provided a partial answer in the Delta. But the plan wasn't bolstered by the honesty, efficiency and skill it needed; instead, all the weaknesses of the system were brought out. Of the thirteen province chiefs in the Delta, few were from the South or had any understanding of the Southerners' temperament and affection for their land, and only two of the chiefs seemed to have grasped the psychological concept of the program—that a mystique had to be created to make the peasant *want* to come into the hamlet. One hundred such people, not one hundred kilometers of barbed wire, could resist the Vietcong.

The dream envisaged remained only on paper, for Mr. Nhu saw it as a means of population control instead and put his people in charge of the program. Province chiefs competed with one another over the number of hamlets they could build. The more hamlets they built, the more they were in favor with Nhu and the more U.S. aid they received; consequently, one problem for the American mission was the tendency of Vietnamese officials to divide a hamlet in half and count it as two, thereby getting twice the aid. Each chief engaged in a mad scramble to build hamlets faster than the next: "If you stand still long enough down there, they'll throw a piece of barbed wire around you and call you a strategic hamlet," one American said.

But the success of the program in the Delta rested largely on the strategy of building hamlets slowly, starting with one secure area and then slowly branching out and gathering other villages into a protective umbrella, thus creating a sense of mutual protection through the interlocking units. But this type of construction never took place. Instead, hamlets went up helter-skelter, lacking any overall, Delta-wide plan of priorities. Vast numbers of troops who should have been on mobile duty were tied up building and defending hamlets, so that eighteen months after Maxwell Taylor had described the desperate need to increase the percentage of mobile troops, there were more of them in static positions than ever before.

As a result of this rush of construction, both Americans and Vietnamese boasted loudly that the program was far ahead of schedule and that it would be completed sooner than expected. The American military high command was a willing partner in this self-delusion; it was only too glad to listen to favorable statistics. In April, when an American general visited a Delta province, he was given an enthusiastic briefing by a Vietnamese officer to the effect that seventy-two hamlets had already been built and that many more were on the way, while in reality only thirteen were really secure. When an American told him this, the general became angry at the American officer and immediately accused him of lying. But the numbers games went on, while beneath the surface the hamlet program in the Delta was an inflated, jerry-built structure. Inside the villages—which could not protect themselves from attack in any case—the people were either passive about having been shoved around or actively angry about the broken promises of medical and educational services. "Sometimes all you found representing the Government inside these hamlets were the Cong An—the local police officials working for Nhu—usually ill trained, men who were there because they were related to someone in Saigon, who were ignorant and tough, and who abused the population. No wonder the Vietcong looked like Robin Hoods when they began to hit the hamlets," one high civilian official in the Delta told me.

In 1964, a year after the plan had failed and Diem had fallen, an amazingly frank report on the hamlet program by USOM (the local term for the Agency for International Development) said, "From the very inception it was apparent that many of the provincial officials did not fully understand the concept and were so frightened by the pressures from the President and his brother that they would employ any measures, from forced labor and confiscation to false reporting, to achieve the quantitative goals set."

Thus, in June and July of 1963, when the Vietcong began to assault the Delta hamlets, they were attacking what was essentially a paper program. With the exception of Kien Hoa, where the province chief understood the meaning of the program, they encountered only a thin defense—a few local militiamen, most of whom lacked the will to resist and many of whom had been infiltrated earlier. In many hamlets the local workers had not been paid as promised; in others the sons of officials had been exempted from service. Because of hundreds of such abuses, the discontent and lack of commitment made the enemy's task easy. Rather, the Government's presence was too often felt by the fear it generated among the peasants. The Saigon *Post*, which is an English-language paper run by the Vietnamese, said plaintively, on January 10, 1964, when for the first time since Diem's fall free speech was allowed in the Vietnamese press:

> Yet these indirect causes are forgivable. What cannot be forgiven is the sad but commonplace case of abuse by district chiefs—more often by their chiefs for security. Name a single Delta province where the deputy's name is not whispered with fear among the peasant population and with a furtive, over-the-shoulder glance.
>
> On the answers to these questions depend whether the peasant will look to the Government for protection of his person, his rights and his property, or to the Vietcong. And we must not forget that as long as there is one aggrieved peasant, there are ten potential Vietcong sympathizers and as many potential recruits. And every new case of abuse will widen this gap between this essential war factor and the Government.

Even in Kien Hoa Province the Vietcong forged a remarkable record. During a long period of time in 1962 and early 1963, when they were laying low militarily, they had steadily and successfully built up shadow governments in the villages and hamlets of this province, and recruited peasants. An American officer in Kien Hoa told me that between April and

June 1963 the guerrillas were able to recruit two thousand men, and to form and equip two new battalions of six hundred men each, besides expanding to full strength the single battalion which had previously operated in the province.

Thus, the strategic hamlet program never really affected the Vietcong's ability to handle the population, for it never separated the guerrillas from the source of their greatest strength: young men.

The Vietcong approach to the program as a whole was extremely clever and once again showed their understanding of the nature of the war. The Americans and the Government had hoped that the hamlet concept would force the Vietcong to attack the people; this would enrage the population and encourage them to defend themselves against the guerrillas; at the very least it was thought that it would turn the peasants against the enemy and put them on the side of the Government.

But it did not work out that way. The Vietcong were not hungry, and they did not need to prey off the villagers. Since they were usually local Southerners, often from the region in which they were bivouacked, they knew the area well—and they had infiltrated the hamlets. When they attacked, they attacked only the symbols of the Government: the armory or command post of the hamlet, the hamlet chief or the youth leaders (who were particularly hated because they were Nhu's men). They rarely harmed the population, and so the people of a village, who saw that the Government had not kept its promises and could not protect them, often sided with the Vietcong after a raid.

With Vann gone, the pressure on his successors in dealing with the press was enormous in June and July; knowledgeable American advisers would often just turn away from reporters when asked about conditions. As the situation deteriorated in an atmosphere of military secrecy during these months, we became dependent on lower-echelon officers for first-hand observations, and on American civilian officials connected with the hamlet program—the latter being under less pressure to conform than their military counterparts.

During those two summer months we watched the Vietcong winning by default in the Delta. A year after the American build-up of weaponry and personnel had reached its peak, it was clear that the Government had lost the initiative, that the enemy had benefited more from the weapons than we had, that his capacity had increased more than the ARVN's the past year, and that with the failure of the Government civic program the guerrillas' tactical position was also superior.

The implications of all this were extremely serious. The American build-up, which had been prompted by a deteriorating situation in late 1961, had lost its edge and momentum; the Communists had learned to react, and thanks to the outposts the enemy had been able to use the Government as a supply store. In 1962 the Government's main strength had been its main-force units and their weaponry; now even this advantage was gone. By July 1963 some of the enemy battalions had over five hundred troops; the 514th, which had caused so much trouble, had six hundred trained soldiers and 57- and 75-mm. recoilless-rifle sections, 81- and 60-mm. mortar sections and .50-caliber machine guns. By August the Government battalions which, with the exception of the Marine and air-borne units, rarely had more than three hundred and thirty effective troops, were no match for the Vietcong main-force units. Not only were the guerrilla units bigger, but they used their weapons better and had better NCO's. As a result, though the Government still had a superiority in artillery, they were now openly afraid to tangle with the enemy. In a war which was so largely psychological and in which the opinion of the populace was so important, this was disastrous.

Colonel Pham Van Dong, one of the most knowledgeable men in the country, and who had commanded a regimental combat team under the French, returned in dismay to Saigon from a tour of the Delta in July. "It's just like the Indochina war, only worse. The VC are preparing for hard-hitting mobile warfare, with battalions as well-equipped as the Government's, and perhaps bigger," he said. A Vietnamese general allowed Sheehan and me to see the private figures of the Vietnamese Joint General Staff; even such statistics as these— which I distrusted as being too optimistic—showed that the trend was going in the wrong direction. Whereas the Delta figures for the last six months of 1962 had been relatively favorable in comparison with the past—thanks largely to the impact of the new American gear—there was a sharp drop for the first six months of 1963. This indicated that the enemy had learned how to counter the new techniques. According to these figures, Government weapons losses had risen about 20 percent and Vietcong weapons losses had dropped about 25 percent. One of the most important statistics indicated that the Government had lost eighty crew-served weapons (meaning BAR's, machine guns, mortars or recoilless rifles), an increase of about thirty; in comparison, Vietcong losses of these vital weapons had dropped from one hundred and fifteen to fifteen. These figures are important, because each side gives up these weapons reluctantly; their loss is a very good indication of the effectiveness of each opponent's first-line fighting. If there is a tide in the war, the exchange rate of such weapons will reflect it immediately.

This deterioration was taking place at a period when the Buddhist crisis was in full swing, and so we were not able to follow it up as closely as I would have liked. Due to lack of time, preparing a story on the decline in the Delta became a joint task among Sheehan and Perry and myself. We interviewed our Vietnamese sources, American civilians and the younger American officers. By now many high-ranking officers—division advisers, say—were under great pressure not to talk to reporters, and so we would have to consult their captains, trusted friends of ours, to discover what their superiors were thinking. One captain who had been in Vietnam for a little over a year was told by his colonel, "You're going home just in time. This whole place is collapsing."

The story we were after entailed vast amounts of leg work, and all the knowledge and contacts we had developed in our many months in the country. Only someone who had been there could know what the situation had been a year before, or could have developed the confidence of such good sources.

Time never used the material in Perry's file, and Sheehan was never able to complete his story because of faster-breaking news, but on August 15, 1963, the *Times* published my long piece. It began: "South Vietnam's military situation in the vital Mekong Delta has deteriorated in the past year, and informed officials are warning of ominous signs. Essentially, these military sources say, a Communist Vietcong build-up is taking place in the Delta. They find it particularly disturbing because it has persisted since an American build-up twenty months ago." The story went on to state that the Vietcong were engaging in "a sizable military offensive" and were preparing large beefed-up battalions for mobile warfare.

No story I ever wrote drew a more violent reaction. The President of the United States was angry, his generals were angry and his civilian officials were angry. At a press conference Dean Rusk specifically criticized the story. I still have the cable the *Times* sent me about his conference:

RUSK AT FRIDAY NEWS CONFERENCE TOOK EXCEPTION TO REPORTS OF DETERIORATING MILITARY SITUATION IN VIET-NAM STOP HE CITED DECLINE IN SABOTAGE AND PROPA-GANDA INCIDENTS AS WELL AS LARGE-SCALE ATTACKS AND SAID ADDITIONAL AREAS WERE COMING UNDER GOVERN-MENT CONTROL WITH STRATEGIC HAMLET PROGRAM MOV-ING FORWARD STOP DOES THIS WARRANT STORY FROM YOU?

I answered that it didn't, that unfortunately our story still stood and that I was sorry that Rusk didn't believe it.

In Washington some officials in the Pentagon compared my story to Vann's written brief (I had not seen Vann or heard from him in four months, but our views on the Delta were basically the same) and felt that the similarity might be in-criminating—that perhaps he had been leaking intelligence to me.

In Saigon, where Military Assistance Command Vietnam was receiving all kinds of jolts about the story from higher command, the job of disproving it fell to Major General Richard Stilwell, the operations chief of MACV. Disprove it he did, according to his lights. He later assured me that he had lost a good deal of sleep over it. In a briefing several days later, to a room filled with visiting reporters, he attacked both the story and me by name, and he produced a lot of figures that showed how well the war was going in the Delta.

I've since been told that after Stilwell finished with it, my story went back to Washington with virtually every word circled and with a prolonged brief "disproving" every point made. Several months later, when the decay in the Delta was more obvious, a friend of mine, a high-ranking civilian who worked for the Pentagon, asked a member of the MACV staff who had been right, the reporters or the generals. "Oh, the reporters were," the staff man said casually.

There were also attempts to contradict my story through a few visiting reporters who were then writing remarkably optimistic views of the war in Vietnam. One of the most important of these was written by Miss Marguerite Higgins, then a reporter for the New York *Herald Tribune*. Miss Higgins, who had been in Vietnam for a brief time, wrote on August 28:

> . . . But as of the moment General Harkins and his staff flatly contradict published reports that South Vietnam's U.S.-backed fight against the Communists—particularly in the rice-rich Delta—is "deteriorating" and that a Vietcong build-up is taking place to the point where the Communists will be able to conduct mobile warfare with battalions as well equipped as the Government's.
>
> "What is mobility?" interjected one of the general's corps advisers. "Mobility means vehicles and aircraft. You have seen the way our Vietnamese units are armed—fifty radios, thirty or forty vehicles, rockets and mortars and airplanes. The Vietcong have no vehicles and no airplanes. How can they be mobile?"

Presumably Miss Higgins was quoting a corps adviser in the Delta. In any case, the statement seems to me particularly revealing, for it sums up the incredible arrogance of the upper-level American military establishment in this crisis, and

shows how little the Americans had learned from the French.
To be sure, the Vietcong did not have mobility by Western
technological standards. But they had an Asian ability to filter
quietly through the countryside unobserved, to move twenty-
five miles a night on foot, or in sampans with excellent local
guides, to gather and strike quickly and then disperse before
the Government could retaliate. That was the only kind of
mobility they had, but it was a far better kind than the Government's, and too many American generals never understood it.

My *Times* story also revealed the handicaps for a visiting
reporter. Even if such a journalist were seriously interested
in writing a piece about the situation in the countryside, his
limited background might well betray him if he attempted to
write a long interpretative story. When he talked to a corps
adviser, did he know that he was being fed the opinions of
General Harkins and Colonel Cao? Was he aware of the difficulty in getting along with Cao, the resultant paralysis and
loss of American freedom? Had he heard of Vann's and Porter's dissents?

Even that autumn a visiting journalist could go down to
the Delta and be told that the war was going well. There were
plenty of people willing to reassure him. "We're killing plenty
of VC down here," Colonel Connor, Porter's replacement,
revealed to visiting reporters in October—and as an added
fillip pronounced Cao an aggressive commander.

About that time I saw Denis Warner, the Australian correspondent, who told me: "The American generals are talking about the Mekong Delta just the way the French generals
talked about the Red River Delta in 1951 and 1952. I bet I
could go back to my old notebooks and find the same quotes
from the French generals that the Americans are telling now."

XIII

Early in the spring of 1963 I was privately criticized by experienced colleagues for not writing more about the political problems of Vietnam. I had been concentrating on the Delta; that was fine, my friends said, and it was good that I went out on operations, but such stories only indicated one facet of the country's malaise.

I agreed with my critics, but the fact was that the political situation in Vietnam at that time was difficult to describe, for there were few pegs for stories. (In the vernacular of the trade, a "peg" is an event which provides a vehicle or an angle for a reporter to write about a trend that has been developing slowly.)

In all the time I had been in Vietnam there had been no major new developments—no attempted coups, no mass rebellions—simply a hardening of attitudes. Diem's trips to the countryside were infrequent; his relations with the Americans remained strained and tenuous (they had been idyllic as long as the Americans wanted nothing); the Government was increasingly dominated by the Nhus, who were coming more and more under public scrutiny.

There were indeed few events in these developments from which to fashion a specific story, and besides, in the atmosphere of Saigon there were additional problems. In the spring

of 1963 the USIS, which had been making the newsreels for
the Government, got into a hassle with the Diem Administration and stopped doing the news films. In a country where
movie-going was a main form of entertainment, these newsreels were a potent force, and the Nhus had become more
and more insistent that they be featured in them. The American film makers refused, pointing out that Nhu's only title
was political counselor and that the original assignment had
been to star Diem. They felt that propagandizing for the Nhus
would only backfire with the population, and they did not
feel that the United States should be caught in the middle. So
the Government had begun to make its own newsreels, in
which the Nhus seemed to be on camera all the time.

But my source of information would have been obvious,
and I was unable to write it up. The essence of the political
situation was that Vietnam was a country ruled by a clumsy
and heavy-handed government, whose population had a latent
sense of discontent. The resentment was palpably there—
anyone could feel it—but it did not lend itself to daily reporting; there were no elections by which it could be tested,
no criticism in the newspapers, no deputies standing up in
the Assembly to speak.

The result was a surface control of a seemingly passive
people. Yet even the lack of enthusiasm was damning enough
for a government charged with winning a war. In the Phil-
ippine insurgency the war against the Huks had gone badly until
Ramon Magsaysay, a popular leader, had rallied his people;
in Malaya the Communist insurgency had done well until the
British promised the Malayans independence. In Vietnam
there was no organized opposition, simply and only because
there was no focus of protest. All the outspoken, anti-
Communist, anti-Diem leaders had left the country or were
imprisoned; the intellectuals who remained were harried and
divided, talking ineffectually in hushed voices in private
homes; even those Catholics who wrote what verged on criticism of Diem in their little papers were quickly silenced by
the Government. Thousands of political leaders were in
prison, and opposition to the Vietnamese government was
only expressed surreptitiously.

This state of affairs ended with the Buddhist crisis, which began in the spring of 1963.

On May 9 I received a phone call from the Vietnamese Director General of Information, who said that there would be a special press conference that afternoon. When I asked why, he said that the Vietcong had murdered nine Buddhists in Hué. I was immediately suspicious, because it was highly unusual for the Government to take the initiative in press matters; when it did, it was usually trying to conceal something rather than enlighten us. Other reporters were equally cynical, and it turned out that our doubts were justified. The conference had been called because Nick Turner of Reuters had gotten wind of the real story, and this had frightened the Vietnamese bureaucracy.

At that time, few of us knew much about Buddhism in general, or its Vietnamese particulars, other than that it was the major religion in Vietnam and that about 70 percent of the population subscribed to it. (Later, during the actual Buddhist crisis, there was a concerted effort on the part of the Nhu family, and forces sympathetic to it, to belittle this percentage—Madame claiming that it was only 15 percent—but this was belied by a Government brochure handed out by the Vietnamese embassy in Washington, which said that the nation was 90 percent Buddhist. Actually, about ten and a half million Vietnamese called themselves Buddhists, although about half of these were basically ancestor worshipers and half were practicing Buddhists; of the rest of the country's fourteen million people only about one and a half million were Catholics.)

There had been persistent reports of discrimination and some persecution of Buddhist priests in the central coastal region, and it was known that many Buddhists felt that if they were to get ahead in Vietnam they had to become Catholics—which produced a group of converts known as "1955 Catholics." But we reporters knew little else; to us the Buddhist monks were strange little men in orange robes—distant, faceless little Asians. Like other Americans in Vietnam, we were concerned with the war. After eight months there, I knew no

Buddhist priests, knew little about Vietnamese Buddhism and had never been in a pagoda.

I missed that first press conference; I was tired after eight months of digging for stories and was on my way to Hong Kong for a two-week rest on the day the conference was called. It was good to be getting away; let the others put the story together.

They did. The incident had taken placed in Hué, near the Seventeenth Parallel. The lovely old imperial capital of Annam, Hué lies on the bank of the Perfume River, in the central coastal region of Vietnam, and it is the most Oriental city in the country. It was still the home of Ngo Dinh Can, the President's brother who was the feudal overlord of the central region; more important, it was the see of Archbishop Ngo Dinh Thuc, Diem's most respected and eldest living brother. Because of Thuc's position and because of his strong role in the family, the Church had become much involved in temporal affairs—so much so that Ngo Dinh Can had reportedly complained to some Buddhist leaders and to the military that he was tired of demands by Thuc's young priests for troops and trucks to work on one Church project after another.

But Hué was also the center of Vietnamese Buddhism and Buddhist teaching. In precolonial days the greatest flowering of Buddhism in Vietnam had taken place there, and much of this aura lingered on in the form of a longing for the past. In this region approximately 80 percent of the population was Buddhist; moreover, in contrast to the rest of Vietnam, where Buddhism was fragmented and disorganized, it was militant, well organized and extremely well led in Hué. And whereas in most parts of the country there was a modicum of religious tolerance, in the central coastal region, and particularly in Hué, the very strong religious feelings had practically brought the Buddhists and the Catholics to the verge of a religious war. Correspondents talking to young Catholic priests in Hué were stunned by the venom with which they described the Buddhists and their religion; talking with Buddhists, the same correspondents came away frightened about what would happen if a Buddhist government ever took over in Saigon. It is hardly surprising that even after the fall of Diem, whose family exacerbated the tension, this religious conflict has continued, with both sides claiming that the Government is favoring the other.

As far as can be determined, what provoked the Buddhist crisis in Hué was a series of coincidences. Several days before the outbreak, Archbishop Thuc had celebrated his twenty-fifth year as bishop. It was a great occasion, and both the Government and Vatican flags were flown from rooftops and church steeples. Diem attended the festivities, and when he saw the flags, which violated a Government law proclaiming that only the Vietnamese flag could fly in public, he issued a statement calling attention to this ordinance.

Unfortunately, Buddha's birthday—his 2587th—came only a few days after this announcement, and the Buddhists in Hué wanted to fly their flag too. The Government prohibited this, and also denied a Buddhist request that their leader, Thich Tri Quang, be allowed to speak on the local radio. The Buddhists, aroused and well organized, marched on the radio station, where they were turned away. At this, thousands of angry, militant Buddhists massed in a square in the middle of the city, and the police could not break up the demonstration. Finally, Government troops were brought in; the major in command ordered them to fire, and they shot into the crowd. No intermediate step, such as firing over the heads of the crowd or using tear gas, was taken. Nine people were killed, and an armored car rolled over some of the victims.

The first official version of the incident was the Government's; it stated that a Vietcong agent had thrown a grenade into the crowd. But this account was slowly discredited as more details became known; a group of West German doctors, working in Hué as part of an exchange program, produced eyewitness and photographic evidence that supported the subsequent Buddhist version. The Government quickly buried the victims without performing any autopsies, and stuck steadfastly to its grenade story—one more example of its policy of blaming anything awkward on the Vietcong. Conflicting reports continued to filter in; the American consulate in Hué reported to Saigon that the Buddhist version was correct and that the Government's was completely inaccurate.

During all of this I sat in Hong Kong, admiring the scenery and being glad that I was out of Saigon. Bob Trumbull, then the *Times*' chief correspondent in Southeast Asia, with headquarters in Hong Kong, and a wise and thoughtful man with more than two decades of experience in the area, said, "This is the kind of thing which gets going in Asia and then keeps on building. It sounds like the students in Korea. Vietnam may be ripe for it."

But Charley Mohr, who at that time was the *Time* bureau chief in Hong Kong, came closest to putting his finger on the situation. "It's the same old story. Diem can't admit he's wrong, and so the Government will pretend it didn't happen, and they'll lie and make a hell of a lot of people angry."

It was hardly surprising that the Government's pride and sense of infallibility expanded what should only have been an ugly incident into a crisis that rocked the country. An American intelligence officer was with Bui Van Luong, the Minister of the Interior, when he was sent by Diem to Hué in order to give the President a personal report on the situation. The facts soon became apparent, and the American suggested that the remedy was simple: reparations of about five hundred thousand piasters (about seven thousand dollars), and an immediate public statement admitting that the Government troops were at fault. The minister reportedly answered, "The money is all right, but we can't issue the statement. We can't admit that we did it." Because Bui Van Luong was so afraid to tell Diem the truth, he returned to Saigon and told Diem that the Government version of the incident was correct—that the Vietcong had engineered the incident. Once again the carefully rigged system of the Palace had done its job; Diem, completely separated from reality, was permitted to think what he wanted to think.

Thus began the Buddhist crisis. It was to last for four months, and it was finally to create the atmosphere in which the Government fell. In the beginning it was primarily religious, with limited objectives; in the end it was primarily a political movement clearly trying to bring down the Government, to which all dissident elements in the country had rallied. It was to encompass all the problems of the Government: its inability to rule its own people; the failure of the American mission to influence Diem; the growing power of the Nhus; and the Government's totally unrealistic assessment of the population. Observing the Government during those four months was like watching a government trying to commit suicide.

In dealing with the Buddhist crisis, the Government was limited by its previous attitudes and by its estrangement from the masses. The kind of simple gestures which would have settled the crisis immediately—such as a propitiatory appearance by Diem at a pagoda, which would have generated some badly needed popularity—were alien to its character. Moreover, almost as soon as the crisis reached its peak, in the fourth week, such a gambit became impossible, for by that time it would have been interpreted not as a sign of generosity—for this was a government which had never operated generously before and had never shown itself willing to compromise—but as a sign of weakness.

In the Buddhist crisis the Government was not dealing with Americans who would naïvely accept its words and signed pieces of paper at face value, but with its own shrewd people, who knew more about the Government than *it* knew about *them*, who could predict Government reactions and who could behave on the assumption that these reactions would certainly be clumsy.

The religious division between Catholics and Buddhists had begun at the time of the partition of the country in 1954. At that time about seven hundred thousand Catholic refugees, many led by their priests, fled from the North to South Vietnam because they feared reprisals and persecution at the hands of the Communists. A lonely, undesirable minority as far as most Southerners were concerned, they found a friend in Diem, became his most enthusiastic supporters and established their own communities. Diem, suspicious of Buddhists

and of Southerners, felt that he could trust the newcomers;
after all, they were refugees and Catholics, and they had no
one to turn to but him. Catholic priests naturally encouraged
the relationship and thus became a vital part of the Government; Diem in turn used his religion to prop up his weak
administration. Favoritism and abuses inevitably resulted;
members of the faith became village leaders, and soon most
district and province chiefs were Catholics—often in a province whose population was completely Buddhist. So many
members of the trusted secret police apparatus were also of
the Church that in central Vietnam the hated local security
men were first and foremost thought of as Catholics, not as
Government officials.

Anxious and desperate to support Diem, the Americans
encouraged some of these practices. As early as 1955, Graham Greene wrote in a newspaper article, ''Mr. Diem's general piety has been exploited by his American advisers until
the Church is in danger of sharing the unpopularity of the
U.S.A. . . . Diem's ministers are not all Catholics, but Diem,
justifiably suspicious of many of his supporters, has confined
the actual Government to himself and members of his family.
Diem may well leave his tolerant country a legacy of anti-
Catholicism.'' Catholics benefited from the relief and aid
programs, received priority to build schools and permission
to cut and sell lumber from carefully protected national re-
serves, and were granted special commercial-trade benefits.
Because priests interceded for them, in the Government's
land-development schemes Catholics often were given the best
lands, and during the building of the strategic hamlets they
were often exempted from the physical labor performed by
Buddhists. In 1957 and 1958, when the Government opened
land-development centers in the central highlands, the province chiefs in the central coastal region forced Buddhists to
move to them, but Catholics were often exempted. In some
areas there was mass conversion of villages to avoid this up-
rooting. In addition, young Buddhist priests were harassed
and often forbidden by the authorities to travel in the interior,
and there were persistent reports that several of them had
been murdered. (After the November 1, 1963, coup, the Bud-

dhist inhabitants of many of these land-development areas returned to their former villages, and one of General Khanh's first orders after taking power in 1964 granted them permission to do so.)

Yet official religious discrimination was the exception. What the situation boiled down to was that an authoritarian Government, which was more mandarin than Catholic, nonetheless seemed to the Buddhists to be *Catholic*-authoritarian, particularly because in the central coastal region young priests were taking advantage of the prevailing sentiment in Saigon and indulging in the kind of abuses that Diem himself would never have countenanced.

Thus, the religious dispute was as much a product of the regime's shakiness as a cause, and its explosiveness could be traced to the fact that the Americans had backed a man whose minority religion was regarded by many Vietnamese as the religion of the West and of colonialism. The Buddhists resented the fact that they were second-class citizens in a country where their religion had once flowered and dominated. They felt that since foreign powers had come to play a major role in Vietnam, they had been neglected; this had been true under the French, and now the Buddhists never saw the American ambassador or a reporter, and they never won fellowships to the United States.

These grievances had been smoldering when the incident took place in Hué. The Buddhists considered theirs the majority religion, and it was true that the Catholics held power and office far out of proportion to their number but that was partly because of necessity. In general they were wealthier, better educated and better trained because of their advantages under the French, and they had been quicker in spotting the nature and the threat of Communism in Vietnam—for obvious reasons they had more motivation to oppose it. Lastly, in any society, and particularly in a new one, education and wealth give the privileged a head start, so naturally, the elite do their best to perpetuate the status quo.

During the latter years of Diem's regime, however, Buddhism began to attract many Vietnamese who were opposed to the Ngos. There was no political opposition party, and the family controlled virtually every organization in the country. In these circumstances Buddhism had an attraction because it was *not* Catholic, *not* under the auspices of the Ngo family—and because it was traditionally Vietnamese. Almost as soon as the incident in Hué took place, before a protest movement was even under way, a Vietnamese professor told Sheehan: "You Americans look around and see that the Vietnamese are orderly and quiet, and you think everything is all right here. But this is not so. We Vietnamese have been living under oppression for centuries. When the time is right, the people express themselves in one way or another. Today they dare not make outright political protests, so they express their feeling through religion."

Early in May a group of Buddhist elders went to see Diem. They were representative of the older and more moderate Buddhist leadership, and they wanted to discuss the Hué incident and several other, long-standing grievances, such as the right to fly the flag. Diem met with them for several hours, then authorized his spokesman to issue a statement to the reporters that he had told the Buddhists they were "damn fools" to be concerned about religious freedom; the constitution of the country guaranteed it, and *he* was the constitution. After the meeting the Buddhists had a statement of their own; they said quietly that the President had been very nice, but that they were not satisfied with his answers.

To most reporters and observers, that seemed the end of that: the Buddhists would return to their pagodas in anger, another element of the restless population would be outraged by the Government, the American mission would say that Diem had treated the Buddhists with firmness, thus gaining their respect, and business would continue as usual.

We were wrong. The first thing we learned about the Buddhist leaders was that they were remarkably tough. On occasion they were passive and unworldly, at other times they were overly suspicious or too calculating for their own good, but always they were resolute and committed. There was no bluff to them; they had considerable popular support and their followers would do almost anything they wanted; and they never indulged in empty threats.

At the time of that first meeting the Government held that the Buddhist protest was to be taken not as a legitimate grievance of the population worthy of investigation, but as an affront to the president. The Government line of reasoning was very simple: protesting the lack of religious freedom was an insult to Diem because he ruled the country and he was against such discrimination. In effect, the Buddhists were saying that he was unjust, but this was not so. Besides, he was very well informed about what had happened in Hué and how the population felt. Why, his own Minister of the Interior had confirmed that the Communists had thrown a grenade, and his officials here in Saigon knew that the people were with him, and that the trouble was being caused by some radical priests whom the population would know better than to follow.

But this new challenge posed complicated problems that Diem was ill prepared to meet. He could not satisfy them with empty promises—as he could the Americans; or play one faction against another—as he could with the Army; or cut off any funds, since such a threat meant nothing to the Buddhists. He could not imprison them as he would a group of political leaders; to arrest priests was more difficult, more dangerous and would have vast international implications— quite apart from the fact that trying to check aroused Buddhists is like trying to stop quicksilver. The Buddhists also turned out to have an extremely effective intelligence system, for there were many of them in clerical and menial jobs throughout the key areas of the Administration, who provided the latest information on what the Government was doing and thinking.

Diem continued to be ill informed. Midway through the Buddhist crisis he summoned Lieutenant Colonel Pham Ngoc Tao, an extremely bright officer who had once served as province chief in Kien Hoa. He was a former Vietminh leader and his brother was Hanoi's ambassador to East Germany. Because of Palace intrigues, Tao had been transferred to a relatively unimportant job inspecting strategic hamlets, but this duty took him regularly into the countryside. He and Diem retained a mutual personal affection for each other—though it later turned out that at that very moment he was one of the chief plotters in the young officers' coup because he felt that the Government was completely out of control.

After greeting Tao, Diem immediately asked him what the people in the countryside were thinking. Fully aware of the populace's discontent and realizing what Diem's reaction would be, Tao quickly changed the subject. The two men chatted for a few minutes and then Diem repeated the question. Again Colonel Tao evaded answering.

But Diem would not be put off. "What do the people think?" he said.

"Well, Mr. President," Colonel Tao said as diplomatically as he could, "the people are not very happy."

At which Diem charged out of his chair in a rage and said angrily, "It is all Communist propaganda."

I returned from vacation on May 28; by then any normal government would have settled the Buddhist incident, but in Vietnam it was just beginning. It the early afternoon of my first day back several hundred monks suddenly materialized in front of the old opera house—which was where the National Assembly convened—to draw attention to the start of a two-day hunger strike. The monks showed considerable organizational ability; obviously they were going to be formidable foes. Closely watched at their pagodas by secret police, they had quietly slipped into four buses (with drawn shades) in different parts of town, had circled separately all over the city and had disembarked in the central square at exactly 2 P.M., to begin their protest. They stayed there for three hours and then marched back to their pagodas at 5 P.M., just as many Vietnamese were returning from work. This demonstration made a profound impression: people were startled and moved, for no open protest against the Government had been held in Saigon for many years.

Thus were we reporters initiated into a new world, that of Vietnamese Buddhism, a world in sharp contrast to the Vietnam we knew. We spent endless hours waiting at pagodas and sparring verbally with agile Vietnamese spokesmen; we drank innumerable cups of tea served with the penetrating odor of rotting cabbage wafting in the background (even today when I am offered tea, I automatically sniff for the smell of boiling cabbage). Unlike the Vietnamese we knew best— the lean, rugged Army officers whose lined faces were eloquent evidence that they had survived two decades of warfare, or the sharp-faced Vietnamese newsmen who had lived by their wits and survived intrigue—the Buddhist monks looked like people who have been sheltered from the world. Their faces were smooth and unlined, almost a little sickly, and their hands were soft. Unlike many educated Vietnamese, they had had little contact with the Western world. Only one of them had been to the United States, for a year of study at Yale; because of this, he had once met Ambassador Nolting and was known among his peers as "the American Buddhist." If a priest spoke French or English, he automatically became a spokesman.

At times the Buddhists monks were incredibly naïve about the outside world, but they were also cynical and quick to suspect the worst of everyone. Once I asked Duc Nghiep, one of their spokesmen, his opinion of Madame Nhu. "She is the Vietnamese Lady Macbeth," he answered. "She and her husband want to kill the King of England." A little later he said that many of the Buddhists wanted to burn themselves to death to protest the lack of religious freedom. I asked him why he didn't set fire to himself. "Every priest has his job to do," he answered seriously. "Some priests burn themselves; my job is to talk to you."

If an American reporter wrote a story that displeased the Buddhists they were not only apt to hold press conferences denouncing him, but they were sure that he must have been bought by the Ngo family. They did not understand the function of a free press, but they quickly sensed that it could be used and that it gave them some protection. Early in the crisis reporters received an anonymous tip that Buddhists distributing literature had been arrested by the police. When newsmen arrived on the scene they found only a few monks. Where were the police, the reporters asked. "Oh, we told them that we had called the foreign press, and so they let us go," one of the monks said. Thereafter a deputation of us called on one of the Buddhist leaders to explain that reporters were not policemen or bodyguards.

On another occasion during the middle of the crisis we were all gathered at the Xa Loi pagoda because we'd heard that something was going to happen. Duc Nghiep walked up to us and suggested that we go home. "There will be no human sacrifice today, gentlemen," he said. Half an hour after we had departed, the Buddhists charged out of Xa Loi and held a large demonstration in front of the residence of Ambassador Nolting. Later one of the reporters asked Duc Nghiep why he had sent us away. "Ah," said the Buddhist, "because when you left, the secret police left too, and when they were gone we could leave the pagoda and demonstrate."

Diem regarded the Buddhists with a certain amount of tolerance—though he felt more at ease with Catholics around him—probably because he did not consider Buddhism a truly serious religion. But in this struggle he was a victim of his own vanity—and very much a prisoner of his family. Archbishop Thuc and the Nhus all urged a hard line against the Buddhists; since the crisis had emanated from his own area, Thuc felt that concessions to the monks would be a slap at him. The Nhus opposed conciliation simply on principle and were openly contemptuous of Buddhists—Mrs. Nhu going so far as to state publicly that they were Communist-dominated. She also felt that culturally they were beneath the Ngo family and Catholics in general. "It is embarrassing to see people so uncultured claiming to be leaders," she told me. In another and quite revealing interview with Charley Mohr, she said that there were few devout Buddhists, and that worried Buddhist leaders were using the crisis to try to convert people to Buddhism, "otherwise they fear that eighty percent of the country would become Catholic."

Of all the members of the family, only Ngo Dinh Can, ruler of Hué, was reported to be urging a conciliatory approach. Considered by many people to be the most practical of all the brothers and the most Vietnamese (he was very limited in foreign languages and never saw Western visitors), he was rumored to keep a very accurate intelligence service on what the population in his province were doing and thinking, and he knew enough to be worried about the growing strength of the Buddhists.

The country was ripe for a group which would stand up to the family. As the protest continued, it seemed to be gaining strength and enthusiasm and a wider base of support. On June 4, I wrote that what had started as a religious protest had become ''predominantly political,'' and that the Buddhists were providing ''a spearhead for other discontented elements.'' By June 11, I was reporting that the dispute ''had become a full-scale political protest,'' and by July 2, I was writing that ''Diem and his family are now engaged in an all-out fight for political survival . . . Before, there was no organized dissent. Now a small patch of yellow cloth, normally a sign of Buddhist loyalty, is worn widely and defiantly as a badge of political opposition . . . The younger priests now give the impression of trying to keep the dispute simmering so that eventually someone else will capitalize on the feeling of protest . . .''

At the beginning of the crisis the priests had seemed frightened and a little unsure of themselves, but then they grew more confident; they were well aware that at least two groups were plotting coups. By the end of June the family was tightening its security measures, and the tension was building in Saigon.

Throughout all of this the American embassy was the unhappy partner of the Government. Day after day, as the Buddhist protests increased and received world-wide publicity, the Americans became more embarrassed. The image—largely created by the Americans—of Diem leading a widespread, solid national movement toward certain victory was being shattered, and so was the idea that the Americans could influence the Ngo family. Every day the embassy urged a quick settlement; every day it received a chilly response. ''The longer this goes on, the more Diem turns toward the bosom of his family,'' one foreign service officer told me. The Americans were also angered by Madame Nhu's anti-

Buddhist statements, and they urged Diem to control her.
"The Americans want this to go away. They want to make
everyone happy," Madame Nhu later told me. "Trueheart
[William Trueheart, the deputy chief of mission in charge of
the embassy during Nolting's absence on home leave] told the
President that if I was not silenced they would have to with-
draw support. The Americans were trying to blackmail me."

Of course this was an exaggeration; the Americans were
merely hoping desperately for some kind of reconciliation.
Trueheart was in a peculiar position. He was a Nolting protégé; the two were close friends; Nolting had asked that
Trueheart be assigned to Saigon as his Number Two man.
Until the Buddhist crisis, Trueheart had gone along with the
American policy, but during this prolonged demonstration of
Ngo-family ineptitude he had become appalled by the Government's lack of competence, and had become increasingly dispassionate—had, in fact, begun to sound like an American
embassy official in any other country. His resultant disen-
chantment with the Ngo family was responsible for a cooling
of his personal friendship with Nolting, who was far more
committed to the family and the policy. (Afterward, close
personal friends of Nolting felt Trueheart had let Nolting
down, while friends of Trueheart felt that Nolting had entered
a less than favorable efficiency report on Trueheart; they
claimed that several officials in the State Department inserted
letters of commendation in Trueheart's file to counter the effect.) By mid-June, Trueheart believed that the crisis would
grow, since he saw little hope that the Government would be
able to reach an accommodation with the Buddhists. Recog-
nizing that this was a situation where the Government could
easily turn adversity into an advantage by placating the Buddhists and bringing them into the fold, he felt that it was more
likely that force would be used to crush them.

In this crisis, with our international prestige linked to Vietnam, all the weaknesses of the American tactics toward Diem
became evident. Basically Nolting's idea had been the
"money in the bank" policy—that is, he would go along with
Diem as often as possible in order to gain the President's
confidence, in the hope that when the embassy wanted to

make a stand on a matter truly important to American interests it would have "credit in the bank." The policy backfired, however; Diem trusted Nolting personally, but there would be no credit for the ambassador to draw on. A particularly humiliating example was when Jim Robinson of NBC was expelled for calling the family a "clique"; Nolting spent more than three hours arguing the expulsion unsuccessfully with Diem. Later, American policy opposed Diem's decision to break off relations with Laos, but Nolting could not change the ruler's mind. Finally, the embassy was never able to persuade Diem to make the kind of concessions to Prince Sihanouk, the Cambodian leader, that the United States felt were desirable for peaceful relations between the two countries.

At times Nolting would gain minor victories, but despite his good will and good intentions the relationship between the two men was undermined by the fundamental differences between their two governments. The psychology and outlook of the Ngo family were so completely alien to those of Washington that the alliance was almost doomed from the start. At best the two administrations could have had a paper agreement; in theory they might agree; but in practice they were talking about different problems, different beliefs, different worlds, and—despite their mutual fear of Communism—different enemies. The Vietnamese were not really interested in what the Americans thought about the Buddhist crisis; they knew that their ally was nervous about the international implications of that struggle and that the Americans' chief concern was the war, not the survival of the family and its conception of domestic balance. The Ngos felt that their basic duty was to stay in power; they did not want American advice in any area—particularly in what they considered a domestic problem. The Americans, on the other hand, disapproved of the Government's position in the Buddhist crisis, and saw it as an opportunity to reunite the people and instill a sense of national purpose. They received assurances from Diem that he was working toward a conciliation, but looked in vain for such a gesture.

During these weeks, when the Americans were obviously trapped by their own policy, reporters talking to embassy officials were surprised by how poorly, particularly in the beginning, the mission was informed about developments in the Government and among the Buddhists. At the same time, because American policy heretofore had deliberately included inordinate praise of the family, Washington was also circumscribed. It could put little effective pressure on Diem behind the scenes; yet any public statement dissociating the United States even slightly was extremely awkward, because it would contrast so sharply with previous statements and would have a profound effect on Vietnamese domestic politics. The turmoil in Saigon during those days was such that any whisper of withdrawal of American support for Diem might easily have touched off a coup. Thus, the American officials had little room to maneuver in, and while they coaxed the family they watched American prestige being dragged down with it.

But even as the Americans were attempting to persuade Diem to make a move of conciliation toward the Buddhists, the Nhus were countering with pressures of their own. On June 8, Madame Nhu issued a strong statement in direct contradiction to the stated Government policy of reconciliation. Madame said that the Buddhists had been infiltrated by Communists and that they were being duped, and she threatened strong Government action against them. Once again this was an example of the power and shrewdness of the Nhus; they often announced policy without consulting Diem, knowing that he would never contradict them publicly or rebuke them privately. They also realized that if they seized the initiative he would eventually come around to their position.

"If that's policy, it's a disaster," said one American embassy official after her speech. But to the Buddhists it *was* policy, for they had to live in the country and were subject to the whims and beliefs of the family. Since Madame Nhu's remarks helped to convince the Buddhists that they would be captives of the Nhus, the price of reconciliation went up immediately.

While the Buddhist movement had been gathering momentum, its leaders had talked to reporters about the possibility of such dramatic protests as a monk burning himself to death; none of us, however, took such threats seriously. On the morning of June 11, I was sleeping late when I got a panicky call from Nguyen Ngoc Rao, the Vietnamese reporter for UPI. His voice was almost out of control; all I could understand was that I should get to the corner of Le Van Duyet and Phan Dinh Phung streets as quickly as possible. I grabbed Ray Herndon of UPI, who was staying at the house, and we dashed for the corner six blocks away. As we arrived we saw a crowd of chanting Buddhists in their orange robes. Just another demonstration, I thought; we had become so used to these by then that I silently cursed Rao for waking me up. But at that moment I looked into the center of the circle and saw a man burning himself to death.

I was to see that sight again, but once was enough. Flames were coming from a human being; his body was slowly withering and shriveling up, his head blackening and charring. In the air was the smell of burning flesh; human beings burn surprisingly quickly. Behind me I could hear the sobbing of the Vietnamese who were now gathering. I was too shocked to cry, too confused to take notes or ask questions, too bewildered to even think.

Later we learned that the man was a priest named Thich Quang Duc who had come to the square as part of a Buddhist procession, had been doused with gasoline by two other priests, had then assumed the cross-legged "lotus" position and had set a match to himself. As he burned he never moved a muscle, never uttered a sound, his outward composure in sharp contrast to the wailing people around him. I had never felt such conflicting emotions: one part of me wanted to extinguish the fire, another warned that I had no right to interfere, another told me that it was too late, another asked whether I was a reporter or a human being. All around this scene of medieval horror were the signs of modern times: a young Buddhist priest with a microphone saying calmly over and over again in Vietnamese and English, "A Buddhist priest burns himself to death. A Buddhist priest becomes a martyr." Pictures were being taken of the immolation; Malcolm Browne and Bill Ha Van Tran had been tipped off earlier, and both had taken dramatic photos of the burning.

To Madame Nhu this event was simply a barbecue and an affront, but to thousands of Vietnamese it was an emotional and momentous occasion. The Buddhist leaders played this reaction skillfully; they took Quang Duc's heart to the pagoda and placed it in a jar, claiming that since the heart did not burn, Quang Duc had left this world unsatisfied. This simply added to the legend; Quang Duc had become a martyr for the people in many parts of Vietnam.

The Government, now very much on the defensive, began to circulate rumors: that Quang Duc's fellow priests had set him on fire, and that he had been unable to feel any pain because he had been heavily dosed with morphine. These reports simply made the population angrier; no Vietnamese and few Americans believed them.

For whether the Government liked it or not, the Quang Duc suicide had electrified the population, though the dramatic effect was somewhat mitigated later when other Buddhists rushed to burn themselves to death too. Whatever complaint an individual Vietnamese harbored against the Government, he was sure—however irrationally—that Quang Duc had killed himself for *his* particular grievance.

The United States was staggered by the suicide and by the world's reaction to it, and Washington redoubled its efforts for a settlement. It quietly warned the Ngo family that it might have to dissociate itself from the Government unless it made peace with the Buddhists. Under this unwanted pressure from the Americans, the Government finally met with the Buddhists, and on June 16 the two sides produced a joint communiqué. It was a curious mixture of the views of both sides, but on the most crucial of the five Buddhist demands— the admission of responsibility for the Hué incident—the announcement simply stated that an all-government commission would investigate the circumstances of the deaths. The communiqué was signed by President Diem; at the bottom he added a special notation saying that he had believed in these points all along—thus saving face by implying that he was conceding nothing.

The joint communiqué pleased neither side; it simply hardened the disagreement and changed the complexion of the protest. For it was only a piece of paper; it had no more meaning than the good will of both parties, and simply the act of signing angered the Nhus and disturbed the younger Buddhist priests

The communiqué was signed early in the morning, and according to a reliable Palace source the Ngo family was having chicken soup for lunch when Madame Nhu read it. She berated Diem for cowardice and called him a jellyfish for even negotiating. "You defeated the Binh Xuyen, you defeated the Hoa Hao [two sects], you defeated the paratroopers, and now you have lost to a few miserable unarmed bonzes," she said. "You are a coward."

Diem allegedly answered, "You do not understand this affair. It has international implications. We had to settle it."

At this point, it is said, Madame Nhu picked up the tureen of soup and threw it across the table. "And so, there was no chicken soup for lunch," said my Palace informant.

Among the Buddhists the reaction toward the document was one of deep suspicion. On the morning the communiqué was issued, several reporters drove to the Xa Loi pagoda to talk with Duc Nghiep. "When I tell some of the other priests what has been signed they will be very angry," he confided.

Suspicions increased in the following days. Not only were there no gestures of reconciliation; just the opposite began to take place. First Nhu issued a secret memorandum to his Cong Hoa Youth movement, calling the Buddhists rebels and Communist-infiltrated, and suggesting that the group urge the Government not to accept the joint communiqué. (The Government almost never made a step without this kind of elaborate sham of popular backing. Although Diem was the head of the Government and had signed the communiqué, Nhu was playing his usual game of telling one of his groups to demand what he had intended all along. He would then tell Diem that the people wanted the Government to turn against the Buddhists, and the family could proceed to do as it wished—in response, of course, to popular demand.)

The attacks on the Buddhists in the English-language newspaper, which was the mouthpiece of the Nhus, worried the Buddhists. Moreover, reporters and diplomatic officials were informed by their Palace sources that the communiqué was not to be interpreted as a sign of weakness; the Government simply intended to wait until the fuss died down and would then arrest some of the Buddhist leaders. Through their own intelligence sources the Buddhists began to glean quite detailed accounts of the Government's plans.

At this time there was a marked change in the Buddhist leadership. Until then the leaders had been the older monks more conscious of tradition, generally more conservative and not as interested in politics as the younger priests. Young Buddhists had been a force in the dispute but the older men had been able to control them up to the signing of the communiqué. Now, however, in late June, the younger leaders, realizing that they were in the movement too deeply for an easy retreat, knowing that they were marked men—and not unhappy about the fact, for they wanted the Government to fall and they wanted to be political—took over. It was easy enough for them to do so; the older Buddhists had been undercut by the Government's behavior since the signing of the communiqué, and their role in Buddhist councils had been weakened.

The young priests represented a new force in Vietnamese politics. Generally in their thirties and early forties, they were men who were clearly affected by living in a nation which had undergone thirty years of political revolution and war. They had grown up in a country in which the mandarin way of doing things had almost always failed, and they had noted the appeal to the population of the Vietminh's dramatic techniques. They were highly skilled in politics, and they had a keen insight about the psychology of their people. Foreigners were always awed at the way the priests could move their people, whether joking with them or inciting them; their mass meetings, in which they encouraged the Buddhist population to participate, resembled the civil rights rallies in Southern Negro churches. They were articulate, brilliant men; the Vietnamese Buddhist movement was clearly one of the few in the country where men of true talent, instead of second-raters, had risen to the top. They could discuss the populace, the war, the family and American foreign policy skillfully and with originality.

Once I told one of the most brilliant of these priests that a friend of mine sympathized fully with their cause, but that he felt they were bad Buddhists. Good Buddhists, my friend had said, were interested in another time and place, not in worldly events. Duc Nghiep looked at me and snapped, "Tell your friend that on his way to the next world a Buddhist priest has responsibilities in this one." He explained further: it was wrong that President Diem had lost the confidence of his people and that his soldiers were like mercenaries who fought with their bodies but not with their souls. Then he looked sad (the Buddhists were always very good at looking sad), and said, "I am a refugee from the North. I know the Vietminh, and I know what they do to religion. Ho Chi Minh is my real enemy, but he is more clever than Ngo Dinh Diem. When Ho Chi Minh stands in front of me he is always shaking my hand and smiling, and when he stabs me it is from behind. But this government is clumsy, and it is trying to stab me from the front. It is all very sad."

President Diem was sixty-two years old, a Catholic, a product of a different generation and of a respectable conservative order; his Buddhist opponents were different in every sense. I believe that the Buddhist crisis was a conflict of generations; it was also a protest against an authoritarian regime, a conflict of two religions, a conflict between the haves and have-nots, but more than anything else it seemed to me a conflict between twentieth-century Asians and the generation that had preceded them. One generation was stiff and righteous in its attempts to cope with new forces by relying on tradition; the other was young and facile, acutely attuned to the rising expectations and aspirations of a repressed population. The young Buddhists resembled the men coming to power everywhere throughout the underdeveloped world, leaders who despite great political and economic problems were able to hold power because of their ability to sense their people's wants.

In the weeks that followed, these leaders skillfully played on the Government's weaknesses. Gradually they turned to provoking it. "We shall throw them the banana peel for them to fall on," one priest told a group of Buddhist youth. They seized the initiative; the Government reacted to *them*, rather than the reverse. Often the Government broke up their demonstrations with violence and bloodshed, and as Bull Connor and his police dogs in Birmingham were to etch indelibly the civil rights movement in the minds of millions of Americans, so the Buddhists used the Government's repeated clumsiness to commit their people further to their cause and to strengthen the movement. "There is blood on the orange robes," a spokesman would say at a demonstration, and the emotional response was always astonishing.

In response, the Government had no policy and no initiative; Diem was too proud. In any case, it was too late to make the kind of gestures which earlier would have ended the conflict; on the other hand, he had promised the Americans that he would not do what he and the Nhus wanted to do— crush the Buddhists.

By late June the Ngo family knew it was in a fight for survival, and that coups were no longer merely being discussed but were actually developing. Stricter security precautions were taken; streets around the Palace were blocked off, security policemen with radiophones were stationed at key spots, all unusual movements were watched and the various secret police agencies were on constant alert. Certain units whose loyalty was considered questionable, such as the airborne, were ordered on operations designed primarily to keep them out of Saigon. Diem suddenly promoted a large number of young officers, but for some reason he promoted staff officers rather than field commanders. Early in July, Nguyen Ngoc Tho, the Vice-President, announced that a preliminary investigation of the Hué incident confirmed the Government account that the Vietcong were responsible for the deaths. Buddhist leaders in Hué retorted that there had been no investigation—or at least, no Buddhists had been interviewed. Saigon hummed with rumors of intrigue. Watching this slow process of disintegration, it was inconceivable to us reporters that it could be settled without bloodshed.

In mid-July, Ambassador Nolting rushed back from his vacation to try and settle the Buddhist crisis once and for all; reportedly he had been instructed by President Kennedy to "go back there and see if you can't get that guy to play ball."

At the airport he made a brief statement which reaffirmed the American belief in religious freedom and failed to mention Diem by name. Later that day Nolting met with reporters at his office. He said he had returned to try to convince Diem to "change his image, both here and overseas." (I remembered the words because it seemed so characteristic of American policy to be worried about images at this moment.) I asked Nolting if he didn't think that in trying to get Diem to change his image the ambassador would be in conflict with Mr. and Mrs. Nhu. The ambassador thought for a moment, and then said no, he didn't.

Nolting's return had little effect; neither side could turn back. Gradually the crisis began to spill into the countryside, and the Americans became even more alarmed. Buddhists demonstrating in Saigon in mid-July were badly roughed up and their pagodas were closed. In an audience with Diem, Nolting urged him to announce a dramatic new policy; the Americans were hoping desperately for that new image. Finally, on July 19, Diem spoke on the radio for about two minutes, and in a cold, brief statement granted one minor concession about the flying of flags. He had little else to say except that the population should respect him, that he would be fair, and that he was forming a special Government committee to investigate Buddhist complaints. But even as he spoke the pagodas were still sealed off with barbed wire.

Of course Diem's broadcast did not have the desired effect on the population or on the Buddhists in particular. In this situation Nolting was almost powerless. He had committed himself totally to Diem; his whole policy was based on his personal relationship with the President and on his ability to influence him. The policy had failed, not because of the ambassador's lack of dedication or skill as a diplomat, but simply because his faith was never reciprocated; it was accepted, but never returned. Now it was rumored that Washington suspected that the policy had failed in other areas, too, and that Nolting would be replaced by a new ambassador. Friends of Nolting's felt he had been badly treated; for months he had not been told whether his tour would be extended. On his departure for home leave at the beginning of the Buddhist crisis, he had told reporters that he was coming back, although at the time Saigon was rife with informed reports that he was through—that he would return only to pick up his suitcases. Eventually it turned out that Nolting apparently was given almost no advance notice of Henry Cabot Lodge's appointment.

At this moment Nolting, cornered, was to involve himself in Vietnamese politics one more time. In late July the most important aspect of the Buddhist crisis was not whether the "good" Buddhists or the "wicked" Government were at fault; the real question—and everyone in Saigon and Washington knew it—was whether the Government was competent to handle the discord, or whether its clumsiness and short-sightedness would allow the Buddhists to become a major and unpredictable force in Vietnamese politics.

It was at this point that Nolting stepped in gratuitously. He said in an interview that he had never seen any evidence of religious persecution in Vietnam; taking matters a step further, he added that he was tired of everyone's tendency to take "his eye off the ball" by spending too much time and energy on the Buddhist question. The crisis was a side issue, the ambassador said; the important thing was to win the war.

Wittingly or unwittingly, with this statement Nolting placed the United States squarely behind Diem in the crisis. The Nhu forces were delighted with the interview: the *Times of Vietnam*, the English-language daily which faithfully reflected the views of Mr. and Mrs. Nhu, headlined the story and labeled Nolting "the first American ambassador to Vietnam really worthy of being addressed by his title." Ambassador Lodge, the paper added, "has mighty big shoes to fill."

Rarely had I seen my Vietnamese friends so angry. They were almost irrational about Nolting, not because he had claimed not to have seen any evidence of discrimination, but because the whole interview seemed to them to symbolize the United States' disregard for their country and problems. "It is always the same with you goddamn Americans," one Vietnamese told me. "During the French Indochina war you told us that if we fought the Communists for the French, you would see that we got independence very soon. Now you tell us to fight the Communists for Diem, and that when there is peace you will get us a good government. We are no longer interested in your goddamn advice."

The Buddhists were no longer interested in Nolting. Duc Nghiep said, "It is only the last present of Mr. Nolting to Mr. Diem. I do not think Mr. Cabolodge [rhymes with camouflage] will be President Diem's cup of tea."

Apparently Nolting realized belatedly what a tempest he had created with his inadvertent and revealing slip. Two days later a CBS television team who had come to his office for an interview watched in amazement as Nolting told an aide to replace the portrait of Jefferson on the wall behind his desk with one of Washington, who, he said, was "less controversial."

Before Nolting departed, Nhu told him that he wanted to name a strategic hamlet after the ambassador at a public ceremony. Since this was obviously a scheme to associate the Americans even more fully with the Nhus in the public mind, Nolting tried to get out of it gracefully by pleading a heavy schedule. But the Nhus were very determined people; Nhu told Nolting to pick any day that would be convenient for him, and the ambassador, trapped, had to give in.

The day was a disaster. A helicopter had killed a little girl in the village the day before while preparations for the ceremonies were being made, and a truck in the caravan ran over another child on the day of the event. The villagers were all carrying small American flags, but their enthusiasm was as ersatz as the occasion itself; they looked pathetically confused and frightened, and with good reason—naming the hamlet after an American ambassador would make it a prime target for the Vietcong.

The reporters who covered the ceremony all noted in their stories that Nolting had done his best to avoid the whole business. Angrily Nolting called up John Mecklin, his public affairs officer, demanded to know how we had gotten that information, and then accused Mecklin of leaking the story. Mecklin replied that no leak was involved, that the story was true, that any reporter with a modicum of intuition would have suspected it and then confirmed it easily, and that the best thing the reporters could have done for Nolting was to publicize his distaste for the affair. Everyone in Saigon, Mecklin said, knew that the ceremony was a fraud; how could anyone take seriously the story that the villagers were supposed to have competed for the honor of having their hamlet named after Nolting by writing the best essay about what the ambassador had done for their country?

Later Nolting called Mecklin back and apologized.

On August 5 the burnings started again, apparently without the knowledge of the Buddhist leadership in Saigon. On that day a monk burned himself to death in Phan Thiet, a small seaport north of the capital. The Government carried off the body.

The suicide in Phan Thiet brought forth more bitter comments from Madame Nhu; she said that she hoped there would be more burnings and that she would clap her hands if there were; the Buddhists should be beaten ten times harder for their behavior, she added. Her comments only provoked further horror. On Monday, August 15, another Buddhist burned himself to death in Hué; the Government troops, using bayonets and swinging steel helmets like billy clubs, snatched the body from the other priests. This in turn bred more death; three days later a Buddhist nun burned herself to death in the seacoast town of Ninh Hoa, allegedly to protest the Government's seizing the body of the Hué priest.

On that very day, Nolting left Vietnam. In the past, airport departures or arrivals had reflected the mood of the mission and of "the team." Such scenes had usually resembled one of Saigon's private parties; senior officers were very much in evidence, reporters were isolated and junior officers avoided being seen with them. But on this day there was a curious change. There was so much bitterness in the American embassy, so many civilians were so fed up with our policy and its equivocations, and so tired of the family's arrogance that we correspondents were now sought out, even welcomed. For the first time officials talked openly with us; no longer were we the enemy, no longer were they worried about being seen with us.

Nolting seemed lonely. In a prepared statement he talked of the mutual bonds of "humility and tolerance, respect for others and a deep sense of social justice" which united the Vietnamese—born of different religions, he emphasized—and the Americans. He added that during his time in Vietnam, progress had been made in education, agriculture and commerce, and in "the inculcation of democratic principles."

Early the next morning a fifty-year-old Buddhist priest burned himself to death. Within a week Nhu raided the pagodas.

XIV

By August it was clear that it was only a matter of time before one of two things happened: either there would be a coup d'état, or Nhu would strike against the pagodas. There was also the possibility of a Nhu coup, which would include an attempt to crush the Buddhist movement.

It was in this tense atmosphere that the Central Intelligence Agency began to take on considerable importance. Just as the other divisions of the American mission had failed—the embassy in converting Diem, the military in having its advice accepted and in assessing the war correctly—the CIA was doomed to fail in its intelligence role.

Although essentially the CIA's lack of success was due to the broad failure of our whole Vietnamese policy, that old problem of the CIA's—whether it was simply an intelligence-gathering agency or whether it was to implement policy as well—was also partially to blame. By and large the CIA's inadequacies in Vietnam were minor compared to the failings of the military mission and the embassy; yet since returning to this country I have been surprised by the public suspicion of its role in general, and of its performance in Vietnam in particular. There still remains a feeling that the CIA was somehow responsible for the continuation of Diem's rule long after it was obvious that he was not the right man for the job.

This is not true; admittedly the CIA had something to do with early American support of Diem, but at the time this seemed to be a wise appraisal. Nor is it true, at least during the time I was in Saigon, that the CIA was in conflict with other parts of the mission, that it was foiling the plans of more honorable and better-behaved agencies. Indeed, just the opposite is true, and that was precisely the trouble: there was no conflict between the various elements of the mission at all. The CIA was not a dispassionate analyst of the situation; it was actively on the team.

I suspect that part of the inherent suspicion of the CIA is the outgrowth of its bogeyman image among liberals; the other side of the coin is the conservatives' suspicion of foreign aid programs. Both of these concerns are products of the frustration of trying to promote America's interests in a complex world where the best intentioned and most enlightened of policies, often carried out by the ablest of public servants, do not necessarily work. When these policies fall short of success, as they frequently do, U.S. citizens tend to look for scapegoats and conspiracies; naturally they seek these largely according to their own political predilections, and inevitably they are apt to find the philosophy they are against in domestic affairs conspiring against our policy overseas.

But the world and our foreign policy are not that simple. By and large, domestic ideologies are not effective in foreign countries, and the leaders we support abroad have the unpleasant habit of not conforming as Republicans or Democrats would wish. Diem, for instance, was not the conservative Vietnamese that many Americans think he was. He was suspicious of businessmen and capitalism, and his influential brother Nhu was probably inclined toward socialism, but the Government was mandarin rather than right or left wing.

What happened to the CIA in Vietnam sheds some light on the immensely difficult task it has, and on the conflict between this country's traditional view of itself, its policies and the necessities forced on it by the Cold War. I am not familiar with the intricacies of CIA operations or techniques, and I am not an intelligence expert. But many CIA agents in Saigon were my friends, and I considered them among the

ablest Americans I had seen overseas or at home. They were
placed in the most difficult jobs, often victims of the enormous disparity between their own high ideals and the vastly
different motivations of their Asian ally. Writing only as a
layman who was on the scene, I will try to give the best
account I can of the role of the agency, culminating in its
failure to predict and analyze correctly the crackdown on the
pagodas.

Within weeks of my arrival in Saigon in 1962 I had lunch
with John Richardson, the chief of the CIA in Vietnam. He
was a good man, honest and dedicated, and in his personal
philosophy he leaned toward the viewpoint of the American
right—though this was not by any means reflected in his
operatives. Our talk was pleasant that day, but peculiarly
involved in a long, abstract discussion on the nature of
counterinsurgency. I was never quite sure that I understood
Richardson correctly, for our terms and points of reference
were so different.

One part of that first conversation I remember distinctly:
our discussion of the Nhus. Nhu, Richardson said, was a
great nationalist. When I mentioned some of Nhu's anti-
American remarks and the resentment many anti-Communists
felt toward him, Richardson said that the anti-Americanism
was simply a product of Nhu's nationalism. He was a proud
Asian, but he was also for us; more important, he was the
one man who understood the strategic hamlet program. As
for Mrs. Nhu, she too was a nationalist, according to Richardson—perhaps a bit extreme occasionally, and sometimes
a little emotional, but that was typical of women who entered
politics—look at Mrs. Roosevelt.

I was new in Saigon at the time, but I was not that new.
On the way back to town our host, one of the embassy officials, suggested that I write a story about what he termed the
change in Nhu: "The new Nhu." I said that I would wait.

What happened in the following months convinced me that
Nhu was anything but a nationalist: he seemed to me to be a
born intriguer, suspicious of his ally, taking great delight in

dividing his people and in controlling the population—altogether a brilliant but warped man.

The disparity between Richardson's and my views evolved in part from the different nature of our jobs. The CIA was not simply a group of sophisticated young Americans who were predicting events in a somewhat predictable nation. Had this been its role it would have accomplished it handily—but it would also have exposed the weakness of our policy. The fact was, the CIA was not in Saigon just to analyze and evaluate, it was a participant in some of our programs, trying to make them work in order to turn our overall policy into a success. I am not familiar with the full extent of the CIA's responsibilities in Vietnam, but I do know that it was directly involved in the montagnard arming and training program, as well as in the operation of the strategic hamlet program in some areas. Also, part of Richardson's assignment was "to get close to Nhu." Since Nhu was the key man in the Ngo family, and therefore of the Government, it followed that in Vietnam part of the CIA's role was to influence the Government in the direction we wanted it to take.

In Vietnam there were two major problems facing the CIA in the execution of its basic function—that of gathering intelligence. The first was that no man, once his career and prestige are committed to working for the success of a policy—and once he has told his superiors that such a policy will work—retains his objectivity. From then on, to justify his participation, he is apt to do his utmost to *make* the policy work, regardless of the consequences—witness Nolting's remarkable statements at the end of his tour. Events and indices tending to show that the policy is not working are shrugged off in favor of those which show that it is; agents or individuals who consistently report to the contrary are disregarded in favor of those who are committed to the same vision. Consciously or subconsciously, intelligence becomes tailored to fit the policy.

Richardson, who enthusiastically believed in the policy, had the assignment to gain Nhu's trust, and this constituted the second problem. In Richardson's eyes Nhu was the most influential man in the country (which perhaps he was), not

the most hated man (which he certainly was). In staying close
to Nhu, Richardson had to pay the price of taking Nhu's words
for an event, even of seeing the situation through his eyes.
Consequently, it would have placed his position with Nhu in
jeopardy if his agents were working the other side of the
street and gleaning intelligence—as they should have been—
from anti-Nhu sources. Furthermore, since Nhu and his wife
were hated and feared in Vietnam, the fact that our intelligence chief was close to Nhu placed a considerable damper
on the gathering of intelligence. One of the most frequent
criticisms about the CIA by responsible Vietnamese—indeed
about the entire American mission—was that information
given Americans about the Ngos went right back to the Palace, apparently in an attempt to buy confidence from the suspicious family. (An American professor in this country told
me recently that in September of 1963 he had a student who
was the son of a high Vietnamese official. After the pagoda
crackdown the official had written his son a letter giving details about Nhu's plans, and the student had shown it to the
professor. Sensing that the information was important and
significant, the professor passed it on to the State Department. Evidently the information was then turned over to the
CIA, because the professor—who had thought he was acting
in confidence—was accosted by a very angry Vietnamese student several days later. The boy had a letter from his father
saying that a high CIA official had visited him in Saigon with
an official cable referring to the professor's call to Washington
and asking him to confirm or deny the information.)

Thus, with the onset of the American build-up the CIA
was operating under considerable pressure in Saigon. As the
situation there became more tense, many wary Vietnamese
would tell reporters or young political officers what they were
hesitant to take to higher embassy officials or the CIA. This
was the penalty suffered by an agency whose top members
were part of the team.

As the Buddhist crisis developed, the tension and uncertainty
in Saigon continued to build. Amid all the rumors it became
obvious that two main coups were in the works. It pointed up

the degree of the Government's alienation that both revolts
were headed by men who until recently had been among the
last of Diem's loyal followers. One coup was the senior officers' plot, headed by Duong Van Minh, Le Van Kim and
Tran Van Don; the other was the junior officers' coup, and
during early August this seemed the more likely one to materialize. Eventually, under somewhat different circumstances, the latter did take place as the Nguyen Khanh coup
replacing the older officers' junta, but at the time many of us
thought it would take place immediately because its planning
was extremely advanced and its leaders impressed us as being
bolder than the generals. However, the generals had a habit
of ordering key battalions out of town every time the young
Turks were ready to strike.

One day in August an important Vietnamese whom I
trusted said he wanted me to have lunch with him and one of
his friends. After lunch we repaired to the friend's house in
Cholon, the Chinese section of Saigon, where I was told that
my two companions were part of the young officers' group
which was planning a coup. I was surprised to be given this
information, but even more surprised when they told me that
they wanted me to cover the story from the inside. They could
guarantee nothing if things went sour. Certainly, if the coup
failed I would have to leave the country, and there might be
even more unpleasant results.

I left them to consider the proposal for a while, talked with
Sheehan, decided that journalistically it was worth the risk
for such a story, and agreed. Burt Glinn, a photographer then
in Saigon for the *Saturday Evening Post*, was also told of the
plan, and he too was ready to try his luck. The leaders of the
coup gave us a military radio and we were assigned a band
and call numbers. We were to be "kidnaped" by the coup
plotters and taken to their headquarters; they thought that this
would give us a measure of protection if the coup backfired.
After that, there was nothing to do but sit back and wait
nervously. On several occasions during the next few weeks
we were alerted, but each time the generals, now preparing
their own coup, switched battalions on the plotters.

But during this same period CIA agents were telling me

that their superiors in Vietnam were still so optimistic that they were not taking the turmoil and unrest very seriously. Yet it was well known that the Nhus were angry over what they felt was Diem's weak handling of the Buddhists, and there were reliable reports that Nhu was planning a coup of his own, which would begin with an attack on the Buddhists and would end by making him the strongest man in the country. Finally this became more than a rumor; details of the plan began to filter down. Hearing these, Nick Turner of Reuters went to see Nhu. "I hear you are planning a coup and that you will raze Xa Loi," Nick said. (Only a Reuters man can make a statement like that and get away with it.)

Nhu smiled. At first he denied it; then he began to talk. He said that if the Buddhist question were not solved, it would soon lead to a coup which would be anti-American, anti-Buddhist and anti-weak Government. If such a coup took place, say, at midnight, Xa Loi would be razed by 2 A.M. (Actually Nhu's timing was slightly off; the raid on Xa Loi began at 12:30 A.M. and ended at 2:30 A.M.) There was only one man capable of leading such a coup: Nhu himself. After Turner filed his remarkable story, he was called to the American embassy and asked if he believed Nhu was serious; he answered that he was 99 percent certain.

By this time Nhu had brought his personal military arm, the special forces under Colonel Le Quang Tung, into the city. Tung's troops were an American brain child. Selected for their physique, specially trained, specially well paid, they were conceived by the American military as an elite force to be employed in counterguerrilla warfare. But the Ngo family had seen fit to make them the political and protective private army of the family, and they had done very little guerrilla fighting. Two battalions of these troops had quietly been brought into Saigon in July, making a total of four in the city.

On August 17, I cabled my office and suggested to my editors that they use every single word coming out of Saigon. Something was on the way, I said, and it was not just Henry Cabot Lodge.

The Buddhists themselves appeared to be at least as much aware of all developments, and their protest seemed to have a mounting intensity. On Sunday, August 18, they put on one of their most impressive demonstrations. Fifteen thousand enthusiastic people, many of them young, flocked to the Xa Loi pagoda. Nguyen Ngoc Rao, the UPI reporter, said that it was the only emotional crowd he could recall since the early days of Diem. The streets were jammed, and when it began to rain the people refused to go home.

It was also a joyous, boisterous crowd. Filming the proceedings on top of the pagoda were two ABC-TV reporters, one of whom was Charles P. Arnot. Suddenly a priest gestured toward the two reporters and spoke a few words; a tremendous roar of laughter went up from the mob. "Thich Quang Do has just told the Buddhists that the foreign correspondents have pledged to go on a day-long hunger strike," Rao whispered to me. Then Quang Do asked the correspondents to address the crowd. Arnot replied that he would be delighted to, but that he would have to cable New York for permission.

The mood of the demonstration was buoyant, but if the priests had said the word, fifteen thousand Buddhists would have marched on Gia Long Palace immediately. However, Lodge was due in a week, and the Buddhists were clearly holding their fire for his arrival. As I wrote two days later—on the eve of what was to be the pagoda crackdown—the Buddhists were playing "a fast and dangerous game."

On Monday, August 19, a Vietnamese friend called; he was much more cautious than usual, and we made an appointment to walk together along the river front. There he told me that Nhu planned to raid the pagodas and that Colonel Tung's troops would be used. That same day we learned that Nhu had held a meeting of the generals and had chastised them for not taking sufficient precautions against a coup. He told them that one was likely to take place, and that if it did, the family planned to evacuate to a hiding place outside the city while the generals surrounded the capital and razed it with artillery instead of fighting at close quarters. If there was a coup, Nhu said, it would be inspired by the intellectuals and would have Western support. (Incidentally, this was the second time that Nhu had talked to the generals about the

possibility of a coup; on the first occasion he said that he
heard rumors of one, and that perhaps some of them knew
about it. If so, he suggested that they stay and talk with him
after the meeting. None stayed.)

That night I filed complete details, including verbatim di-
alogue, about Nhu's second meeting with the generals, which
had taken place only thirty-six hours earlier. I asked a Vietnamese friend what Nhu's reaction would be to the story.

"It will make him glad," the Vietnamese said.

"Why?"

"Because it will make him think that he can't trust the
generals," the Vietnamese said. I still did not understand.

"He already distrusts the generals, and this will convince
him that he is right and that he is brilliant," the Vietnamese
answered.

On the surface, Saigon went its charming, attractive, corrupt way; the security precautions remained tight, the girls
remained pretty, and a reporter could write whatever kind
of mood piece he wanted ("In this tense city . . ." "In
this happy city where tension lurks beneath the tranquil surface . . ." "The tense surface of Saigon today belies . . .")
By this time Sheehan, Perry, Turner, Rao, An and myself
had created a small but first-rate intelligence network. Each
of us had a different specialty and area: An, for instance, had
the best military contacts in the country, since he had served
in the Army with many of the majors and lieutenant colonels
as a young officer; Rao, by courage and endless hard work,
had built a network within Diem's secret police force—such
a good network, in fact, that after the coup he was ineffective
as a reporter for several weeks because all of his sources were
in hiding. We had long suspected that a showdown was coming, and each of us had carefully been cultivating sources so
that we could be ready for it. Now, that Monday, a long
afternoon of checking on the part of all of us indicated that
something was imminent—Rao, for instance, had found that
the secret and combat police were on some sort of alert—but
we failed to find out exactly what it was. We were all exhausted; for the past five days Sheehan, Turner and I had
taken turns staying up all night in order to warn the others in

case something broke. Tired and irritable, that evening we decided that the strike would have to come to us.

But on Tuesday afternoon, August 20, I had a drink with Dang Duc Khoi, Diem's information officer who had long since become disenchanted with the President and tired of all the intrigue. "On that matter you inquired about yesterday [the raid on the pagodas]," he said, "I think it will come tonight or tomorrow." I checked another source and received confirmation, then returned to the office and filed a story which said that despite all of the American and Vietnamese officials' talk about the dispute having ended, nothing had been settled, that the Government and the Buddhists were further apart than ever, that the Buddhists were not eager for a settlement, that the Government's initiative had been reduced to deciding whether or not it should keep the bodies of burned monks, that Nhu was restless—and that a showdown was near.

We prepared for a long wait; not sure whether the climax would come that night, the next day or at all, we decided to carry on as if the situation were normal. Several of us were eating at the Faas-Halberstam villa when Mert Perry arrived in a cab. An anonymous Buddhist had just called our office and warned that the crackdown was coming that night. The Buddhists, it turned out later, were tipped off by two sources. First, the Buddhist wives of some of the combat police had called and said that their husbands were going to arrest the Buddhist leaders that night; second, people living in areas around the pagodas had warned that secret policemen had been moving into the neighborhood all day. This was an excellent example of the advantage of having the population on your side in a political war.

The group split up and we each started checking different areas. Mert and I toured the pagodas. They were all tightly locked; they were expecting the raid, and the streets around them were deserted and quiet. At the An Quang pagoda the young priests were overjoyed to see us; they must have thought that our presence meant protection. At Xa Loi everything was calm, and some of the leaders were asleep. When we woke them they told us that they knew about the raid, and then went back to bed. Mert and I hurried out; we suspected that the attack was near, and we didn't want to be caught in it.

Mert returned to the office and I to the house, but I had no sooner settled down than Sheehan raced up the driveway in a cab, shouting that he had just seen three trucks filled with troops roar past the house headed in the direction of the An Quang pagoda. I leaped into his cab and we headed for Xa Loi, which was four blocks in the other direction. On the way we passed the Third District police station; in the lot by the headquarters were hundreds of troops in full battle gear and about twenty trucks, some of which were already setting out in the direction of Xa Loi.

It was a warm and pleasant night. I had that rubbery feeling that comes to an athlete before a game, or that one feels in the last few minutes before a helicopter assault—a period when one's senses are frighteningly acute. I can remember Sheehan cursing and shouting at the driver in Vietnamese, *"Di di. Di di!"* like a man in a harness race. We sped toward Xa Loi, our driver terrified of being involved in whatever was going to happen, but almost equally terrified of his passengers.

We arrived at the pagoda as convoys converged from every direction; it was like being caught in the middle of a vast military operation. Though two hundred troops could have accomplished the mission, several thousand seemed to have been assigned. We were caught in a sea of soldiers; a block and a half from the pagoda there was a traffic jam of troop trucks, and we jumped out of the cab. I later learned that Sheehan, racing to find a phone to try to start emergency filing (we assumed, correctly, that the regular cable facilities would be closed), managed to worm his way into the United States Operation Mission next to the pagoda, and from this vantage point saw and heard much of the action. I could only get to within a block of the pagoda; I could see most of what went on, but every time I tried to edge up closer I was pushed back by a tide of police.

What followed was a horror spectacle. Had Nhu wanted to arrest the Buddhist leaders it could have been accomplished efficiently in a few moments, but these troops were enacting a passion play of revenge and terror. Hundreds of them charged inside, and the night was filled with a discordant jumble of the screams of the Buddhists, the shouts and cries of the attackers, the shattering of glass, the cracking of pistols and occasional explosions—all this punctuated by the sound of the gong on top of the pagoda being struck wildly back and forth, clanging desperately in the dark. Around me Vietnamese officers barked orders; unit after unit moved up and charged into the pagoda as if they were sure that the Buddhists had a battalion inside and reinforcements were needed.

There was one particularly chilling sight. A squad of Colonel Tung's special forces, identifiable by their berets and their size, trotted forward in a V-form riot formation, each carrying submachine guns at high port. As they pranced into the pagoda, looking something like a smart football team coming up to the line of scrimmage, the mark of American instruction was all over them, and the endless clanging of that gong seemed to me to signal the end of a foreign policy.

At that moment, similar units were breaking into pagodas in Hué, smashing the giant statue of Buddha and killing, according to the American consul, thirty priests and students. But as I stood listening to the screams in Saigon and watching Buddhists being carried out, it was impossible for me to tell how many were killed and injured; later I learned that several monks were listed as missing and that about thirty were injured or wounded, but the true toll was never known.

At one point three troopers came up and started shoving me back. As they became more insistent I feared that they would arrest me, so I used a trick I had learned from Jean Louis Arnaud, an Agence France Presse reporter in the Congo. Once during the fighting in Katanga, Arnaud was being pushed around by road guards demanding cigarettes; Arnaud suddenly turned on his tormentors and asked *them* for a cigarette. The Congolese, first stunned and then delighted, produced a whole pack and insisted that Arnaud take it, and immediately the manhandling ceased. Now I borrowed a cigarette from the Vietnamese troopers, smiled, talked fast and convinced them that I was not supposed to move.

The orgy lasted for about two hours because many Buddhists had barricaded themselves inside various rooms of the pagoda and the troops had to take doors off hinges to reach their victims. Though the Buddhists were certainly not cooperating in their arrest, I was puzzled that some of the leaders had not fled to a hiding place, once they knew that the strike was coming. After the coup I asked Thich Quang Do about this, and he answered, "We had done nothing wrong; therefore we could not flee. If we had, it would have been an admission that we were guilty." But my own impression was that the Buddhists were ready to have some martyrs and also that they might have miscalculated the extent of the crackdown; that night raids were conducted not only in Hué and Saigon, but in every major city in the central coastal region; thousands of priests were picked up. There was another possibility: an expectation on the part of the leadership that at the last minute there would be a countercoup by the generals or junior officers.

At this point my problems changed: I had the story, but wasn't sure how to get it out. I slipped away and returned to Sheehan's office. It was two-thirty in the morning, which meant that it was two-thirty in the afternoon in New York. Neil and I compared notes; his vantage point had been better and he had more details than I did. Then we began to try to file. Neil managed to reach the U.S. Army's communications system and was able to talk a specialist there into sending out about a hundred and fifty words—complete with pistol shots and screams—that gave him a world beat. Then we went to the embassy to see what we could find out from them, and whether they would file our stories for us.

There was nothing to learn there, for to our astonishment the embassy had been caught completely unaware by the raids. Another good story, I thought. One of the top officials asked, "Why didn't you tell us?" It seemed incredible that all those people who had been tipping us off for the last thirty-six hours had either not called the embassy—or that if they had, the report had not reached the top officials who were still being assured by the Ngos that there would be no raids. But what happened in the next few days was even more astounding: the raids having taken place, the embassy was unable to learn what had happened or who had been responsible.

Through one more private channel Sheehan and I sent out brief additional reports of three hundred words on what was at least a fifteen-hundred-word story. While this was enough to satisfy my editors in New York, I felt terribly frustrated; there was so much more to report. Even in that first story, however, I had noted that the raids bore the stamp of Ngo Dinh Nhu; I felt that I had never made a safer assumption.

At about four-thirty we returned to Sheehan's office. There we found an exhausted Rao lying on the bed, listening to troop movements which were being broadcast on the military radio that had been given to me earlier. On a map of Saigon he had marked tank companies and battalion after battalion as they took up positions ringing the city. Was this a coup? Rao stayed behind, tracing the moves, while Sheehan and I toured the city. We saw the tanks and troops, but of course we could not tell who was ordering their movements. When we returned to the office a couple of hours later, there were new developments: martial law had been proclaimed, as well as curfew, the Army had allegedly taken over all civilian functions, and strict censorship was enforced. We found out later that way back in July the generals had decided that one way to get troops into the city for their own coup was to impose a state of martial law; they figured that after Diem had declared it, the troops which would be moved into the city to enforce it could stage their revolt. But when this idea was suggested to the brothers, Nhu, who had been planning the pagoda crackdown, saw it as a perfect cover for his own plot. Adopting the generals' plan in part, he raided the pagodas, using only his own special troops; the Army had taken the initial blame, and the generals had been beaten to the punch.

Early in the morning Major General Tran Van Don broadcast several new orders as part of the martial-law regulations. He claimed that the Army was assuming command of the country because enemies of the people were working hand in hand with the Communists and imperialists. Supposedly General Don was in charge, but later we were told that he had said to General Dinh, the one general with any power, "Tomorrow you may be giving the order to have me arrested. Be good to me, eh? Get me a nice cell and put a pretty girl in it."

Plastered to store fronts in Saigon was a long and involved handbill, supposedly written by the Army, which announced that its day of nationalism had finally come. Though the tone of this broadside sounded like something that Nhu, not the Army, had written, everyone's confusion at this point was understandable. The city was filled with troops, and the declaration of martial law and the alleged role of the Army were matters we hadn't counted on and which had to be explained. In our stories written on August 21 we reported the martial law, but added that the exact role of the Army was unclear and that Nhu had obviously played a strong part in what had taken place.

At noon on August 21, under the most difficult conditions—after almost no sleep, with tension everywhere, great fear on the part of our best Vietnamese sources, the curfew which made travel at night impossible, and no communication lines—we went to work to track down the real story.

It was a time of rumors, and thus a time not to be too hasty at the typewriter. In such circumstances a prominent person who has not been seen is often alleged to be either in power or dead, and a reporter can dig up anything he wants to hear. Information is everywhere; it is the evaluation both of that intelligence and of the people who give it which becomes all-important. In trying to determine what had happened and who was in power, our appraisal of the facts as we knew them went something like this:

1) The strike had all the characteristics of the one proposed by Nhu and repeated to us by knowledgeable friends. In addition, the Buddhist sources had confirmed that virtually the same plan was to be executed at that particular moment. Moreover, on the night of the raids I had identified Tung's special forces and two of Nhu's top aides directing actions at Xa Loi. Lastly, one of our Vietnamese friends had talked to an air-borne soldier who was very angry because many of

Tung's troops were wearing air-borne uniforms that night. The implications of this disguise were obvious.

2) It seemed very unlikely to us that the Army would have staged a coup with a blood bath. Though there might be some officers who were annoyed with the Buddhists, one of the first things the Army would seek if it came to power was a rapprochement with the Buddhists.

3) The Ngo family distrusted, feared and felt contempt for the Army, and the purpose of much of its intrigue was to divide it. Yet according to the announcement, the Army and the Ngo family were now sharing power. It was not like the Ngo family to share power with anyone, or any institution—least of all the Army.

4) One correspondent had an interview with Madame Nhu on the day after the pagoda raids. She was in a state of euphoria, chattering like a schoolgirl after a prom. She told the reporter that the Government had crushed the Communist-Buddhists, and referred to this as "the happiest day in my life since we crushed the Binh Xuyen in 1955." In many ways Madame Nhu was the most forthright member of the family, and she could not possibly have been overjoyed at the idea of the family turning over part of its power to the military. Since for a long time she had been the most active proponent of a strong policy against the Buddhists, it seemed probable that she was celebrating the Ngo family's victory.

5) I knew General Tran Van Don fairly well, and had spent some time with him in Da Nang. He had impressed me as a thoughtful, candid man with a considerable amount of integrity; he had even permitted me to use his name in an interview I had with him—a highly unusual circumstance. He was very much the Vietnamese aristocrat, urbane, born and educated in France, and it was hard to believe that he had authorized the pagoda strike.

6) There were constant humiliations of American officials on the day after the raids. Telephone lines to the houses of the top officials were cut, and the car of the head of the USOM, Joe Brant, was stopped and searched at the entrance on his way to and from work. Other Americans were kept waiting interminably for appointments with Government of-

ficials and in securing permits to drive after curfew hours. If
the Army had really been in charge, it would immediately
have moved to reassure the Americans that it wanted them
there and that it needed their support. (Indeed, the Army did
exactly this after the November 1 coup; it was so public-
relations conscious that it withheld from distribution the photographs of the bodies of Diem and Nhu because it feared
they might offend American and world opinion, even though
there was tremendous pressure to release the pictures to prove
to the population, who doubted that the two brothers would
ever die, that their rule was over at last.)

All of these factors were in my mind when I started my
leg work; it would take very hard evidence indeed to convince me that the pagoda raids had been the Army's show.
On the morning of August 22 everything pointed in the other
direction.

One of the first conversations I had that morning was with
John Richardson, who had asked to see me. In the first hours
after the pagoda raids there was already a rumor spreading
around among responsible Vietnamese that the CIA had
known of the crackdown, indeed had given its approval, and
that the event had been specifically timed to occur between
American ambassadors so that the United States would not
be embarrassed by the affair. In Vietnamese minds this was
a logical extension of Richardson's close relationship with
Nhu and the CIA's with Colonel Tung. It was inconceivable
to the Vietnamese that the CIA had not known of the raid,
and they were therefore sure that the CIA had sponsored it
indirectly or at the very least permitted it. The Vietnamese
were ready and anxious to believe the very worst about the
Americans at that time.

That morning Richardson was a tired and shaken man. He
refuted the rumor immediately. "It's not true," he said. "We
just didn't know. We just didn't *know*, I can assure you."

After I left Richardson's office, I continued to check details. Soon a pattern began to develop. Shortly I met an
American intelligence friend and asked him who was responsible.

"Nhu and Colonel Tung," he said, and then listed the

units which had been involved. "It didn't have a damned thing to do with the Army," he said.

"Why didn't you know?" I asked.

"We should have known," he said. "We had every damn warning you can get. We kept telling *them*"—meaning his CIA superiors—"that Tung had his special forces in town and that something like this might happen. We could have been spared this. We could have headed it off."

Like every other American at this moment he was bitter and angry. The violence of the pagoda raids had come as a shock to almost all the Westerners in Vietnam, and now, as people had time to think, the implications of the event were becoming clear. It meant the death of a policy; it was the end of trying to fool ourselves about our conciliatory effect on Diem, for now the Government would be even more under the influence of the Nhus. Further, since American equipment and American-trained troops had been used, the population would have even less confidence in the United States.

Finally, the violation of sacred promises was a direct slap at the Americans, and since this humiliation had come just as a new American ambassador was on his way, it limited his actions by presenting him with a *fait accompli*. (On the night of August 22, General Ton That Dinh, the one general who had been in on the planning of the strike, told a friend of mine, "I, Dinh, am a great national hero. I have defeated the American Cabot Lodge. He was on his way here to pull a coup d'état, but I, Dinh, the hero, have foiled him.")

However, gathering news and writing it was by then a secondary problem. All normal means of communication were now useless because of the heavy-handed censorship of the regime, and no serious reporter wanted his name to appear over a story which had been strained through censorship. So that day we began to use pigeons: civilians or military personnel flying to other Asian cities who could carry our copy out and then relay it to our home offices. From then on, this meant late-morning deadlines in order to catch the plane, which in turn meant that we had to be at work by 7 A.M., rushing to see sources, often allowing not more than thirty minutes for the actual writing of a story, and then racing to the airport to smuggle out the copy with the passenger. Fortunately most of the airport security men were fed up with the regime; our biggest problem was with our own military mission. Colonel Basil Lee Baker, the chief PIO, who had never been considered the reporters' best friend, was true to form during these frantic days. On one occasion, hearing that we were trying to send stories out with servicemen who were flying to Bangkok on a military plane, he called Major General Richard Weede, Harkins' chief of staff, to find out if regulations permitted this. The answer was no, so Baker sent an officer out to the airport to board the plane and announce that it was a court-martial offense to carry out press packets; the officers had no choice but to return the material to us. The incident did not serve to strengthen the existing bonds between Colonel Baker and the reporters; thereafter we had to resort to commercial transport only.

On August 22 we worked all day to put together a full picture of what had happened. Back at the office Sheehan and I swapped notes and then began writing. It seemed obvious that Nhu had used the Army as a front for his strike, in order to hide his own hand and to give the impression that the raid enjoyed far broader backing than it did—that this was an action of national unity. The story caused the *Times* some confusion because it conflicted directly with what the State Department was telling Washington reporters. The *Times* editors fretted for a while and then ran the two stories side by side on the front page under a headline reading: "Two Versions of the Crisis in Vietnam; One Lays Plot to Nhu, Other to Army." The paper introduced the two pieces with a statement which said:

> The confused situation in South Vietnam was reflected yesterday in conflicting versions of the role played by the Army high command in the Saigon regime's attacks this week against the Buddhists. A dispatch from Saigon quoted reliable sources there as having said that the drive had been planned and executed in its initial stage without the knowledge of the Army. But information received in Washington pictured South Vietnam's Army commanders

as having put pressure on President Ngo Dinh Diem to persuade him to act.

My story began: "Highly reliable sources here said today that the decision to attack Buddhist pagodas in South Vietnam was planned and executed by Nhu," that the Army had not seized power and in fact knew nothing about it until the raids were well under way. It said that the troops involved were under the command of Colonel Tung, and that Nhu had acted to teach the Buddhists and the Americans a lesson, and to present Lodge with a *fait accompli*.

Our Washington story showed that Nhu had succeeded in confusing the issue by his use of the Army, for it stated that it was the generals who had pressured Diem into acting.

That night we went to the airport to greet Lodge. The PIO's had spent the whole day getting permission for us to violate the curfew by watching the arrival of the new ambassador. We were herded into a special bus, and on reaching the airport found the heads of the American mission awaiting the new chief. At this point we still had no idea that the mission was accepting Nhu's account. While waiting for Lodge at the airport I was talking to Bob Trumbull, my chief from Hong Kong who had arrived earlier that day to beef up the bureau during the crisis, when I saw a high member of the American mission. I introduced Trumbull to him; in the conversation that followed I made it clear that I thought the raid had been engineered by Nhu, but the official said that he believed the Army had forced Nhu's hand. My private reaction was one of anger; it had never occurred to me that the American mission still believed this, and I assumed that it was said for the benefit of a newly arrived reporter—that it was more of the same old policy line, which I had felt sure was out of date at last. For once I should have taken the line at face value; the fact was that the embassy had misreported the raid.

When Lodge arrived shortly before midnight he was immediately presented with a curfew pass so that he could travel at night. He shook hands with Harkins and Trueheart and then turned toward us. "Where are the gentlemen of the press?'' he asked. Clearly the attitude toward us had begun to change.

When we returned to the censor's office to file, every reference indicating that there was any unrest in the country in my brief story on Lodge's arrival was stricken out. All our attempts to slip out the news that Vu Van Mau, the Foreign Minister, had resigned were caught except Mal Browne's; Mal got it through by typing the news onto the caption of a photo of some soldiers and sending it out by wirephoto.

Sheehan, Rao and I spent the night at Mecklin's immense house. There was a reason for this; we had been warned that we were now high on Nhu's list, and both our Vietnamese and American intelligence sources told us that grenades might be thrown into our living quarters. Sheehan lived in the back room of a small apartment with only one exit, and the villa Faas and I had just moved into was away from the center of town and had no telephone.

The next morning Lee Griggs of *Time* flew to Manila, and since he was a reliable pigeon who would make sure that all the copy got out, I sent four stories with him. One, written just before he left, was the daily story on the latest events and maneuverings, and on Lodge's arrival. A second piece described the situation in which Lodge found himself, how it had gotten that way and how serious it was; it was used in the "News of the Week in Review" section on the following Sunday. The third story was a profile of Colonel Tung and how he had come to power. "He has shown over the years that he can be absolutely trusted, that he carries out all orders faithfully, that he has no power impulses of his own and that he keeps his mouth shut," the story said. This ran as a "Man in the News" profile.

The fourth piece, an analysis of the American mission, which ran beside the one on Tung, connected our policy over the past two years to the failures surrounding the pagoda raids. Though it was written in ignorance of the fact that the embassy had blamed the raids on the Army, it said that our mission's lack of knowledge about what was going on in the country could be traced to the fact that it had cut off normal channels of intelligence, had depended excessively on official accounts and had not listened to its junior officers and young civilians. The story continued:

The entire episode has underlined what some sources here consider to be one of the gravest sicknesses of the huge and talented mission here—a vast divergence between what the people in the field are seeing and reporting and what the highest Americans are reporting, because of the ties of the Ngo family to the chiefs of the mission. The fact that Ngo Dinh Nhu with Colonel Tung as his military arm was planning something was not really a secret. Whether it would materialize was another question, because certain aspects of the planning were hard to believe. What was particularly humiliating was that Colonel Tung and his special forces were an American brain child: they were an American idea, to be the proud Vietnamese counterpart of our own elite Special Forces, better equipped and better paid than regular troops. We financed them, we paid them, and we had advisers with them.

With those four stories out, I relaxed a little; a year's hard work had just paid off, and we had told our readers what they needed to know.

That night I had drinks with two friends in the CIA. They were exceptionally bitter, and though they didn't blame any single individual for the agency's failure, they clearly were not happy with Richardson. We discussed the problem of service in a faraway country about which few United States citizens knew or cared. They were both dedicated men, and the risks that they had to take and the immense personal sacrifices they had to make meant a deep commitment on their part. But in this corner of the world such dedication often was not matched by the Asians, and in an atmosphere of despair there was sometimes a tendency to listen too much to Vietnamese who reflected what you wanted to hear.

My two friends were also angry because they felt that the CIA would be blamed unfairly for our whole policy. They were sure that the fault was more Washington's than Saigon's, and they were quite explicit in explaining why. Periodically, as if he were sure that no one would ever believe it, one or the other would say wearily, "Goddamn it! We told them it would happen." I assumed that "them" meant Saigon; it was clear that they felt that Saigon had been caught in Washington's trap. He added, "You give every goddamn thing you have, and you end up with this. I came halfway around the world to get my face rubbed in ——." Altogether, it was a sad conversation; it revealed to me how difficult such a job was, and it made me glad that I was a reporter.

Later Sheehan and I tried as best we could to reconstruct what had happened in the embassy after the raid.

In general the inclination—indeed, the policy—had been to believe what the Ngo family said. With Nolting gone, Richardson was probably the most influential American in the mission; Diem would not see Trueheart, but Nhu would talk to Richardson. Undoubtedly Nhu fed Richardson his version of the pagoda raids—that the generals had forced the hand of the brothers. The Vietnamese generals had almost no confidence in General Harkins; evidently they were not able to state their case strongly enough to the American military mission and had to turn to lower-ranking CIA agents.

Richardson had always seen events as Nhu wanted him to; like Harkins, the CIA chief felt that our policy was working and the war being won. While high American officials were very unhappy about the pagoda raids, they realized—consciously or subconsciously—that a rejection of Nhu's version meant a complete re-evaluation of our stand. Since these American officials were very much a part of that policy and had publicly committed their careers to it, they were in no hurry to write it off. Moreover, Richardson did not have the private sources which would refute Nhu's story, for to have listened to such voices earlier would have been to doubt the effectiveness of the policy. And so Saigon misinformed Washington. It was the last stammer of the old guard.

Meanwhile we reporters continued to file stories in a vacuum; we didn't know what was getting out, what was being printed or what play it was getting if a story was used. Then, four days later, Lee Griggs returned from Manila with a folder filled with messages. My pieces were getting into the paper, it turned out, and there were some complimentary notes, including a particularly nice cable from James Reston: KEEP GOING BECAUSE WE'RE ONLY GETTING PROPAGANDA THIS END. I also received my first inkling that Washington had been wrong on what had happened: YOUR STORY ON NHU TWINED WITH SZULCS WASHINGTON SAYS GENERALS FORCED NHU TO SILENCE BUDDHISTS. Finally, there was a cable from our foreign desk: STATE DEPARTMENT NOW COMING AROUND TO YOUR VIEW WHAT HAPPENED AND WHO DID IT AT PAGODAS STOP CHEERS AND MORE CHEERS.

Sitting in the office, I clutched the cables and yelled for Sheehan. Hearing the commotion, Mert Perry came downstairs and read the message; together the three of us laughed and laughed. Mert said that it appeared that Washington had finally got the little picture, and went upstairs to get beer for us. Charley Mohr said, "You guys are the first reporters I've ever known who scooped the State Department by four days."

Holding up the cables proudly, I said to Charley, "Well, that's the end of the press controversy out here. We've finally broken through. Now they'll understand."

I was wrong; the stakes were simply bigger from then on, and the press controversy had just begun. No one would find this out quite so clearly as Charley Mohr and Mert Perry.

XV

Henry Cabot Lodge did not really switch policies when he arrived in Vietnam, but a new policy needed to be evolved. The old policy lay shattered in the Xa Loi pagoda, in the broken promises handed Nolting by Diem, and in the phony version of the raids given the embassy by Nhu. The old policy had not ended at the behest of the Americans; it had been violated so outrageously by the Ngo family that one Western ambassador referred to the pagoda crackdown as "the end of the gallant American effort here."

Only a handful of the most faithful remained loyal to the Ngo family; in Washington the Vietnamese ambassador—Madame Nhu's father—and all but one member of his staff resigned, and her mother, the Vietnamese observer at the UN, also resigned.

The Army, embittered because it had been slandered by being blamed for the raids, was more confused and divided than ever. The brothers offered cash bonuses to some generals as a means to appease them and to cause further dissension; nominally the cash was "to be divided among the troops for their valor," but no one was naïve enough to believe that it would ever reach even a general's chief of staff.

Government workers felt dejected, and American hamlet officials noted that they were having a harder time than ever getting Vietnamese civil servants to go out in the field. The populace itself was angry, not just at the family, but at the United States. In Vietnam, as elsewhere, the tendency is always to blame someone else, and the majority believed that since the special forces troops had been paid for and trained by the United States, the Americans must have been in on the planning.

Saigon had become a city of fear. Nhu's Cong Hoa Youth, who were nothing but armed civil servants, marched through the city's slum areas warning the people that if they participated in any anti-Government activity they would be arrested. Many Vietnamese officials took to sleeping in different houses every night and communicating with one another only by courier. Americans with close Vietnamese friends were unable to see them; many high civilian Vietnamese were arrested; a few fled the country. Some key military men were placed under full-time surveillance by the Government, and the Marine commander, warned that he would be imprisoned if he stayed in Saigon, promptly took his troops out on a series of operations to avoid this.

The Americans in Saigon were confused and unsure of the next step. For despite all the warning signs, the American mission had little in the way of contingency plans; they had really believed their own words about there being no alternative to the Ngo family.

A couple of days later a statement broadcast over the Voice of America, a carefully calculated reference to the fact that the United States now absolved the generals from the pagoda raids and blamed them on Nhu, was perhaps a subtle hint that Washington was no longer fully committed to the Ngos. But the mission had few strong contacts with the Vietnamese Army at this point, and it was certainly not trusted by the dissident elements of the military. The generals were uncertain about American intentions, for no groundwork had been laid. The ordinary Vietnamese were no surer of what the United States planned to do; the last American face they had seen was that of an embarrassed Ambassador Nolting having a hamlet named after him, and the last public comment had been that of General Harkins saying that the strategic hamlet program was working and that victory was near. Thus, the Voice of America broadcast reached unreceptive ears.

In the middle of all this confusion, the Nhus were happy and

confident. Diem was little heard from or seen, and the Nhus
dominated the Government. Cong Hoa officials told reporters
that there were plans for a huge mass meeting at which Nhu
would be urged to take power. Eventually this was postponed
because of the frigid American reaction to the idea; at that point
the Americans were exerting considerable pressure on the Nhus
to leave the Government. But Nhu and his agents continued to
be active. More arrests followed—of professors, lawyers, civil
servants, and some key young officers who were reportedly imprisoned primarily as a warning to their superiors. Nhu seemed
to be completely carried away with himself. A few days after
the raids he sent out a directive to all civil servants demanding
that they confess their thoughts during the Buddhist crisis and
the martial-law period.

"You are asked to confess sincerely and with a sense of responsibility and honor," the directive said. Typical questions
were: "What ideas did you have when the 'the Buddhist affair'
flared up in Hué until the joint communiqué was signed (ideas
about the acts of the Government and those of the Buddhist
extremists)?" Then followed an extraordinary sentence: "This
part of the directive will be devoted to self-confession about your
behavior without time limits. The self-confessor will comment
on his behavior since his acts were related to [*sic*] the following
items: Your sense of responsibility and your way of serving.
Your bad habits. You are requested to outline a method to elim-
inate your listed drawbacks." Lastly, each civil servant was directed to sign with the following notation: "I certify that this
self-confession is sincere."

In an interview with a Canadian reporter, Nhu stated that it
was "extremely unpleasant, a real martyrship for me to engage
in politics," but that his country's needs demanded it. He also
said that even if the Americans cut off aid to Vietnam, the war
would be won because of the strategic hamlet program and because of the hamlet cadres "who are loyal to me."

Nhu and Diem had always triumphed in the past because they
were almost the only men in Saigon, Asian or Western, who
knew exactly what they wanted. Other Vietnamese had been
divided, irresolute or naïve; as for the Americans, potentially
they could have wielded a great deal of influence, but since they

did not have to live under the Government they were supporting, they had used this power without much discipline, almost idly, and had not taken the day-to-day political developments as seriously as their position and responsibilities called for. Now Nhu, who was sure that he was winning the war, thanks to the twisted reports of his hand-picked men, really believed that he had triumphed over his two other enemies as well—the United States and the Buddhists.

In all of Saigon there was only one loud voice of protest: in the days after the pagoda raids, the Buddhists' place as demonstrators was taken by the students. Saigon's students, traditionally disinterested in politics, living in comfort far removed from the grimness of the guerrilla war, became the new protesters against the Government by going on strike at the schools and inviting mass arrests. First it was the university students, and thousands of them were arrested; when they were gone, their places were taken by the high school students, and thousands of them were arrested. For a week the Saigon streets were filled with students being carted off to indoctrination centers.

The Government reacted in the only way it knew how—by beating some of the leaders and arresting most of the followers. Of course the regime charged that the students had been infiltrated by Communists, and a press conference was held in which two alleged Communist teen-agers confessed that they had corrupted an entire high school. But if they were Communist-influenced, these students came from the most unlikely backgrounds: at the universities they came from Saigon's best homes, and most of the rebellious high schools were in neighborhoods composed primarily of Catholic refugees from North Vietnam, Army officers and upper-echelon civil servants. Again and again we reporters saw high Army officers trying to negotiate the release of a son from a compound, and most of the students also had brothers or friends who were Army officers. The Government was handling the situation as it had handled other protests, but each time it was cornered, the wall behind it was closer.

This was the situation into which our new ambassador was thrust. As any housewife with a television set knows, Lodge is a hand-

some man, the image of the perfect American ambassador. He
is not unaware of this. His background is patrician, and he is
always conscious of his reputation and his dignity; but while he
can be extremely charming, he can also be quite rude. He is a
total politician in the best sense; that is, he is attuned to the
needs, ambitions and motivations of others. Yet his background,
coolness and reserve mark him as essentially different from
other, more genial and back-slapping politicians. Some of this
reserve is inherent—the product of his breeding, education and
prestige, but I suspect that some of it is deliberate—Lodge's way
of emphasizing his variance from the norm. Because of this
distant attitude he does not have the best reputation among Republican politicians, and he was not beloved by the press corps
at the UN.

In Vietnam all this was different. Lodge became known as a
difficult, demanding man to work for, but he had the respect of
his subordinates and of the reporters. He turned out to be a
shrewd, tough operator, very much a match for the Ngo family.
He was absolutely single-minded, he worked hard and did his
homework, and he had no illusions about the task facing the
United States. He quickly analyzed the situation in Saigon, and
today in Washington he is considered to have been the best ambassador we have ever had there. Above all, he wanted to know
what was going on in the country, even when it looked like bad
news. He also played his hand very close to the vest. "He doesn't
trust anyone," one aide told me, "and because of that he's never
had any confidences broken." Sheehan, who comes from Mas-
sachusetts, said, "Lodge is what my Irish mother would call a
crafty Yankee."

The pagoda crackdown, which in a sense was a slap in the
face to Lodge, had taken place while he was en route to Saigon.
But I don't believe that it affected his attitude toward the family;
it became evident that even before he left Washington he had
learned enough to believe that the family was incapable of ruling
the country and of prosecuting a difficult war. Shortly after he
had taken up his new post, Lodge had lunch with a journalist
and questioned him closely for more than an hour on the family
and on the war. The reporter gave him a pessimistic report, and
then asked, "And what's your impression, Mr. Ambassador?"

"About the same as yours," Lodge answered coolly.

Though Lodge did not believe the war was going well, or even being fought very hard, the fact that Harkins was an old family friend from Boston days placed him in a difficult position, since Harkins would never admit that things were not running smoothly. However, this did not deter Lodge from speaking his mind on several occasions. Once after spending several hours with Diem, he told his embassy aides that the man couldn't possibly rule the country; the President couldn't even speak coherently. While Lodge had ticked off American grievances and recommendations, his host had stared at the ceiling, and when the ambassador was finished the President poured out a babble of words about something totally unrelated. Lodge was told that this always took place whenever the Americans asked for anything.

Lodge soon found out that the feeling among the different sections of the mission about the need for a radical change in policy far exceeded that of the Washington people concerned with the area. Without experiencing the situation first-hand, the State Department could not perceive the sense of crisis and bitterness and frustration which existed in the mission. On his arrival Lodge had found a virtually mutinous embassy on his hands; the Americans had had enough of the Ngo family, of our acceptance of Ngo dictums and of official pretenses covering up failures of policy. At a meeting with AID officials Lodge was stunned by their vehemence. William Flippen, for six years a key official in Saigon, deputy chief of the AID mission and one of the ranking members of the American staff, delivered a bitter attack on our previous policy. Flippen added that the American military had been consistently wrong in its reports and interpretations ever since he arrived in Vietnam, and stated flatly that the war was being lost. The chief of the strategic hamlet program, Rufus Phillips, told Lodge that the program was in serious trouble and that the war was going particularly badly in the Delta. One after another, Americans spoke of the deterioration in their areas of responsibility.

At the USIS the new ambassador received a similarly cold analysis of the Government and the attitude of the population from some of the service's most knowledgeable field workers.

"Maybe USOM can sell its pig program in the countryside," one USIS officer said, "but we can't sell this Government to the people, and we only bring ourselves down to its level when we try."

In the CIA most of the young agents were also brutally frank about the Government's unpopularity and its inability to fight a war. There was only one man—Richardson—who did not agree with these assessments; the CIA chief was too much a part of the old policy to change his opinion at this date. Reportedly Richardson believed that it was unrealistic to switch governments now and that at least Nhu had shown that he was smarter than the generals.

Richardson's attitude reflected the dilemma of the U.S. Administration—a dilemma of its own making which did not concern Lodge. Throughout the bad times Washington had claimed publicly that all was well, that corners were being turned and that victory was in sight. If the war was being won, why the change? Conversely, if things were not going well, why had the Administration claimed that they were? The policy makers found themselves prisoners of their own news managing. For the past American optimism had come primarily from our military mission, and the people most identified with it were the generals in Saigon and the high officials in the Pentagon. Their statistics had "proved" that we were winning, their careers were tied to these predictions, and understandably they believed both in their careers and in their predictions. These generals were not interested in the politics of Vietnam—Buddhists, students, arrests and such like—but in the business of fighting and killing the Vietcong. After all, the war was still going on; perhaps operations had slowed down a bit during the last week in August when a lot of troops were tied up with the pagoda situation, but that was unusual.

What we saw in Saigon was some evidence of the alignments which at this time were taking place in Washington. There, too, the military stuck to their previous position, but some civilians had expressed doubts even before the Buddhist crisis: "That's a very fragile situation out there—it could go either way," one notoriously optimistic—in public—high official had told Sheehan privately in April 1963. The religious controversy and the

Government's inability to cope with it strengthened the doubts of these civilians: how could a regime unable to settle the Buddhist crisis be effective in administering the hamlet program and in fighting the war?

Thus, by the summer of 1963 some high State Department people had already become receptive to the idea of change. This included men like Averell Harriman, the Undersecretary of State, and Roger Hilsman, the Assistant Secretary of State for Far Eastern Affairs. Curiously, the Secretary of State himself, Dean Rusk, never chose to play a major part in this continuing foreign-policy crisis; the foremost civilian role was McNamara's.

According to some of his advisers, President Kennedy had ambivalent feelings. Privately he did not believe the glowing reports handed in by the military; he was angered and irritated by the Ngo family—particularly by Madame Nhu—and yet he was reluctant to act. But the crackdown on the pagodas enraged the President personally. He and other Washington officials considered it not only the end of a policy, but a betrayal by an ally as well. And as the Buddhist crisis continued, it inevitably undercut those spokesmen who had praised Diem's political acumen. Thereafter, according to friends, Kennedy began to think that change was inevitable. "His position became one of hoping to bring others—particularly McNamara and the military—along with him, and to do it as subtly as he could," one White House aide said.

Immediately after the strike on the pagodas, Washington received information from some Vietnamese generals that Nhu was reportedly dealing with Hanoi; if this were true, the generals said, they must act, and they wanted to know the position of the United States. It was a very blunt question.

At virtually the same time the Americans accepted Nhu's version of the raids and blamed them on the generals. When this news went out over the Voice of America, reports reached Washington of complaints from the generals that the United States was unfairly blackening the name of the Vietnamese Army, and that the Americans should issue a correction. Also,

Admiral Felt in Honolulu allegedly told the State Department that a revised statement was desirable. As a result, on August 24 a cable was sent to Saigon for Lodge's approval. It said in effect that State was planning a press briefing to say that the pagoda strike had been carried out by Nhu and his special forces. In the same cable the State Department reportedly also instructed Lodge to tell the generals that their question about action in the event of Nhu dealing with Hanoi was of course hypothetical, but that the United States was always interested in supporting anti-Communist governments.

This message received broad support: by Roswell Gilpatric, the Undersecretary of Defense, by Richard Helms, the deputy at CIA (since it was a Saturday, many of the top men were not in their offices), by Rusk and George Ball at the State Department and by the President at the White House. When Mike Forrestal, head of the Vietnam Task Force who was drafting the cable, called General Krulak at the Pentagon about Taylor's position, Krulak verbally gave Taylor's approval. (All of this is significant, because a month later, when the military hardened on its basic position—that the status quo was the best platform from which to wage the war—an attempt was made to show that Hilsman and the State Department had gone ahead without Defense Department approval.) By 4 P.M. the next day Lodge had responded affirmatively to the cable, and State Department reporters were given the new and accurate version of the pagoda raids.

But the second half of the cable produced no dramatic changes in Saigon. The generals, divided and frightened, were still unsure of the American position, and for the moment Nhu was very much in charge of the city.

Thus, in early September, when there was no real change in the internal situation in Vietnam, the White House began an agonizing reappraisal of our policy. The President was receiving a barrage of reports: journalistic ones, traditionally pessimistic; from Lodge and the State Department, now suddenly pessimistic; from Nolting, now back in Washington after being replaced—cold-shouldered, bitter and angry but as optimistic as ever, siding with the rosy Defense Department view; and finally, there were the military reports quoting endless statistics on how well the war was going.

In these circumstances the President once more was deceived by the American military. In order to weigh as best he could the conflicting reports he was receiving, he sent, in early September, two men to Vietnam. Joe Mendenhall, the former Number Two man in the American embassy in Saigon and now a member of the State Department's policy staff, was to report back to Kennedy on the civilian situation; the military reporter was once again General Krulak, a two-star Marine general who was rumored to be the next commandant of the Corps.

The two men spent less than a week in Saigon. As they were leaving, Mendenhall told one American civilian, "Well, I know how bad it is, but I think I'm going to have trouble with Krulak."

He had more than trouble. When the two gave their reports before a group of top policy makers, including the President, Mendenhall expressed his deep pessimism. Krulak, however, was glowingly optimistic and talked about the growth of the strategic hamlet program and the number of operations Government troops were conducting. When both had finished, President Kennedy turned to them and said, "Are you gentlemen sure you visited the same country?"

Fortunately, at this time the President received one more key report on the deterioration in the Delta, and it was from an impeccable source: Rufus Phillips, the young civilian in charge of the strategic hamlet program. A 1951 graduate of Yale, Phillips had served as a young Army officer in Vietnam, where, in 1956, he had met Colonel Lansdale during the latter's years as adviser to Diem. Phillips had become a protégé of Lansdale's; like the colonel, he believed that there was a good chance of making Vietnam a stable country. In 1962, when the American build-up took place, Lansdale was unable to return to Vietnam. The reasons why are not clear; some say that he was too pessimistic, some that he had created too many enemies within the military establishment. Still, young Phillips was chosen to head the hamlet program.

When I first met him, Phillips was very much a member of the team; he was optimistic, and he generated idealism to his civilian staff working as advisers in each province. He and I

differed sharply on the effectiveness of that effort, but I always
enjoyed talking to him; he struck me as having the greatest
knowledge of Vietnam of all the high officials of the civilian
mission, and he discussed the country and the war in more than
clichés and with great feeling. By July 1963 his own associates
in the Delta, including Ralph Harwood, his deputy in the Delta,
were warning Saigon that the program was not working and that
in many of the lowland areas the Vietcong were taking over
virtually unchallenged. By August the reports were increasingly
ominous, and when Phillips went down to the Delta, took a look
and decided that the situation was indeed grim, he did what most
of his colleagues in the upper reaches of the mission would not
do: he admitted that he had been wrong and that the program
was failing. It was to be an act of considerable personal courage.

In early September Phillips returned to Washington and
warned the President about the hamlet program in the Delta; he
said that Nhu had tricked the Americans, that in two key provinces, Dinh Tuong and Long An, it was largely a paper program
and that the Vietcong were making great headway. Phillips was
immediately and bitterly challenged by Krulak, who doubted
his veracity and his competence, but the expert testimony of the
young civilian undoubtedly convinced the President of what he
already suspected—that the military was reporting the war in-
accurately.

Unfortunately, Phillips paid a high price for his honesty; the
wrath of the military establishment descended on him. Since his
father was dying in Washington at the time, he did not return
immediately to Saigon. But for the first time a member of the
team, an honest and expert one, had challenged the Army's
reporting.

I heard about Phillips' dissent and visit to Washington in an
unusual way. I was talking to a friend of mine at the USIS when
his wife, who had just had lunch with the wife of one of the
generals, came in. She told us that her friend had said that her
husband was "going to get that ——Rufus Phillips if it was the
last thing he did." From that it was easy to piece the story
together.

* * *

Back in Saigon we watched the rapid development of a split between the civilian and military missions. Reporters found that at MACV they were still treated coldly, whereas they were not only treated well at the embassy, but from time to time were even tipped off by its officials about Government defeats.

A similar division was taking place in Washington. Finally, in late September, President Kennedy decided to send his two top Pentagon officials, Secretary McNamara and General Taylor, to Saigon for one more special report on the country. Though Kennedy aides were later to explain that this was part of the President's attempt to coax the military, it looked like a whitewash to outsiders. Why send the two top Defense Department officials if not to back up the military, who were already reporting so optimistically?

The visit looked even more like a whitewash when, on September 25, after less than twenty-four hours in the country and after the first meetings with American officials, Arthur Sylvester, the assistant secretary for public affairs, told us at a briefing that the war was "getting better and better, rather than worse and worse." Indeed, he added, the Government was "rapidly approaching" the point militarily where the "goals set will be reached relatively shortly."

There must have been a reaction to this blatant news management both in Saigon and Washington, because two days later Sylvester noted that his first briefing might have "tended to throw things out of focus"; in fact, he admitted it was possible that his remarks "were tending to suggest I was trying to plaster things over with a pretty brush."

Behind all this double talk an absorbing behind-the-scenes struggle was taking place between Harkins and Lodge, each of whom was trying to press his views on the two visitors. Lodge was ready for his first move even before the jet bringing the Washington officials had landed. As the two men were descending the ramp, Lodge assigned two of his aides to block Harkins so that the ambassador would be the first to greet the Secretary. Harkins was caught in a trap as the crowd surged forward, and we could hear him shouting plaintively from behind a group of photographers, "Please, gentlemen, please let me through to greet the Secretary."

Harkins had one advantage: the trip was under the auspices of MACV, and therefore he could arrange the schedule of what the two visitors would see. On the other hand, the Secretary was staying with Lodge, and the ambassador had the opportunity to work on McNamara each morning at breakfast and each night when the daily inspections were over. Lodge deliberately gave Harkins a head start; for the first three days the Secretary and his party flew to various corps areas where the military was in charge. With little variation he was given the standard briefings and statistics—except in the Delta, where the Americans were considerably more cautious.

But midway through their stay Lodge began his campaign; he disagreed forcefully with the conclusions of the military and he expressed strong doubts about the progress of the war. Key civilian personnel working in the Delta in different capacities were quietly brought up to Saigon to meet the Secretary.

This conflict was something new for McNamara. He had been to Saigon before, and he had met frequently in Honolulu with the Saigon team. Each time he had been given the team report: MACV would say that the war was being won; the embassy would say that the war was being won and that Diem was coming around; the CIA would say that things were going well and that the montagnards were coming around. Then, if it was a Saigon visit, McNamara would go to the Palace and be told in a five-hour monologue that the war was being won and that the Americans finally understood its nature. Lastly, he would visit a couple of specially selected sites where the news was good. Duly impressed with the effectiveness of the programs and the team, he would leave Saigon a less wise man than when he arrived.

In my opinion McNamara may well be this country's most distinguished civil servant of the last decade. Brilliant and tireless, he rides herd over the vast and tangled responsibilities of the Pentagon, where he must involve himself daily with awesome problems that are almost beyond human comprehension. He is the final civilian control over a center of power whose strength is expanding at the same rate that the complexity of its weaponry is increasing. Yet one of McNamara's most fervent admirers among the Pentagon "whiz kids," the group of bright young civilians that McNamara has gathered around him, notes

that his chief is interested in everything "but men and ideas."
Unfortunately, the war in Vietnam was little else. In addition, I
don't think McNamara's political ear is tuned to the quiet voices,
and I don't think he fully realized why he was getting such
unanimity—American and Vietnamese—of official opinion. He
had spent a lifetime looking for facts and figures and depending
on them—in the past they had not let him down. Sheehan recalls
that in May 1962 he went on a visit to the first of a series of the
hamlets which were later to prove such a flop. McNamara, Harkins, General Lyman Lemnitzer, Nolting and then Brigadier
General Nguyen Khanh, McNamara's escort officer, were tour-
ing an area that had been under Vietcong control. To Sheehan
the population seemed very unfriendly; all the people stayed
indoors except for one old man who strolled out to look at the
foreigners. After talking with the old man, McNamara inspected
the nearly completed fortifications around the hamlet as Nolting
explained their purpose. They watched a group of obviously
hostile peasants digging a moat under Government supervision.
The peasants kept their backs to the Americans, but "I had the
feeling that they would have enjoyed cutting our throats and
burying us in that ditch," Sheehan said. McNamara, who asked
a barrage of questions, wanted to know where the peasants would
hide when the Vietcong attacked. There was a long pause while
the generals tried to think of a plausible answer; the Vietnamese
had privately told American reporters that there were few young
men in the hamlet because most of them were out fighting with
the Vietcong, and that a number of the remaining families in
the hamlet were sympathetic to the guerrillas. Finally General
Khanh told McNamara that the people could take refuge in the
blockhouses with the Civil Guard troops. But this did not satisfy
the Secretary of Defense, so Khanh invented the story that if the
hamlet was attacked the peasants would lie down on the floor in
their huts to avoid the gunfire.

Apparently such weird explanations and lame answers had
satisfied McNamara in the past. Now, even as late as September
1963, he showed his insensivity to the situation on a tour of the
country by asking all his questions in the presence of General
Harkins, thus talking only to largely inhibited officers.

In the Pentagon much of McNamara's success has been the

result of selecting a group of bright civilians who examined
military goals and priorities and gave him objective viewpoints
and alternatives. In Vietnam this technique could not be applied;
McNamara had no civilian eyes with him and he was entirely
dependent on the Harkins line. If he'd had a civilian "whiz kid"
in Saigon reporting directly to him, things might have been different; perhaps McNamara trusted the advice he was getting and
felt that the war was a place for military expertise only, or perhaps the military would have resented the presence of a civilian
reporting back to their chief. In any case, when Lodge disagreed
flatly with Harkins, McNamara for the first time ran into real
dissent from sources that he respected.

The tip-off on the struggle between Harkins and Lodge came
the next to the last day of the trip, when McNamara canceled a
final military tour of the countryside, sent Taylor off by himself,
and stayed behind for more talks with civilians. The next day,
when McNamara and Taylor left, the word was out; for the first
time the Secretary had not only been thoroughly briefed on the
political chaos in the country, but had been given a dark picture
of the progress of the war. Lodge was satisfied that he had broken through (a high officer in the embassy who did not like
Lodge personally called it "a goddamn *tour de force*").

When McNamara returned to Washington he reportedly told
Kennedy that the military had been wrong, that the war was not
going well and that the official version of military events was
inaccurate. Out of this came a curious statement which expressed concern about the political situation, urged the Vietnamese to continue the fight and further said that the Americans
hoped to bring home most of their advisers by 1965. Lodge was
surprised by the statement, but in Saigon it was written off as
election-year rhetoric. What was important was that behind the
scenes Lodge's viewpoint had prevailed. The Kennedy Administration no longer believed that the war was being won, and the
United States intended to slowly reverse its total commitment
to Diem. Ironically—and not entirely by chance—the key men
in this movement to disengage ourselves gradually from a government which so loudly proclaimed its anti-Communist stand
were two Republicans, Lodge and McNamara. Taylor never
changed his position, but President Kennedy, aided by Lodge,

had been largely successful in bringing McNamara around to his own opinion.

At the time of the McNamara-Taylor visit, the Government had been tidying up loose ends in an attempt to placate the Americans in Saigon; such surface gestures had always satisfied them in the past. The curfew, still in force, was gradually pushed back, and finally martial law itself, which had never been anything but Nhu's way of harassing his opponents, was rescinded. President Diem issued a statement saying that the Buddhist problem had been solved; the Vietnam press announced that Foreign Minister Vu Van Mau, who had been arrested on his way out of the country, had not been arrested at all but simply unavoidably detained; Ambassador Tran Van Chuong in Washington had not resigned, as everyone (including him) had thought: he had been discharged and it was only because of an unfortunate delay in communications from Saigon that the news did not reach him in time.

But Lodge was not interested in such gestures. Step by step he and Washington had been moving to demonstrate to the Vietnamese population that we no longer considered the Ngo family indispensable to the war, and that our future support would be given to the country and to the people, not to the Ngo family. Ever since his arrival Lodge had shown this in a number of small ways which differed sharply from the actions of his predecessor. On the night the pagodas were sacked, two young Buddhists had taken refuge in the USOM building next door to Xa Loi. Twice the Government asked that they be returned, and twice Lodge refused; in fact, on one of his first public trips in Saigon he paid a call on the two Buddhists. When Thich Tri Quang, the enigmatic leader of the Buddhist movement, received asylum at the U.S. embassy, Lodge not only refused to return him to the Government, but in an attempt to counter some of the hostility toward the United States, which had been engendered by the pagoda raids, let it be known that we were "delighted" to be his hosts—thus producing the curious situation of supposed allies fighting a war against Communism and bickering over the harboring of a "Communist agent" by one of them.

When Madame Nhu on a trip in Europe criticized American junior officers for acting like "little soldiers of fortune," Lodge deliberately and publicly took exception to her words as "shocking and cruel." This was the first public statement Lodge made after his arrival in Saigon, and it was received with relief by almost every American there who had heard Madame attack everything from our soldiers to our Bill of Rights. Lodge's defense of our soldiers was certainly understandable, but it was also the first step in the United States' long-awaited confrontation with Diem. The President resented the criticism deeply. At that moment a team of Hearst reporters, headed by William R. Hearst, Jr., was in Saigon for the purpose of writing stories favorable to the regime. During an interview with Diem one of the journalists of the Hearst task force mentioned that many people in the United States were sympathetic to Diem and his cause, but were disturbed over Madame Nhu's statement about the junior officers—perhaps Diem would like to take this opportunity to repudiate it? Diem begged off, giving the strange excuse that he did not know enough about the junior officers and therefore could not comment.

Besides being blunt in public, Lodge talked scornfully about the family in private, knowing full well that in a city where there were no secrets, his words would soon be all over town. Also, certain U.S. aid was being withheld; lastly, Richardson, Nhu's greatest American ally, had been sent home.

A few weeks after his arrival Lodge had decided to get rid of Richardson for several reasons. First, the new ambassador did not want a dissenter who was a holdover from another policy. Second, he felt that as long as Richardson was in charge of the CIA, intelligence would not move freely and the Vietnamese would doubt that American policy had in fact changed. Finally, Lodge reportedly believed strongly that the intelligence-gathering and operative functions of the CIA should be separated. For all these reasons Richardson went home early in October—but only after a silent struggle both in Saigon and Washington, for John McCone, head of the CIA, was understandably reluctant to have his organization made the scapegoat for the mess in Saigon.

Perhaps another ambassador might not have been so determined to get his way in this unpleasant situation, but Lodge was no ordinary ambassador. He carried unusual credentials, and he had arrived at the very time when it was fortunate to have as mission chief a man of reputation who was not a career officer worried so much about his next assignment as the job at hand. Lodge could talk directly to the White House whenever he wanted, and his requests merited special attention. As an American of national reputation, and as a former Republican nominee for Vice-President, his presence gave a handsome bipartisan veneer to our troubled policy in Vietnam. Moreover, if he were not treated with respect, he might resign in a huff and give the Republicans a major campaign issue. Needless to say, he received every consideration from Washington.

There was another reason why Lodge's personal credentials were a particular advantage in this unusual situation. A career diplomat might have regarded the inevitable decision about the Ngo family with some fear and trepidation; there were still shadows from the McCarthy era. A career man might have been in more of a quandary about the choice to be made; perhaps the status quo might have seemed more desirable than a potential future attack for being too liberal.

But Lodge's reputation in this regard was impeccable, and in him the Kennedy Administration had not only a man willing to take a risk, but an ideal political buffer for the possible consequences of this new policy. Aside from bearing a great Republican name, hadn't no less an authority than Richard Nixon once said that he had stood up to the Russians more than any other American? No one in the mainstream of American politics was likely to charge Lodge with being soft on Communists. (This was clearly shown by *Time* after the November 1 coup. While the magazine was unhappy about the turn of events, it was always careful to skip over Lodge's role in it; indeed, when Lodge won the New Hampshire primary and loomed as a serious Republican presidential nominee, his role in Vietnam was hailed by *Time*. A career diplomat, however, might not have been treated so kindly by Henry Luce's skillful team.)

* * *

The new policy being fashioned by Lodge and by Washington was to support the war effort fully but to disengage the United States from anything that could be interpreted as a personal commitment to the family. "Anything that helps the war we support; everything that hurts the war we oppose" was the phrase used. Thus were we moving steadily toward creating an atmosphere in which a coup d'état could take place, for the all-out support which had previously been thrown to the Ngo family was now directed exclusively to the anti-Communist war effort.

In starting afresh, Washington and Lodge were on shaky ground, for they could expect potentially vast repercussions in American domestic politics; in the middle of a war they were facing the unknown in preference to a government which had publicly proclaimed that it was anti-Communist. The Ngo brothers had always played this card well in the past, but now the feeling was growing in Saigon and Washington that the United States could no longer afford to be blackmailed into endless support of a government simply because it was anti-Communist.

At this time a key Vietnamese in Saigon was Colonel Le Quang Tung, the head of the special forces. The Americans had been backing him as part of our policy, but to both the Army and the population he was a symbol of the Ngo regime. As long as the United States continued to support the Nhu-Tung private little army, any policy demanding change would be ineffective.

Sheehan and I had come on this controversy in early September. That was a fascinating time for a reporter in Vietnam, because everyone was talking. The departure of Nolting, the arrival of Lodge, the failure of our past policy and the disgust of most Americans for it had opened many mouths. My office, knowing that I was exhausted after covering the crisis for more than four months, offered me a long break in Tokyo, but I turned it down; there were many subsurface stories, and it was no time to pull a man out who had been building up his sources. My visa had little enough time to go, and I had better stay in Saigon as long as I could.

During this period Sheehan and I were following up on a hunch, and in talking to a friend I casually asked about Colonel Tung's relations with the U.S. mission; I knew that we had been financing Tung in the past, but I did not know the details. Our friend smiled and said, "Well, they almost cut the little bastard off the other day." Since he was an old friend and since it was the time of the great thaw, he began to talk.

It turned out that one of the central debates within the American mission was: what to do about Tung. To Americans he was the most obvious symbol of the treachery of that night; but more than that, to the Vietnamese military he was a symbol of the family's political control of the Army. The Americans were arguing among themselves that the Vietnamese officers would never believe that there was any change of heart on the part of the United States as long as Tung was financed.

Our basic information, coming from several sources close to the CIA was that the agency had originally organized and paid for Tung's operation to the tune of a quarter of a million dollars a month, and that it was still paying this sum. Sheehan and I checked hard, had this figure confirmed to us, and used it in our story. But more than a year later, another CIA friend claimed that by the time the pagoda crackdown took place, the agency no longer financed all of Tung's operation. By then, he said, the CIA paid for only a part of Tung's force, and most of the money now came from regular Military Assistance Program funds. As proof of this, our informant claimed that a few weeks after Washington finally decided to cut Tung off, the news was broken to him, not by a CIA man, but by Major General Stilwell of MACV.

After gathering the information, there was still a question of whether or not to file such a story; this is always a difficult decision, and in this case publication of these facts would certainly affect long-range plans. A considerable public and editorial outcry was going on in the United States about the pagoda sacking, and the State Department had publicly condemned the treatment of the Buddhists; yet the story would publicize the fact that the United States was still deeply involved with those responsible—Nhu and Tung.

But the role of Tung illuminated the basic problem of the American-Ngo relationship. We had initiated certain programs designed to win the war, but they were quickly twisted by the family into a means to bolster their personal power and safeguard their survival. Therefore I decided that I had a legitimate story.

Sheehan and I did two more days of leg work. Neil was convinced that Nhu was not unhappy about our earlier stories of how he had handled the pagoda raids. One of our Palace sources told us that "Nhu will like your pieces because they will show how he has outsmarted the Americans. He will be torn between not wanting to upset the Americans, because he wants more aid, and of wanting everyone in Washington to know how clever he is." But Sheehan felt certain that now Nhu and Tung would be enraged by publication of this story because we were shaking the money tree, and therefore, to protect our sources and ourselves as much as possible, we slipped our dispatches out of the country with a friend en route to the Philippines, and instructed our employers not to use our by-lines. The *Times* ran the story with a Manila dateline, with an adjoining story from Washington, written by Reston, to give the Administration's reaction—which was that it would neither confirm nor deny the stories but that it was extremely angry about them. Washington claimed that the special forces units were fighting the guerrillas, a point I had disputed strongly. The whole argument of my story was that the men who knew Tung best felt that his six battalions were almost never used against the Vietcong—that they were, in fact, a private security force.

The day after our stories were printed, one of our most reliable sources said that Tung was very angry with Sheehan and Halberstam. "You in very big trouble," our man said. Sheehan's idea of dropping the dateline and our by-lines, thereby allowing Tung to save face, appeared to have had no effect. That night when I came home—we were still staying at Mecklin's house—I noticed that there seemed to be an unusually large number of cyclos and taxicab drivers outside the grounds. We knew that all taxicab drivers working under Tung had red paint on the hub of their wheels, but in the last few days we had taken the extra precaution of not using the first cab that came along, but the next; we had noticed that some cabs were waiting for suspiciously prolonged periods in front of our office. When Sheehan returned to the house a few minutes later he said, "There are so many of Tung's cyclo drivers outside that I nearly knocked them over getting here." We went up to the top floor and looked out the window; in the darkness a large number of men were patrolling the street. Both of us were nervous and a little afraid, and nothing is as contagious as someone else's fear and nervousness. We were alone in the house, for Mecklin was back in Washington, and we were tired and worn out. We had spent part of the day checking on a new organization headed by Nhu for which ex-criminals were hired and given guns, to form what the Vietnamese figured would be a suicide squad. Our intelligence friends were taking this seriously, as well as a report that a number of Americans had been placed on an assassination list, and for the moment so were we.

That night we rigged the doors to the upstairs bedroom with a massive Rube Goldberg trip apparatus (shoelaces tied to lamps and shaving-cream cans, designed to fall on plate glass for sound effects). This was to be our DEW line, but we had no defense to fall back to. Fortunately there was no attempt to storm the USIA mansion that night and the only result of our creation was that it shattered the composure of Mecklin's house boy, who was already in a state of nerves.

The Tung story made tangible the U.S. commitment in many areas where we didn't want to be involved. It is very easy to moralize over the responsibilities of the recipient of foreign aid— we seem to do so whenever we give anybody money—but it is important for the giver of aid to be just as responsible, because the donor has power in a country without having to live under the regime he supports. The impression I had was that we were not nearly thoughtful enough in this regard, and that too often we left ourselves open to abuse.

In late October the Administration quietly made a new decision about Colonel Tung. No longer would there be "business as usual." On October 19 he was notified that his troops would only receive pay if they were used against the Vietcong, and then only if they notified their American advisers about every movement.

"The cut," I wrote that day, "will probably have more psychological and political than economic impact. Observers here believed that the cutback was bound to increase the growing tension between the United States and the ruling Ngo family, who are currently cooperating in an uneasy alliance against Communist guerrillas.''

Colonel Tung was very angry when told of the new plan. When Sheehan called him up and tried to get an interview, the colonel said, ''I am a soldier and I do not interfere with politics,'' and hung up. But immediately our phone began to buzz so loudly that we couldn't use it for two days.

XVI

In the middle of all this I had gotten a letter from a friend in New York in early September, enclosing a column about me from the New York *Journal-American*. Among other things it said that I was soft on Communism and that I was paving the way for a bearded Vietnamese Fidel Castro. When I showed it to a friend at the embassy, he said, "Well, I think you have to expect this sort of thing. There may be more."

There was more. A few days later Joseph Alsop, after a brief visit to Vietnam, wrote a column which attacked a group of "young crusaders" of the press corps in Vietnam who were responsible for the peculiar state of psychosis which existed among the inhabitants of Gia Long Palace. Suddenly reporters who had covered the complex evolution of the Buddhist crisis for four long months, who had realized that the monks were an emerging political force long before the American embassy did, found themselves charged by one visiting reporter with not having understood the movement's political implications; reporters who had been covering the disintegration in the Delta for more than a year and a half and had gone on more than thirty missions there were surprised to see themselves accused by Mr. Alsop of not having visited what he quaintly referred to as "the front." Though at this time Lodge was slowly changing the policy to an anti-

Diem stance, Alsop withheld any criticism of the more prestigious Lodge. However, being criticized by Alsop is no small
honor in our profession, and we felt that our stock was rising.
The so-called "press controversy" of Vietnam had begun.

Indeed, suddenly there was no shortage of criticism. One
source of this was the Kennedy Administration, which, when
finally forced to make decisions on Vietnam, was so entan-
gled in conflicting currents within its own establishment that
it was difficult for it to change its position. The Administration was being pressured by mounting forces in the United
States and in Vietnam, and yet it was understandably hesitant
about making changes in the middle of the war. In a speech
to the nation the President told Diem, in effect, to make reforms—or else we could continue supporting him anyway.
("He has tried to change Diem on television and so far he
has failed," James Reston wrote about Kennedy.)

Washington simply did not want to read much of the reporting from Vietnam because it made the situation sound
like a major foreign policy failure, and each day there was
more evidence that the Americans were being led around by
the nose by the Ngo family. In addition, the Administration
was angered by its own ineptitude, first, in letting the pagoda
crackdown take place; second, in not having diagnosed it
correctly; and third, by not having an answer when it finally
did learn what had happened. In some ways Vietnam was
second only to the Bay of Pigs as an Administration failure.
But there was a major difference: the Bay of Pigs debacle had
taken place only ninety miles from home; the bungling was
obvious even to the most myopic, and it could not be hidden
or, in the Washington phrase, "papered over." But Vietnam
was twelve thousand miles away; the situation there was infinitely more complicated, and it required sophistication and
interest for the public to follow it. Therefore it was relatively
easy for Administration spokesmen to make a series of glib
statements about Vietnam, and to attack a handful of young
newspapermen without established reputations.

So the Vietnamese press corps came under fire. White
House reporters were constantly told by Pierre Salinger and
other members of the White House staff that the Vietnamese

reporting was inaccurate and the work of young, emotional correspondents; White House assistants, more interested in the President's political standing at home than the status of the guerrilla war, would explain knowingly that reporters in Vietnam never went out on operations. In the higher reaches of the Pentagon, where the realities of the war rarely penetrated, the criticism was particularly vehement. Defense Department reporters were told by General Victor Krulak, the Pentagon's specialist on counterinsurgency, that they simply couldn't understand what was going on in Vietnam: experienced reporters like Richard Tregaskis and Maggie Higgins had found that the war was being won, but a bunch of young cubs who kept writing about the political side were defeatists.

The general even went so far as to tell a *Time* reporter one of the most peculiar stories to come out of the press controversy: that when Maggie Higgins was in Saigon young Halberstam had met her at a bar, had shown her a photo of some dead bodies, had asked her if she had ever seen dead men, and then had burst into tears. Krulak took great delight in passing this story on to everyone in sight; whether it was his or Miss Higgins' invention I'll never know. "It was a damn good thing you never belonged to any leftwing groups or anything like that," a friend of mine in the State Department told me after the flap was all over, "because they were really looking for stuff like that."

On October 22 Arthur Ochs Sulzberger, the new publisher of the *Times*, went to the White House to pay a courtesy call on the President of the United States. Except for Vietnam, the Administration was riding high. Kennedy was sure that Goldwater would be his opponent in the next year's presidential election and that the Democrats would win easily. Almost the first question from President Kennedy was, "What do you think of your young man in Saigon?" Mr. Sulzberger answered that he thought I was doing fine. The President suggested to the publisher that perhaps I was too close to the story, and too involved—which is the most insidious kind of comment one can make about a reporter. No, said Sulzberger, he did not think that I was too involved. The President then asked if the publisher had been thinking of transferring me to another area. No, said the publisher, the *Times* was quite satisfied with my present assignment. (As a matter of fact, at that particular point I was supposed to go on a breather for a two-week rest, but to its everlasting credit the *Times* immediately canceled the holiday lest it appear to have acquiesced to this pressure.)

Other attacks on us came from varying sources. In the Hearst chain Frank Conniff singled me out in a long article. However, Conniff was by far our most honorable critic; he later came to Vietnam, sensed the military cover-up and wrote quite fairly about us in subsequent columns. The most curious attack of all was that of *Time*, which criticized two of its own reporters in the process.

There had been a long, simmering dispute between *Time* reporters in Vietnam and their editors in New York—a far sharper division than the usual one between field and office. (*Time* employs immensely talented people and puts out a very professional magazine, but I have always observed that *Time* reporters have to do an undue amount of apologizing to news sources about the final product.) These *Time* reporters felt strongly that the magazine was giving too optimistic a view of a war that they saw was barely being fought and in which the enemy was becoming stronger all the time. Not surprisingly, as *Time*'s method of reporting the war paralleled the Pentagon's, so its published accounts paralleled the Pentagon's optimistic version—a case of the chiefs telling the Indians what the Indians had seen.

Periodically Charley Mohr, *Time*'s chief correspondent in Southeast Asia, would return to New York for conferences during which he would argue for tougher coverage on Vietnam. Instead his editors, who had lunched with Secretary McNamara and other Pentagon officials, and had seen the most secret of charts and the most secret of arrows and been given what the Pentagon called "the big picture," would explain patiently to Mohr that he understood only a portion of the big picture. And *Time*'s coverage—paralleling the official version—would continue.

Part of the reason for this, I think, was because of the particular way in which *Time*'s executives view the magazine: to a large degree they see it not just as a magazine of reporting, but as an instrument of policy making. Thus, what *Time*'s editors *want* to happen is as important as what is happening. In Vietnam, where U.S. prestige was staked against a Communist enemy, and the government was Christian and anti-Communist, *Time* had a strong commitment to Diem.

The squabble between the *Time* editors and reporters had started in 1962, but in April 1963, after Dick Clurman, *Time*'s chief of correspondents and one of the foremost defenders of working reporters among the magazine's executives, had visited Saigon, there was a slight improvement. Clurman had met some of the other reporters, had talked with their sources, and had heard Diem and Nhu complain about what was wrong with American advice while at the same time Nolting was telling him there was no disagreement on the advice.

Mohr and Mert Perry felt somewhat encouraged, and during most of the Buddhist crisis they were relatively pleased with the stories that appeared in the magazine. But their journalistic optimism ended in August 1963, with the cover story on Madame Nhu. Mohr, whose file for the story is one of the most brilliant I've ever read, drew rave notices and enthusiastic cables from his home office for his leg work and writing. But he was deeply disappointed with the final results; he felt that it was too flattering and that it overemphasized the personable aspect of Madame (ironically, his lead had begun: "Vietnam is a graveyard of lost hopes, destroyed vanity, glib promises, and good intentions . . .") and played down her destructive influence on the country. Charley and his editors exchanged brief and uncomplimentary letters, and then he went back to work.

Several days later, in mid-August, Mohr was asked for a piece on the Saigon press corps. He filed a long and detailed one, flattering to the reporters, and analyzed the reasons for the controversy. It never appeared in print, but Mohr was extremely busy during those hectic weeks and had little time to think of anything except the story at hand. Although nominally based in Hong Kong, he was spending all his time in

Saigon; he saw his wife Norma only when she flew in from Hong Kong to smuggle out copy.

Mohr is a reporter's reporter. At that time he was thirty-four years old, a man of immense vitality and enthusiasm who was in love with his work and who brought a sense of excitement to everything he did. He was one of *Time*'s stars: White House correspondent at twenty-seven, then chief of the New Delhi bureau, then head of the coveted Southeast Asia bureau. He was a particular favorite of Henry Luce's, who, on introducing him to a gathering of top business executives, had referred to him as "a reporter—and how!" In the course of collecting material for the Madame Nhu story he had charmed the First Lady; she had granted twelve hours of interviews and at one point had said, "I am telling you things I have never told anyone else in my life." A few days before the *Time* story came out, I asked Madame about the forthcoming piece. "I feel like I am sitting on—how do you say it—a volcano," she answered, "but whatever it says, I have decided that the fault will not be that of Mr. Mohr, but of the rewriting man."

Mohr had spent most of 1963 in Vietnam, but he also had a full-time colleague based there. Mert Perry is what in the trade is called a "stringer," which means that he files for a publication and that his copy is often used, but that he does not enjoy staff status. Yet Perry was in every sense a *Time* reporter. He had been sent to Saigon by UPI but had resigned to take the *Time* job, which paid far more money. Trained as a wire-service man, Perry gave *Time* extraordinary coverage. By August 1963 he had been in Vietnam for nearly two years; he knew the Delta well and had been on countless operations in the field, and he had seen adviser after adviser try to grapple with the same problems. Of all the correspondents in Vietnam he was probably the best liked by American officers, and his apartment served as a meeting place for them when they came in from the field—in no small part because his wife Darlene was a very good cook.

In early September, when Washington was still searching for answers, Mohr was asked by his editors to do an exhaustive roundup on the state of the war in Vietnam, including a realistic view of the situation in the Delta. Both Mohr and Perry did a vast amount of leg work for this assignment; they filed twenty-five pages of copy in three days.

Mohr's story, the toughest written to that date by a resident correspondent, began, "The war in Vietnam is being lost." Charley went on to say that not everyone in Vietnam "would be willing to go so far at this point. But those men who know Vietnam best and have given the best of their energies and a portion of their souls to this program are suddenly becoming passionate on this subject." Washington, Mohr noted, had asked all its Saigon officials for detailed reports on what was happening, and had given these officials a chance ". . . to bare their souls. Much of what they write may be diluted by the time it reaches Washington. However, these men realize that they are in the middle of a first-class major foreign policy crisis and that history will be a harsh judge. 'I am laying it on the line,' said one. 'Now is the time for the truth. There are no qualifications in what I write.' Another said: 'I am going on the record in black and white. The war will be lost in a year, but I gave myself some leeway and said three years.' Another said that his program in the countryside is 'dead.' One source said that American military reporting in this country 'has been wrong and false—lies, really. We are now paying the price.' "

This was strong stuff at a time when Washington was trying to make up its mind what to do. The story left no doubt that the American mission had come to the end of one road, and that our past policy had failed. Unfortunately, this was not what the editors of *Time* wanted to hear; in New York, Mohr's file was put aside, and Greg Dunne, a young contributing editor, was told to write an optimistic piece. Dunne refused and announced that he would write no more stories about Vietnam, but others stepped in. Eventually a story was printed which bore no relation to Mohr and Perry's file; among other things, it said that "Government troops are fighting better than ever."

But this type of optimism was so markedly different from most of the other dispatches that Americans were reading or hearing from the *Times*, the AP, UPI, *Newsweek*, CBS and

NBC that an explanation was called for. Otto Fuerbringer, managing editor of *Time*, decided to produce his own interpretation. He summoned a writer to his office, and with what Stanley Karnow, a former *Time* employee, called in the January 1964 issue of *Nieman Reports*, ''nothing but his own preconceptions to guide him, dictated the gist of an article for his magazine's 'Press' section.'' Karnow, Mohr's predecessor as *Time* bureau chief in Southeast Asia, who had quit to work for the *Saturday Evening Post* for just such reasons as this, called the piece ''a devastating compendium of bitter innuendoes and clever generalities, all blatantly impeaching American correspondents in Vietnam for distorting the news.'' The war, the *Time* article hinted, was going better than a small journalistically incestuous group of reporters were saying; these correspondents were nothing but a group of malcontents who sat around the eighth floor of the Caravelle Hotel interviewing each other and never venturing into the countryside.

The printed piece was truly staggering, for it was an indictment not only of us, but of two of *Time*'s own reporters as well. It read as if written by a high Pentagon PIO, and it set off a minor furor in the newspaper world.

In New York, Clurman tried desperately to block publication of the article. Within *Time*'s hierarchy Clurman could not stop the piece on his own; the only man who could overrule Fuerbringer was Henry Luce. But Luce was in Atlanta at a football game, and though he sensed disaster, Clurman could not reach him in time. The article was printed.

In an attempt to keep Mohr, a favorite correspondent, Clurman then made a last-ditch effort. He cabled Charley in Saigon, warning him to meet Clurman in Paris before resigning. But of course when Mohr received the cable—which was the first indication he had of what was afoot—he immediately began thinking about another job. Appalled by the article when he finally saw it, he flew to Paris, where he told Clurman that there was only one thing which could prevent his resignation: equal space in *Time*, under his own by-line, to refute the Fuerbringer attack. Clurman, who knew how important saving face is to Westerners, believed that this would be impossible, but he flew back to New York to talk to his chief.

Luce, who was surprised and embarrassed about the mounting uproar over the "Press" item, was in a tight spot. A refutation of the piece would humiliate his strongest editor, Fuerbringer, a man considered by many of his colleagues to be the architect of *Time*'s dazzling finished product; on the other hand, by doing nothing he would lose a justifiably angry and talented reporter. So he ordered Clurman to go to Saigon to write a *second* "Press" story on the reporters. Mohr, who had handed in his resignation, accompanied Clurman around the city as a sort of *eminence grise*, a façade that cracked whenever Clurman interviewed reporters about their copy and their ideas—at which point Mohr would explode, charging that Clurman, not the reporters, should be on the defensive and answering the questions.

After spending many hours with all of us going over our copy, Clurman became convinced that the "Press" story had been outrageous—but he also realized that a second piece was pointless. Nevertheless, orders were handed down that it be written. Once again there was a struggle between Clurman and Fuerbringer over the tone of the article; at one point Fuerbringer apparently led, then Clurman staged a comeback, but the final version was heavily "Fuerbringerized." Though the piece came as close as *Time* ever ventures in admitting that a mistake had been made, it still claimed that the war was going better than the press corps reported, and it was still an attack on our judgment.

While in Saigon, Clurman had written an article for *Life* on the state of the war; on his return he found it so altered by editors that he insisted on having his by-line removed. But Mohr and Perry had resigned. Since Mohr was a well-known reporter, he had received offers from the *Wall Street Journal, Newsweek* and the *New York Times*; he accepted the *Times* job, returned home, was assigned to cover Barry Goldwater in the '64 campaign, and is now the *New York Times*' White House correspondent. It was more difficult for Perry to resign because he was not so well known as Mohr, but eventually he joined the staff of the Chicago *Daily News*.

The upshot of all the fuss was that *Time*'s reputation with working newspapermen suffered considerably. There was also a certain malicious delight within the profession that Mohr and Perry had caught Fuerbringer red-handed; *Newsweek* and other publications ran pieces about the controversy with great relish.

For all the uproar generated by this teapot tempest, remarkably little light was shed on the roots of the journalistic problems in Vietnam. The traditional right of American journalists to report what they see was at stake here, even though the situation was a particularly sensitive one: ambiguous involvement in a wretched war with a ruthless enemy. Because the news was bad, there were many people who for varying reasons did not want it exposed. Yet an American reporter must believe, if he believes nothing else, that the United States has never survived in times of crisis by playing ostrich. Too much policy and too deep a commitment had already been made in Vietnam on the basis of too little factual information.

Therefore when the Pulitzer Prize for foreign reporting was awarded to Mal Browne and to me in the spring of 1964, it had a very special meaning for me; the Supreme Court within our own profession had upheld the right of a reporter to follow his conscience even in a delicate situation such as this. I think the reason that men such as James Reston went to bat for the Vietnam reporters before the Pulitzer committee was because this principle is so fundamental to journalism.

Much of the criticism of the Saigon press corps had been insidious; for instance, the critics singled out a few of us who were young, and failed to mention older, more established reporters such as Jim Robinson of NBC, Peter Kalischer and Bernie Kalb of CBS, Stan Karnow of the *Saturday Evening Post* and Pepper Martin of *U.S. News and World Report*. Probably most malicious of all was the insinuation that those few Americans who knew the country better than others, who had friends there and who cared the most about the war, were deliberately or capriciously writing pessimistic stories.

Ironically, the real weaknesses of the Saigon press corps

were almost never cited by our critics. What was particularly shocking was that such a major American commitment—this country's only war—was covered by so few reporters. For most of my tour—until late 1963—I was the only full-time staff correspondent of an American daily newspaper. I believe that the *Washington Post*, the New York *Herald Tribune*, the *Baltimore Sun* and other papers which have great influence in the United States failed to meet their obligations during those months in 1962 and early 1963. If some of us had more journalistic power than was merited, it had been granted us purely by default.

Also, though we knew more about Vietnam and the aspirations of the Vietnamese than most official Americans, we were to some degree limited by our nationality. We were there, after all, to cover the war; this was our primary focus and inevitably we judged events through the war's progress or lack of it. We entered the pagodas only after the Buddhist crisis had broken out; we wrote of Nguyen Tuong Tam, the country's most distinguished writer and novelist, only after he had committed suicide—and then only because his death had political connotations; we were aware of the aspirations of the peasants because they were the barometer of the Government's failure and the war's progress, not because we were on the side of the population and against their rulers.

It is not much fun to be pessimistic, and though nobody goes into our business to make friends, it is not much fun being shunned and cursed by high officials of your country in Saigon and Washington. It is not much fun to write grim stories about a country which means a great deal to you and in which your friends are dying. But I think that a reporter's obligation in Vietnam was relatively simple. I believe that the one vision which haunted us all was that of writing the kind of tranquilizer-copy the officials wanted, year after year—until one day the Vietcong would walk into Saigon unannounced. Then our critics could justifiably question the judgment of those young reporters who had told them how well the war was going.

In retrospect, there is one thing that was constantly overlooked in the press controversy: the stanch backing I received from the *Times* and the support Browne and Sheehan received from their offices during those weeks. It was not the kind of imbroglio that any publisher seeks; news executives rightfully believe that reporters should not be seen and that they are most effective when most anonymous. Yet the *Times* stood up quietly to great pressure and treated me very well. Once in the middle of it all, when they queried me on a Maggie Higgins story about how well the war was going in the Delta, I fired off an angry and thoughtless cable threatening to resign. But I was always supported by the great strength of the paper which backed a young reporter despite unrelenting and insidious pressure. It was a hard way to learn how a great newspaper operates under fire, but it was a very good lesson.

XVII

In September and October of 1963 the entire fabric of Vietnam began to come apart. The Communists kept making major advances in the Mekong Delta. In Saigon the Government had turned on its two major sources of support, the Americans and the Army, and had deliberately provoked them. President Kennedy tried first to push for what Washington naïvely called reforms—which in effect meant ousting the Nhus—but this simply provoked fresh outbursts from the Government. The Nhus were not about to oust themselves from the Government.

The *Times of Vietnam* accused the United States of trying to buy coups d'état, specifying the John McCone, head of the CIA, and William Colby, his chief for Southeast Asia, were responsible. The paper quoted a Vietnamese general as saying that though he had rejected the offers of interventionists, "you should have seen what the foreign adventurers offered me." A West-German reporter for the magazine *Der Spiegel*, who was in Madame Nhu's office when she was correcting page proofs of one of the paper's stories about an alleged CIA plot, was stunned to hear her say over the phone, "Yes, but I want you to put Colonel Richardson's name in the story too."

Nhu held a press conference during which he made a pro-

longed attack on the Americans, accusing the United States
"of having caused the process of disintegration in Vietnam."

In Central Vietnam, citizens who were caught listening to
the Voice of America were arrested. Some Americans, particularly those in the USIS, were threatened; after Nhu carefully leaked reports that he planned to raid and bomb the
USIS, Marine guards were put on duty there around the clock
and vital papers were removed.

In mid-October *Newsweek* asked Ambassador Lodge to
pose for a special cover photo; the picture was to be taken
on a main Saigon street. The magazine wanted a student in
the shot, and so the photographer stopped a fifteen-year-old
girl and asked her to stand next to the ambassador. The picture was duly taken, Lodge departed, and the girl was immediately arrested by the secret police.

At this time Nhu let it be openly known that he had entered
into exploratory negotiations with Hanoi; he was doing this
through a French diplomat in North Vietnam who had come
to Saigon on a visit and had been introduced to Nhu by a
Polish member of the International Control Conference. Just
why he was playing this game is hard to determine; in part
he may have been hoping to blackmail the Americans and
make them uneasy, but he probably also considered the strategic hamlet program so successful that he could win the war
without the Americans—and of course, he was fascinated by
the idea of dealing with the Communists.

Next, Nhu summoned a group of American reporters to
tell them that the Vietnamese had "lost faith in America."
He charged that the CIA had tried to instigate two coups
against him; interrogation of the Buddhists proved that CIA
agents were repeatedly urging the monks to stage a revolt.
"It is incomprehensible to me that the CIA, which had backed
a winning program, should reverse itself. I do not believe the
leaders of the CIA really concurred in this," Nhu said.

In this increasingly tense atmosphere there were three major plots: the planned but hitherto unmaterialized coups of
the junior officers and of the generals, and a fake coup to be
staged by Nhu. Nothing can better stress the basic frustrations of American policy in Vietnam than the incredible

amount of intrigue taking place in this country which was, after all, at war. The divisiveness at work in those days would have reduced the closest of relationships to enmity.

Nhu's plot, of which the CIA was well informed, and which was a tribute to his wild and imaginative mind, was scheduled to take place in early November. Nhu was aware of the officers' coups, and he was trying to move to head them off. "Coups," he had told an aide, "are like eggs, and they must be smashed before they are hatched."

Nhu's plan called for some special forces under Colonel Tung to stage a fake revolt in Saigon. Diem, Nhu and certain members of the household would then flee to a refuge prepared in advance at Cape Saint Jacques, the nearby seaside resort, where special communications facilities would have been installed. General Ton That Dinh, one of the trusted generals and a commander of loyal troops, would wait outside Saigon while hired gangsters would run riot in the city for several days, stealing and looting—particularly from Americans. In the confusion Colonel Tung's agents would then announce the formation of a revolutionary government which would include—without their consent—such prominent anti-Diem politicians as former Ambassador Chuong. Thereafter the revolutionary government's radio would attack the Americans, declare that it wanted to end the war against the Communists and indicate that it was sympathetic to a neutralist settlement. After several days of this, Dinh's loyal troops would march into the city and quickly crush the so-called revolt. This false coup would scare the Americans, would prove to them that the only alternative to the Ngo brothers was neutralism, and would demonstrate that the Army still supported the family.

But almost as soon as Nhu began preparing the headquarters at Cape Saint Jacques, the instigators of the other two coups heard of his plans.

The junior officers, who had been plotting for more than a year under various leaders and with different military units, had nearly tried a coup in July, only to have two key battalions ordered out of town at the last moment. This group included men like Lieutenant Colonel Pham Ngoc Tao, in the past one of Diem's brightest and most loyal officers—a man who represented the younger generation and who wanted to wage the war in an entirely new way. Other officers came from some of the elite air-borne and Marine units; there was also Colonel Do Mau, the chief of military security whom Nhu had so mistrusted when he was personally loyal that in desperation he had finally become dissident, and Colonel Tran Thien Khiem, the chief of staff of the Joint General Staff who had saved Diem from the paratroopers in 1960 and had turned on the Government in the spring of 1963.

The junior officers' group had been organized by Dr. Tran Kim Tuyen, the brilliant little man who headed Diem's secret police apparatus until he had a falling out with Madame Nhu in 1961. Tuyen, who had an organization reaching into many units of the Army, was able to gather together a select number of combat units for a coup. But in the middle of the Buddhist crisis Diem suddenly appointed him envoy to the United Arab Republic in order to get him out of the country; the brothers were reportedly loath to arrest the doctor, in the belief that he probably had too much incriminating information on Palace activities. When Tuyen left the country in September, the group was taken over by Colonel Mau, who in turn had a large number of security contacts of his own.

The generals' coup was also headed by men who had long remained close to Diem, who had helped him stave off earlier coups, and whose national loyalties were above suspicion. One of the leaders was General Duong Van Minh—"Big Minh" to Americans and Vietnamese because of his size— the closest approximation to a national hero in the South because he had personally led troops against the Binh Xuyen gangster sect in 1955. Minh had used his great prestige in Diem's first year to rally many other Army officers to the President, but later, because Nhu considered him a possible threat, he had been stripped of his troops and given the meaningless title of military adviser. General Tran Van Don, another highly respected officer, who had been given the nominal title of Chief of the Army and who had no troops directly under him, was also mistrusted by the regime. General Le Van Kim, considered by many Americans to be the

most intelligent of the generals, had been under suspicion
since the 1960 paratrooper coup—not because of any participation in it, but simply because Diem felt that he had not
rallied to his side quickly enough. (Such was the Ngos' paranoia that one officer who had risked his life to save Diem
that night by slipping through rebel lines was thereafter under
great suspicion because the brothers felt he had moved *too*
easily through the enemy units.)

These three generals had started preparing their coup in
June by quietly mustering support. They enjoyed vast prestige
within the Vietnamese Army; in fact, they had everything
they needed for a coup except troops.

In late October tension rose as all three plots grew to fru-
ition. Reportedly the generals tried and failed to coordinate
their coup with that of the junior officers. The latter had set
October 24 as their target date, but the generals, who feared
that the rival group lacked sufficient troops and who wanted
to control the situation themselves, foiled the young Turks
once again by simply sending a key regiment out of town for
the day.

I remember October 24 very distinctly because I had been
tipped off about the impending coup. It was supposed to take
place at 1 P.M., right in the middle of the siesta, when Saigon
would be caught completely off guard. I had lunch with Jerry
King, the *Times* man from Kuala Lumpur who had been sent
to Vietnam to stand by in case I was expelled from the country, Ray Herndon of UPI, and Dick Holbrooke, a young man
attached to USOM who had once worked for the *Times* as a
copy boy. We were sitting in a Chinese restaurant two blocks
from the Palace, and every five minutes during the meal one
of us would get up and make a quick tour of the block. But
nothing happened—which was just as well; when the real
coup came a week later, that particular restaurant was badly
shot up in the first hour of fighting.

In the Vietnamese Army, titles were next to meaningless. The
delicate balance of the Ngo rule rested mainly on two men—
the commanders of the Third and Fourth Corps—who had

been promoted for their loyalty to Diem, not because of merit. The Fourth Corps included the Seventh Division, which was stationed at My Tho, a quick trip down a main highway; the Third Corps had jurisdiction over the troops in and around Saigon, and its headquarters was in the city. The generals commanding these two outfits, Huynh Van Cao of the Fourth Corps, and Ton That Dinh of the Third, were the two Army officers Diem trusted implicitly. Both were of course from the central coastal region, they were members of the Can Lao Party and they were Catholics (Dinh was a convert). Neither was considered competent by his colleagues—militarily Cao was thought to be a catastrophe—but they provided insurance to the family that the troops close to Saigon would not turn against them, and if other units rebelled they could bail Diem out. They also served as a deterrent to coups; thinking about Dinh's and Cao's troops, would-be Nassers were easily discouraged.

The three leaders of the generals' coup, Minh, Kim and Don, counted on Dinh as a key to their success. With Dinh on their side, a coup would be assured; without him, they might win out but it would probably be a bloody and divisive affair. Dinh was Diem's favorite; he considered Dinh virtually an adopted son and had promoted him ahead of senior and more talented officers. Young, cunning, ambitious and vain, Dinh wore a paratrooper's beret at a jaunty angle; his jungle camouflage uniform was skintight, and wherever he went a huge, hulking Cambodian bodyguard who spoke neither French nor Vietnamese lurked menacingly in the background. The general delighted in having newspaper photographers around, and he was often accompanied by his personal Vietnamese cameraman so that there would be a complete record of the days and deeds of Ton That Dinh.

Dinh was the only general who had been given advance warning of the pagoda raids, and he had been told by the brothers that he was the great hero of this anti-American incident. Dinh, who readily believed them, thereafter became military governor of Saigon, and he threw his weight around by letting the other generals know that he might arrest them at any moment.

Dinh summoned a Vietnamese to dinner one night and told him that he—the guest—had been greatly honored. When the guest asked why, General Dinh answered, "Because you are having dinner with a great national hero." "That's nice," said the guest. "Where is he?" "It is me," answered General Dinh. "I have defeated the Americans and saved the country."

During the time when he was riding particularly high, Dinh held a press conference which turned into a farce. He immediately got in over his head by attacking a "certain foreign power"—obviously the United States—which he said had been plotting against his country. When Ray Herndon, who is a tough, brassy reporter, rose and asked what foreign power he was talking about, Dinh stalled. Herndon persisted; surely, he said, anyone who had as much information about the coup as General Dinh must know which country had attempted it. Again Dinh was evasive. "Well," said Herndon, "if you'd like to call your superiors to find out, we'll be delighted to wait." The Americans and the Vietnamese reporters in the audience roared with laughter.

Embarrassed, humiliated, having lost face, Dinh returned to his headquarters, and it was then that the three leaders of the generals' coup sensed that this was the best possible moment to play on his vanity. They were waiting for him at his quarters, and they immediately started telling him what a great hero he was and how the whole country looked up to him. Nhu didn't appreciate him fully, they said; how typical of Nhu! As a national hero he had made a good beginning with his military conduct after the pagoda raids, but now political moves must follow: the people were tired of the listless, ineffectual Cabinet of Ngo Dinh Diem. The country needed active young men in politics, and the Army particularly needed him in the Government to boost its sagging morale. (An indication of the effectiveness of this appeal to Dinh's enormous ego is that the first time Herndon saw him after the November coup, Dinh grabbed his hand and said, "Ah, you are my great friend. You are the one who started it all, who drove me into making the coup. You are the hero of the revolution." Whereupon the general sat down and gave

Ray an exclusive interview—whose main theme seemed to be
that Dinh was "the master of the coup d'état.")

The plotters suggested that Dinh talk to Diem and exert
his great influence to place the military in the Cabinet. Dinh
should become Minister of the Interior, Big Minh should become Minister of Defense, and Tran Van Minh—"Little
Minh"—would make a good Minister of Education who
would keep the students in line. The three leaders also proposed officers for other posts.

The generals were sure that these suggestions would enrage
the brothers and that they would turn on Dinh. The scheme
worked perfectly. In due course Dinh went to see Diem and
proposed a new role for the military and particularly for himself. He, Dinh, the hero of the Republic, was needed by the
people as Minister of the Interior. Diem, who was extremely
touchy about his police apparatus and the role of the military,
was stunned; the last thing he wanted was to have Army
officers in the Cabinet. After giving Dinh an angry lecture
and a blunt rejection, he told him to go to the mountain resort
of Dalat and rest for a while; in effect, Dinh was temporarily
relieved. "Stay out of politics and leave them to me," Diem
told the general.

Dinh returned to the three generals doubly humiliated; not
only had he failed to bring them into the Government, as he
had boasted he could, but in addition he had been sent to
Dalat and told that he wasn't needed. The generals were very
sympathetic. Dinh was being badly treated by the brothers,
they said; it was all Nhu's fault. So began the process of
winning Dinh's participation in the plot. They bribed a for-
tuneteller to tell Dinh that she foresaw a long life of politics
for him, and they constantly played on his vanity by remind-
ing him of the country's need for him. Diem and Nhu made
the plotters' job easier; frightened by Dinh's request, they had
the general watched by security officers. In Saigon's cocoon
of intrigue, Dinh immediately discovered this fact, and it
simply accelerated his drift toward disloyalty.

The generals had slowly brought into their plot other officers of different background and temperament, and after
Dinh's return from Dalat, the generals, moving very cau-

tiously and concealing from him how advanced their plans were—for they did not trust Dinh, not even after he had committed himself to them—began to urge him to stage a coup. By this time they had spent several weeks softening him up, and they felt that he was so bitter against the family that it was safe to tip their hand. They were right; when the generals approached him, Dinh was already drawing up plans for a coup of his own.

The next problem to be faced was that of moving soldiers into the city without alerting Diem and Nhu. This was difficult, because the brothers had developed elaborate means of keeping watch on all troop movement (for instance, Captain Ba of a key armored unit at My Tho had to call the Palace every hour on the hour to report his whereabouts). One early plan called for the generals to feed Diem exaggerated reports of a major Vietcong build-up in D-Zone, just north of Saigon. For some reason Diem had always had a particular fascination for D-Zone operations, and it was hoped that this would allow the generals to move large numbers of troops to a point accessible to the city which would serve as a staging area. With this idea in mind, the leaders set about recruiting units for the coup.

Dinh and his Third Corps troops were of prime importance, but almost equally crucial was the role of the Seventh Division under General Cao's command. Three days before the coup Dinh sent his deputy, Colonel Nguyen Huu Co, to My Tho to talk with some officers whom the plotters thought they might enlist in their cause. The excuse for Co's visit was that under a forthcoming change of corps boundaries, the Seventh Division would be under Dinh's control. In conversations with the deputy division commander, two regimental commanders, the armored-unit commander and the My Tho province chief, Co told them that it was the duty of the Army to overthrow the Ngos because the family had alienated the population and could not govern. To protect his chief as long as possible, he said that every general but Dinh was partici-

pating in the coup, and that Dinh was expected to join it in
the near future.

The entire incident was reported to Diem by the My Tho
province chief the next day. At this point, according to Palace
sources, Diem and Nhu no longer entirely trusted Dinh, but
felt that he could still be used against the other generals because, according to their information, he had not yet fully
committed himself. So the brothers summoned Dinh, and
Diem read him the account of Co's conversation with the My
Tho officials. At this point Dinh put on an emotional show.
He is an explosive man, he can be a very good actor, and on
this occasion he pulled out all stops. Weeping, he put his
head in his hands and wailed, "This is my fault. Because you
have suspected me, I have not really worked for the last fifteen days. I have stayed home because I was sad. But I am
not against you—I was sad because I thought you no longer
trusted me. So Co has profited from my absence to make
trouble." Dinh then calmed down and suggested that Co be
arrested and shot, but Nhu opposed this. He wanted the deputy arrested and interrogated to get the names of the other
plotters.

Taking advantage of his audience with the brothers, Dinh
continued to play the hurt child; he said that some of Nhu's
security men were handing in false reports about him. Nhu
answered that they had not distrusted Dinh; they felt that he
was the most trustworthy man in the country, but they had
been preoccupied with other matters. Indeed, said Nhu, because of Dinh's heroic performance during the Buddhist crisis, they were thinking of promoting him to major general.
They had not quite gotten around to it yet, but now of course
he, Nhu, would take care of it immediately.

At this, Dinh, knowing how Nhu's mind worked, suggested that they plan a counter-coup. Whether Dinh, aware
of the loyalty of the My Tho province chief, deliberately sent
Co down there as bait to leak the plans for the coup to Diem
and Nhu, or whether his proposal for a counter-coup was an
improvisation on the spot to extricate himself from a sticky
situation is not known. No matter, he suggested a massive
show of force: troops and tanks moved into Saigon to crush

the plotters. The idea of a coup within a coup had great appeal to Nhu; the ordinary way of stopping a revolt was much too simple for him. He quickly agreed, and told Dinh to "get together with the other two members of the Can Lao Party," Lieutenant Colonel Nguyen Ngoc Khoi, commander of the Presidential Guard, and Colonel Tung. Diem okayed the plan. "You have full authority to get what you need," he said.

The next day, in a meeting with Tung and Khoi, Dinh told them that a major show of force was necessary and that they must have tanks because "armor is dangerous." Tung and Khoi, who were considered by other Vietnamese officers to be parlor soldiers without combat records, quickly agreed to let Dinh bring in his tanks. But Dinh was worried about the four battalions of special forces troops which Colonel Tung had previously brought into the city at Nhu's order; they would make such a formidable force if added to the Presidential Guard that other units might waver. So he told Tung and Khoi that if all the reserve forces were brought into Saigon, the Americans would be angry and claim that the Vietnamese were not prosecuting the war. "We must fool the Americans," he said to Tung. "You must send your four special forces battalions out of Saigon and tell the Americans that they have been ordered into combat. That will deceive them."

The following day, the one before the coup, Tung moved his four units out of the city after getting the approval of the brothers. Dinh then drew up plans to move large forces into the city, and Diem approved this too, thus legalizing what Nhu called "Operation Bravo Two" ("Bravo One" was Nhu's original fake-coup plan). And so it came about that Ngo Dinh Diem, who had spent so many hours trying to prevent revolts and who had gone to such elaborate lengths to stop this one, made possible the coup that ended his reign.

The three generals, who had been kept fully informed of Dinh's plans, now notified the Americans that they were planning a coup. Reportedly they did not deal with the American military, whom they still distrusted, but with Lodge's office. They did not ask for any assistance, but they said that the coup would be pro-American, and asked the mission not to thwart it. In turn, the embassy did not offer any aid, but it did make arrangements to stay in full communication with the rebels.

Sheehan and I knew that a coup was in the making. While one of our sources was reluctant to talk at any length, he seemed convinced that this time the rebellion would really take place. At this time, in late October, Sheehan's Tokyo office insisted that he take a two-week rest. Sheehan protested vigorously and warned that a coup was coming, but Tokyo ordered him out anyway. However, before he left we worked out a code; in case I learned more details and a definite date, I was to send him a message in Tokyo asking him to buy me a doll. When Sheehan arrived in Tokyo he posted signs all over the UPI cable room giving his hotel number and asking to be called immediately if any cable mentioning a doll arrived for him.

Early on the morning of October 31 a Vietnamese messenger came to the office and asked for Sheehan or me. When I identified myself he turned to one of our assistants and said something in Vietnamese; after being assured that I was indeed Halberstam, the visitor handed me a scrap of paper saying, "Buy me a bottle of whiskey at the PX." This was the agreed-upon signal from one of our sources that the coup was on its way. Immediately I cabled Sheehan to buy me the doll; in Tokyo the clerk at the desk looked at it, casually put it aside, and never called Sheehan.

Earlier I had sent a message to my office indicating that things were growing tense again and expressing the hope that they would run all possible copy from Saigon. Now Ray Herndon and I made some plans for emergency filing, and then went back to work. We learned that the coup was to take place at 1:30 P.M. the next day, Friday, November 1.

Both the CIA and the embassy were sure that there would be a coup; the military, under General Harkins, did not believe it, although a large number of junior officers had warned that a build-up was taking place. On the morning of November 1 the mission sent a coded cable to Washington saying that the coup would come at noon, or rather that State and

CIA predicted it would come, but that MACV did not concur. Later in the afternoon, after the fighting had broken out, an officer at MACV called the embassy and asked that the MACV statement of dissent be stricken. Ironically, the issue of *Pacific Stars and Stripes* which arrived in Saigon that night featured a long interview with General Charles Timmes, the chief of the Military Assistance and Advisory Group, in which Timmes claimed that the Vietnamese troops were "loyal to their government." In the post-coup embarrassment, Timmes claimed that he had been misquoted, that he had said that the troops were loyal "to their *country*" (a point never in doubt), and the offending *Stripes* reporter, Marine Sergeant Steve Stibbens, was quickly bundled off to Tokyo for a rest.

Admiral Harry Felt, the commander of the U.S. Forces in the Pacific, had been in Saigon for a couple of days and happened to be leaving at noon on the first. At 10 A.M. Lodge accompanied Felt on a courtesy call to Diem. It must have been an unusually tense encounter: Lodge knew that a coup was on its way, while Diem believed that his brother's counter-coup was coming. The three men discussed rumors of a revolt, but the meeting was noncommittal.

By midmorning certain troop units were already entering the city. The commander of the Vietnamese Navy, Captain Ho Tan Quyen, was taken out of town and asked to join the revolt; when he refused he was shot in the back of the head. But at noon Tan Son Nhut airport was simply the scene of another VIP departure. In his press conference Admiral Felt praised the nation's leadership and said that the war effort was going well despite the growing Vietcong fire power— about which there was some concern. Someone asked where the arms were coming from, and after an embarrassed silence Admiral Felt smiled and said that perhaps General Don knew. Tran Van Don said that weapons were indeed a major problem, and then he too laughed and said that he did not know where they were coming from either.

As the press conference dragged on, I watched General Don closely because I knew that he was supposed to be one of the leaders of the coup. He was clearly impatient and kept glancing anxiously at his watch. (A week later during an in-

terview I told him that when I had seen him worrying about
the time, I'd had to restrain the impulse to ask more questions
to prolong the press conference. He did not seem amused.)

When Herndon and I left, we drove back to the city by
way of Dinh's Third Corps headquarters, for we had received
a tip that it was swarming with tanks. Our information was
correct; there were troops all over the place, and about fifteen
tanks, some of them being fueled.

We felt more convinced than ever that a coup would take
place, but for the moment there was nothing to do but return
to town and go about our business. It was nearly 12:30; if a
coup occurred we might not eat again for a day, so we had
lunch with Mert Perry and Murray Gart of *Time*. It was a
pleasant, sunny day, and the streets were empty in the center
of Saigon, as they always were during the siesta. Mert was
as close a friend as ever, but our relations with *Time* were
somewhat strained following the attacks on us, particularly
since Gart had replaced our good friend Charley Mohr.

Near the end of the lunch I told Gart that there might be a
coup that day.

"How good is your information?" he asked.

"As good as you ever get," I said and showed him the
scrap of paper with my whiskey order. He took it and later
used it in his file.

As we finished lunch and started to leave, the proprietor
of the restaurant came running up and said that troops were
moving along the waterfront. Just then there was a quick
burst of fire from that direction; we ran over toward the noise
and saw troops taking up positions throughout the city.

We split up. Ray and I went back to the office, where we
found Le Phuoc Ly, one of Sheehan's photographers; he had
been working around his house when a convoy of troops had
driven down the road from Bien Hoa. They had waved to him,
and one of the soldiers who knew him had invited Ly to join
them. "Come along, we are making the coup," the soldier
said.

The rebels had done well. They had managed to move
nearly forty armored vehicles into Saigon and to shift two air-
borne battalions, whose inclinations they doubted, to D-Zone

for the day. They had the troops, the communications and the orders.

Security officials, worried by all the troop movements, had called the Palace, but they had been assured by Nhu that it was all part of a Palace coup. However, at 1:30 two battalions of elite Marines sped into the city and quickly captured the radio station and the police station—but not before the commander of the central police telephoned Nhu, told him the Marines were there and that they were not friendly. For the first time Diem and Nhu were a little worried, and they told a Palace aide to call General Dinh's headquarters. One of Dinh's aides took the call, and though Dinh was there, said that his chief was at General Staff headquarters. Diem demanded that Dinh be told to send troops immediately to the police station.

In the meanwhile, the generals were engineering one more vital part of the coup. Every Friday a luncheon to discuss varied military problems was held by the General Staff. On this occasion Lieutenant Colonel Khoi, head of the Presidential Guard; Colonel Le Quang Tung and his brother and right arm, Major Le Quang Trieu; the garrison commander of Saigon, Nguyen Van La; and Colonel Cao Van Vien, the airborne commander, had been invited by General Don on the pretense of discussing changes in the boundaries of corps areas.

At 1:30, when all were assembled in the dining room, General Don announced that a coup was taking place, and pointedly invited the guests to join. Everyone accepted willingly save Colonel Tung and his brother. At this moment fighting was going on nearby between some of the coup troops and a few of Colonel Tung's soldiers still left in the city. The generals forced the colonel to telephone his officers and order them to surrender; then Tung, the symbol of the family to the other generals and one of the most hated men in the country, was taken outside and executed.

During the early planning of the coup it had been agreed that the Seventh Division must be neutralized. Technically the

Seventh was still under Cao's command, but by coincidence
it was to be transferred on November 1 to the Third Corps,
Dinh's command. Diem had ordered Colonel Lam Van Phat
to take command of the division on October 31, but according
to regulation, Phat could not do so until he had paid a courtesy call on Dinh, his new corps commander. Dinh had refused to see Phat on the thirty-first; instead he told him to
return on November 1 at 2 P.M. In the meantime Dinh asked
General Don to sign orders transferring the command of the
Seventh Division to Colonel Co, his deputy who had been
the contact man earlier in My Tho.

At eleven-thirty on the day of the coup Colonel Co arrived
in My Tho with a small personal staff, quickly rounded up
the division staff officers, locked them in a room and took
command. Then, passing himself off as Phat, Co telephoned
General Cao at Can Tho, the Fourth Corps headquarters,
farther south, to announce that the command change had taken
place as scheduled. Co is from central Vietnam, whereas Phat
is a Southerner, and there is a considerable difference in the
accents of the two regions. For this reason, Co was afraid
that Cao would not be fooled. But evidently Cao has a tin
ear.

Word of what was happening in Saigon had reached the
Fourth Corps headquarters, but Cao had been assured by Nhu
that this was a false coup, designed to expose all the dissident
elements in the country. As a safety precaution, however,
Cao had ordered one regiment and some tanks to stand by to
move if necessary. Of course he did not realize that Co had
already sent most of the Seventh Division's armor up the
highway to help the rebels.

The coup continued to move with clockwork precision. Half
an hour after his first call to Dinh, Diem tried to reach him
again, this time making the call personally. Again he was
informed that Dinh was not there, and the aide talking to the
President heard Diem say to somebody beside him, ''General
Dinh must have been arrested by the other generals.''

Rebel troops quickly surrounded the Presidential Guard

barracks; cut off from the Palace, this small island of Diem supporters could not reach the President. Then the rebels brought up their tanks and blasted away at the barracks, but though the sound of battle was impressive, few men were killed. This strategy of the plotters was deliberate; their superior armor was used almost as psychological warfare, to discourage Vietnamese as much as possible from killing their countrymen.

At 3 P.M. Diem and Nhu began broadcasting from a Palace transmitter on the 49-meter band. The first broadcast called on corps and division commanders and province chiefs to protect the President of the Republic, and the announcer asked for acknowledgments. There were no acknowledgments. Instead, over Radio Saigon, now controlled by the rebels, came pledge after pledge of support from division and corps commanders and commanders of special units. The promises were made by the officers themselves; to anyone who knew them, their voices were identifiable. The lack of support for Diem was stunning; all the division commanders had turned on him, as had three of the four corps commanders. In the end there was only one officer in command of troops who remained loyal to the brothers—Huynh Van Cao. Early Saturday morning Cao realized that Nhu had been outwitted, and he immediately radioed My Tho to order troops to Diem's rescue. This time, however, Colonel Co identified himself. He taunted Cao. "Didn't you recognize my accent?" he asked. Then he told Cao that he had sent all the ferries to the Saigon side of the Mekong River, and that if Cao attempted to cross, "I will send aircraft against you and you will die." With that, Diem's last hope was gone.

During Friday afternoon the generals called Diem and Nhu several times, listing the units and commanders now allied against them, asking them to surrender and promising safe-conduct. But the brothers would not listen to these appeals; instead, they suggested that the generals come to the Palace "for consultations." Remembering that Diem had used these tactics to lull the paratroopers in 1960, the generals were not interested.

By late afternoon the desperate brothers were radioing the province chiefs to send the Civil Guard and irregular units to rescue them. In the last message from the Palace monitored by the rebels that night, Nhu called for the Cong Hoa Youth and the Paramilitary Girls to move into Saigon and save the family. But these personal units of Nhu's and Madame's never appeared; by early Saturday morning their few dedicated members were already hiding their uniforms or visiting relatives out of town.

About four o'clock on Friday, Diem telephoned Ambassador Lodge in his office to tell him that the Army was in rebellion. Lodge, who of course was fully aware of what was going on, reminded Diem that the rebels had offered him safe-conduct, and apparently suggested that the brothers surrender. He also offered Diem and Nhu asylum at the U.S. embassy, saying that he wanted to do everything he could to protect Diem. It is reported that Diem's only reply to this offer was, "I shall try to restore order."

Diem and Nhu still held out some hope that units of the Seventh Division might help them, but in any case, they had long been prepared for an emergency such as this. Under the Palace there was an air-conditioned bomb shelter with a complete communications apparatus. There were also three tunnels, each surfacing far from the Palace in different directions. When the battle for the Palace began early Saturday morning, the rebel troops and the Palace defenders did not know that they were fighting for an empty cage—the birds had flown. At about eight o'clock on Friday evening Diem and Nhu slipped out of the Palace through one of the tunnels, carrying with them a briefcase filled with American dollars. Waiting for them at the other end of the tunnel was a Red Cross car, which took them to the house of Ma Tuyen, a rich Chinese merchant in Cholon. A direct line had been installed between Ma Tuyen's house and the Palace for just such an emergency as this. Cholon is on the south side of Saigon; the brothers were still hoping that the Seventh Division would come to their rescue from that direction.

From Cholon the brothers continued to telephone the generals, not letting on, of course, that they were no longer at the Palace. Sometime after midnight Diem's military aide called Dinh's headquarters again, and this time Dinh came to the phone. He began to curse the brothers in the most insulting Vietnamese phrases. He told the aide, "You are finished. It is all over. I saved them on the twentieth of August, but now they are finished. Tell them to surrender." When they learned of Dinh's defection, the brothers must have realized that they were beaten, for Dinh's troops, added to the other units ranged against them, made their rescue impossible even if the Seventh Division had remained loyal.

Throughout Friday afternoon in Saigon we reporters were scrambling around, trying to determine which units were remaining loyal, which had defected, and what the strategies of each side were. It was quite a difficult job because both sides wore the same uniforms. We were also confused because by midafternoon there appeared to be a lull in the fighting, and it seemed possible that the rebels had lost their nerve. (Actually, they were simply moving more troops into the city and were giving the brothers time to surrender.)

At about five o'clock I hailed a taxi and took a tour through the city. The driver, probably guessing that I was a reporter, made a gesture of slashing his throat with his finger, broke into a wide grin and said, "*Tong Thong* [President Diem] *fini*." As we drove up one thoroughfare I saw columns and columns of air-borne troops marching alongside about twenty armored cars. Vo Huynh of NBC was with them, photographing the advance. I jumped out of the cab and asked him which side these troops were on. "Anti-Diem," he said. I already knew that the Marines were committed to the rebels; if the air-borne with this much armor, some of it from the Seventh Division, was part of the coup, the handwriting was on the wall. Using the facilities of the American military, I immediately sent out a few hundred words, but they never made the paper; the story was simply drowned by the vast amount

of information being released in Washington. The story of
the coup in the *Times* the next day was a Washington story.

The troops moving through Saigon made a striking sight.
The population watched impassively; it had observed scenes
like this before, and it did not believe any of it. The apathy
was broken only by the children. In the center of Saigon one
pro-Diem armored car was roaming the streets shouting at
anything that moved, and sometimes the fire would be returned. As soon as any exchange ended, children would run
out to the armored car and scoop up the brass from the used
cartridges.

On Friday night we watched the shelling of the Presidential
Guard barracks and other engagements in various parts of the
city. Our sources confirmed that the Seventh Division was
helping the rebels, and we wondered why there had not been
any attack on the Palace. Finally one of our Vietnamese assistants learned from a friend at military headquarters that
the assault on it would not come until sometime after three
in the morning. I decided to go to bed and managed to sleep
for about two hours, until the heavy firing around the Palace
woke me up. I joined Herndon, and we took a circuitous
route to the scene. As we watched, one tank after another
moved in, and about two blocks from the building the Marines were advancing in columns in preparation for the attack.
We stayed with them to observe the fire battle between the
opposing armored forces—fought at such close range that a
friend described it as ''like watching two boxers in a closet.''
In short order the superior size and number of the rebel tanks
proved to be overwhelming; several of the Palace tanks were
knocked out, and an entire platoon of Diem's armor surrendered.

At about five o'clock Herndon and I moved up with the
Marines to within a block of the Palace. It was still very dark,
and the night was filled with the noise of heavy tank and
antitank guns; the only light came from two burning tanks.
Suddenly there was a tremendous explosion very close to us.
I was terrified, for I suddenly remembered that one of our
best sources had once told me that Nhu had lined the streets
around the Palace with Claymoor mines, which were to be

detonated electrically in case of a coup. I told Herndon about this, and after consultation we decided to cover the story from a little farther down the block.

At dawn on Saturday a white flag appeared at the Palace, and the firing halted momentarily. The Marines charged across the Palace lawn, with Herndon, myself and Peter Kalischer of CBS right behind them. Suddenly a few defenders who evidently hadn't gotten the word kept firing; caught in the open, we hit the dirt until the last exchange ended. Then it was all over; the Government had fallen. The Marines charging though the Palace grabbed Madame Nhu's negligees and Nhu's whiskey; everything was there but the brothers.

It was a time of jubilation. In the streets around the building, Vietnamese students approached cautiously. When they saw that the Palace had surrendered they crowded around the tanks, hailing the soldiers, lifting them on their shoulders, handing them food and taking pictures of them. Young girls offered bouquets of flowers. The troops accepted what they were given, but they looked slightly confused; they had never been treated this way before by the population. One armored captain later told me he was staggered by the response; it was a nice feeling, he said, for in the past people had always been afraid of the soldiers. Yet there was an air of restraint to the celebration that Saturday morning; it was as if the populace did not—could not—really believe that the Ngo family was no more.

At 8 A.M. the brothers were still alive, and they had been told that the rebels had taken the Palace. By then they must have known that there would be no help from My Tho. There are conflicting reports as to how the rebels discovered the brothers' hiding place. The one I'm inclined to believe is that a member of their own family, who had known of their advance plans and gone with them to Cholon, had betrayed them by getting word out to Colonel Do Mau. This seems to me the most likely version, because I know about some of the extreme precautions that were taken to control the identity of and to protect the alleged betrayer after Diem and Nhu had

been eliminated. According to another account, one of the
officers at the Palace told his captors about the hideout. A
third rumor was that Diem himself, hearing of the capture of
the Palace, telephoned the generals and offered to yield under
certain conditions: that he be allowed to surrender honorably;
that members of his family be allowed to leave the country;
and that he be allowed to remain President for a brief interval
in order to save face and retire gracefully. According to this
version, the rebels agreed to the first two conditions and declined to accept the third, but Diem disclosed his whereabouts nonetheless.

However, the brothers' hiding place was discovered.
Shortly after nine on Saturday morning the rebels sent three
armored cars to a small Catholic church in Cholon near the
merchant's house, where Diem and Nhu had just taken sanc-
tuary. They were arrested and placed in the armored car at
about nine-thirty. They left the church alive; they arrived dead
at General Staff headquarters. Again there are divergent reports of what exactly happened. One story has it that Nhu
antagonized one of his captors so much that the officer, who
had had a friend killed by Nhu, lost his head and stabbed
first Nhu and then Diem. According to another version, the
officer in charge of the armored car was General Mai Huu
Xuan, a former high police official under the French who
hated the brothers so much that he permitted the assassination.

My own feeling is that the brothers were killed because
the generals did not trust either Diem or the Americans
enough. They were afraid that the United States might pro-
pose that Diem be placed at the head of a coalition government, or that Diem might somehow stall them long enough
for his American supporters to exert pressure for a place for
him in a new government. (A high Vietnamese officer once
told me that in a conversation just before the coup, a CIA
man who was obviously trying to find out what the plotters
were doing had said that if there was a coup, they should
avoid killing Diem if possible. In recounting the incident to
me, the officer was angry. "What the hell do the Americans

want—for us to get rid of the Government and then be killed ourselves?'' he said.)

Dinh did not know that the brothers were being assassinated, and apparently asked his fellow conspirators to spare their lives. When he was told over the telephone that they were both dead, he asked the speaker to repeat the news, and then slowly let his hands fall. One of his aides picked up the receiver, and the armored officer on the other side of the line went on to say that the brothers had committed suicide. Dinh's aide asked how this was possible. The officer said that the prisoners had grabbed a rifle from an enlisted man, and when Dinh's aide asked why only one man was guarding them, he was told that ''someone was careless.'' Dinh wept at the news, but he was not so grief-stricken that it prevented him from dancing at a party that night.

The original death certificates contemptuously described Diem not as the head of state, but as ''chief of province,'' one of the jobs he had held under the French as a young man, and Nhu as ''chief of library service,'' one of his early posts. Reportedly they were buried in a small, quiet military ceremony outside of town on Saturday evening.

The death of the brothers was shrouded in secrecy. The generals did not allow the population to see the bodies, out of fear that there would be joyous rioting, so there were still many Vietnamese who doubted that the brothers were dead. Though photos had been taken of the bodies, the generals were afraid to release them because they feared the reaction in the United States. But by Saturday noon the populace of Saigon was accepting the idea that the Government had fallen. Political prisoners telling ugly stories of torture were being released and reunited with their families; at the Xa Loi pagoda the Buddhist leaders, many of them thin and haggard and the victims of beatings, were reunited with thousands of the faithful at a dramatic and highly emotional daylong service. In the streets, mobs of young people had gathered and were attacking vestiges of the old regime which they particularly hated. Singled out were the fraudulent National Assembly, which they tried to destroy, and a giant statue of some legendary Vietnamese heroines built by Madame Nhu, one figure of which, the population believed, had purposely been sculpted to resemble her. The offices of the hated *Times of Vietnam*, and those of another newspaper that also reflected the regime's views, were burned down, and the homes of two ministers close to Nhu and who were part of the secret police apparatus were destroyed.

That night, while countless secret policemen fled their homes, night club after night club opened up and the Vietnamese began twisting again. Throughout the city the photos of Diem, which looked as if he had always been aware of the cameraman, appearing very small and lonely, were torn down. Within days the only traces of the President were the one-piaster coins that remained in circulation, and the bitterness and division which his rule had engendered. It was the end of an era, the end of nine years of the Ngo-family government, and the end of the nine years of American support which had seen our hopes become frailer and our enemies stronger every year.

All Friday and Saturday we had worked—running, filing, checking rumors, and trying to find order in a disorderly city. At midday Saturday when the new military junta released the news that Diem and Nhu had committed suicide we were sure that the story was false. On Saturday night Sheehan, who had just re-entered the country on the first available plane, borrowed a car, and we defied the curfew that had been imposed, to slip out to General Dinh's military headquarters. There a friend told us that the brothers' bodies had arrived, bayoneted and shot. We drove back to the city, and since censorship was again in force, we persuaded an American official to permit us to use official channels to send out a brief paragraph refuting the suicide story.

We returned to the office to find Mert Perry trying to put together a piece for *Time*. As we entered, he looked up from his typewriter and said, "Well, the generals have only one thing going against them."

"What's that?" Sheehan asked.

"They're Vietnamese," said Perry.

XVIII

After the coup d'état I spent the next ten days in Saigon putting together an account of the fall of the Government and the changes taking place. Then friends in the Delta began to telephone and stop by the office, something they hadn't been able to do for a long time. They urged me to come down to My Tho on a visit, for they could talk openly again.

I spent most of the next month traveling through the Delta. It was a sentimental journey, for I knew that I was going home in mid-December, and that I was seeing for the last time the area I knew and liked the best, and where friends of mine had been killed. It was also a sad trip because of the contrast with the countryside I had first seen fourteen months before. Where there had been some hope and momentum then, now all I could see was decay and deterioration on our side, and an improvement in the Vietcong position. It was a bitter trip too, for the steep price necessary for victory a year before had more than doubled now; despite all the bloodshed and all the sacrifices, the winning of the war was further away than ever.

However, for once the job of a reporter in Vietnam was easy. The Vietnamese officers were talking candidly to the American advisers, and both were talking to the reporters. Those first few weeks after the coup were a time of great frankness and soul-searching, of mutual trust in many areas. In mid-November my

old friend Colonel Pham Van Dong, who was now in command
of the Seventh Division, invited me down to his headquarters.
We had known each other well through the long and difficult
months when he was held in great suspicion by Diem; in those
days Sheehan and I had been forced to send messages to him
through a third party. Widely admired by the Americans—one
American colonel said he was the only Vietnamese he knew
who was qualified to lead American troops—Dong was a North
Vietnamese who was considered extremely tough; his appointment had given some of the advisers in the Seventh Division
hope that the tide could still turn.

When I reached My Tho, some advisers took me by helicopter to western Dinh Tuong Province, where he was conducting
an operation that day, just as he had every day the previous
week, keeping his troops moving constantly in an attempt to
seize the initiative from the enemy and to convince a population
which had not seen the ARVN in eight months that the Government still existed. ''We are trying to tell them about the coup
d'état,'' the colonel said when I joined him, ''but the Vietcong
have gotten there first.''

We sat around the command post and talked. The Americans
were in a very good mood; for the first time in months they felt
that they were chasing the enemy—and in an area where the
Government had not been seen for a long time.

Colonel Dong called over the district chief who was in the
command post, and introduced him as a former aide and old
friend. ''I think I trust this one,'' Dong said. Then he turned to
the chief and asked him how many villages there were in his
district.

The district chief said that there were twenty-four.

''How many do you control?'' the colonel asked.

''Eight,'' the chief replied.

Then the colonel smiled and asked, ''And how many did you
report that you controlled?''

The chief looked slightly sheepish and then answered,
''Twenty-four.''

The Americans nodded as Colonel Dong said, ''Mr. Diem
always got a false report. Mr. Cao liked his job, and he and Mr.
Dam always reported that ninety-eight percent of the population

was with Mr. Diem. And so Mr. Dam did not dare make any operations, because if he had casualties, Mr. Diem would ask him why there were any, when all the people were with him, and then Mr. Cao and Mr. Dam would lose their good jobs. Mr. Diem did not like casualties. They made him very angry, and he would transfer commanders, and they would lose their promotions and their money. So the Vietcong did not need to attack the chief towns. All they wanted was control over the rural areas, and so there was no fight and no casualties. When Mr. Diem would ask about the war, Mr. Cao and Mr. Dam would say that it was going well because of Mr. Nhu's strategic hamlet program, and that made Mr. Diem and Mr. Nhu very happy and very flattered. That was how they were winning the war. Once I could drive to My Tho or Can Tho at night without an escort, but while Mr. Diem was winning the war you could not drive without a big escort. It was a very funny way to win a war.''

Then the Americans and Colonel Dong had a discussion about just how much of those two vital provinces, Long An and Dinh Tuong, the Government controlled. It was the kind of conversation almost unheard of in Vietnam, open and frank, with Americans arguing with a Vietnamese for being too optimistic. One of the officers pulled out a list of the hamlets in the two provinces. Of the two hundred and thirteen in Dinh Tuong and the two hundred and nineteen in Long An, Colonel Dong estimated that about 20 percent were politically and militarily controlled by the Government, but some of the Americans felt that 10 percent was more accurate.

Later I asked one of the senior advisers if the situation was really that bad. ''Actually, I think it's worse,'' he said. ''I don't think we've even begun to see the enemy's real capacity—I think they're playing cat and mouse with us. Many of these hamlets have never been hit by the VC, and the reason is that they don't have to hit them—they control them already.''

The adviser went on to say that the hamlets in the Delta had begun to serve as way-stations for the guerrillas. They would slip in at night, eat, and move on the next day. In some areas they made the peasants chop up the endless strands of barbed wire which had virtually become a symbol of Government failure; in others they made the people take the roof off their huts as a sign of obedience. Slowly they were drawing closer to main district and provincial capitals, becoming bolder in their attacks. The noose was being tightened.

For the next three days I went out with the armored personnel carriers as they crisscrossed the Cho Gao area of Dinh Tuong Province, hunting for elements of that old nemesis, the 514th Battalion. I had visited this part before, and now the signs of neglect were as abundant as the coconuts and ducks. In a small village ten miles outside of My Tho we saw the ruins of a strategic hamlet information center; right next to it was a brand-new Vietcong information center with a painting of a guerrilla chasing an American with a bayonet.

Two miles farther on—it was really off the road, because the enemy had cut it so many times that it looked more like a Fort Benning obstacle course than a road ("Damn, they're stealing our road," said one of the Americans)—we rumbled slowly through another village. Usually the sight of troops and vehicles would bring out the children, but here they cowered in doorways; in two huts I saw the parents pulling their children inside. I was riding with a young American captain from Oklahoma who was in the last month of his tour. "I remember this village," he said. "When we came through here before we had to fight off the kids who wanted candy."

That episode was typical of those three days. As we approached one village, the peasants filed out in their Sunday white, anxious that we not confuse them with the Vietcong and eager to have us leave the village as quickly as possible. During the time that we paused there, it appeared that one of the soldiers was stealing a chicken, and one of the advisers sent his interpreter over to prevent this. In a moment the interpreter returned, laughing; the soldier had paid for the bird, but part of the bargain was that he must pretend that he was stealing it, for the peasant was afraid that a neighbor might see him selling something to the Government and report him to the Vietcong.

The whole sortie became something of a nightmare. Three hours later in another village the people seemed unusually friendly. One of the Vietnamese officers talking to the peasants found that they knew nothing about the coup; proudly, he told them about the rebellion in which his unit had played an important part. The Army had taken over the country, the officer said, and now the war against the Vietcong would be fought much harder. The peasants all agreed that this was very good news, and moments later they presented the troops with chickens and rice and grapefruit. But as we left the village, the people asked the soldiers not to tell anyone about the gifts, for the Vietcong would kill them if they learned about their hospitality.

Later my Oklahoma friend told me that he and another U.S. officer had visited a small village in Long An Province about a month before. Outside the village they had found a little Catholic church with a red-and-green Vietcong flag flying from its roof. "I'm not a Catholic, and we don't have too high an opinion of that church down in Oklahoma," the adviser told me, "but I was pretty upset about it." He had sought out the young Vietnamese priest and asked him to explain how this could happen. "It is very simple, Captain," the priest said. "You people come here once every three or four months, and you have tea with me and then leave. But the Vietcong are here every night, and this is the price they exact for the survival of my church."

Two nights later I met one of these brave young priests myself. He was a bright young man with a disarming smile and a good sense of humor, but he was very serious when he told me about the difficulties he had in explaining to his flock the threat of the Vietcong and the fact that it was a Communist-backed and inspired movement. His parishioners did not accept this; they insisted that the Vietcong were nationalists, not Communists. Why, the proof of this was that they permitted the priest to travel safely in an area they controlled; the Communists would not allow that, they told the priest.

"How can I tell them that this is just propaganda?" the priest said to me. "The Vietcong do not want to alarm the peasants now by killing me. They will let me live two more years and then they will kill me. To my people the Vietcong are heroes and revolutionaries, and the Government officials are corrupt and evil."

After three days in the field we headed back to My Tho. The sun had baked the mud covering us and our vehicles, and we were tired and our necks were red, but the advisers were exhilarated by having spent some time in the field and by having used the carriers for the purpose for which they had been intended. The Vietnamese troops were adjusting slowly to the new and—for them—revolutionary attempts to institute a command system in their Army. At one point a young Vietnamese captain had wanted the carriers to move forward, and when one of the NCO's was slow to obey, the officer had pulled out a pistol and pointed it at the sergeant. "Things are heating up a bit," said the Oklahoman, "a good sign."

On the way back to the command post we noticed a young man walking ahead of us as we passed through a village. When the commander in the lead truck told him to stop, he refused; even when challenged again he kept walking. Then they fired a short machine-gun burst over his head, but incredibly he simply strolled on until he reached a small hut. The carrier pulled up in front of the hut, two others pulled up in back, and a squad of troops entered. Inside they found the youth and sixteen other healthy, well-fed young men, their hands uncalloused. A Vietnamese officer said that they were probably part of a regular Vietcong company. They were tied up, and on the way back we watched the other prisoners snarling at the youth who had led us to this windfall. It was nice to learn first-hand that the enemy could make mistakes too.

But such comfort was not to last; in My Tho, to which some of us returned by helicopter, we quickly lost the pleasure of our small victory. There we learned that our convoy had been ambushed only a few miles from My Tho; four vehicles had been allowed to pass, and then the enemy had blown up the fifth, a troop truck. Thirteen regulars had been killed immediately, and seven wounded. Once again the Vietcong had proved their ability to mine the main road in daylight without the population informing on them. Sabotage by mining the roads was on the increase; to the Vietnamese who had fought in the Indochina war this way of intimidating the Government troops and driving them back to the district and provincial capitals was depressingly familiar. "They have us in the caves," Father Hoa, the famous fighting priest of Camau, told me in discussing the new wave of such incidents, "and now they want to keep us there." The prospect of being a cave dweller was not a happy one.

* * *

During the next couple of weeks I learned that the situation in the Delta was even worse than the Americans had realized. The Twenty-first Division, which was operating south of the Seventh, controlled only those areas in which it happened to be; it was nothing more than a mobile outpost. The Seventh Division itself was operating virtually in Vietcong territory. Fourteen months before, the Americans had been saying, "If we could only make them stand and fight." Now the Vietcong were doing just that and the problem was to deploy Government troops in such circumstances so as to avoid prohibitive casualties.

The senior adviser of the Seventh Division called the situation desperate; serious enough at any time, it was catastrophic for men who had been at war for the greater part of two decades. The booster shot had failed; they had seen the Americans come, they had seen the enemy become stronger, and now they were tired.

It is impossible to overestimate the importance the Vietcong placed on psychology in their tactics. It was why they had made their major effort in Long An and Dinh Tuong; while the Government and the Americans had concentrated elsewhere, the enemy had taken two of the richest provinces in the country virtually without a fight. The Vietcong never wasted their assets and always had a good reason for everything they did. In these two territories they would control the lives of more than a million people and the income from immense agricultural resources; they would rule the main highway to Saigon from the Delta, and most important of all, they would have a psychological death grip on Saigon itself. For though the enemy could not control the entire countryside at this time, they could *appear* to control the whole countryside. In the capital this impression of the subjugation of two virtually suburban provinces would have immense effect; it could turn pro-Government elements of the population into fence-sitters, and fence-sitters into active Vietcong sympathizers. Some of the Buddhist leaders, for instance, were not militantly anti-Communist, and because they were interested in the perpetuation of Buddhism and the protection of their followers, they would be apt to decide which side looked like the winner and then try to reach some sort of unofficial rapprochment with it. (Indeed, there is a possibility that some of the Buddhist leaders may have done exactly that in late 1964.) Moreover, surrounding the capital would also create a sense of defeatism among civil servants and the military itself, would encourage neutralist groups, and would affect the thinking of foreign diplomats and military officials.

Until the coup, the mood in the Seventh Division had been one of pessimism. Yet Colonel Dong brought hope with him; the new junta had put its best man on the toughest assignment, and perhaps this was a harbinger of the future. Dong demonstrated what an advisory relationship could be; he asked the Americans to come to his briefings, he made it clear to his own officers that he liked the advisers and their advice, and whenever he telephoned one of his own officers he was punctilious about speaking to the man's American counterpart as well. The result was that the Vietnamese had to be candid with the Americans.

It was a time of brief optimism, however, for if there was any hope in November 1963, it was that something dramatic would happen—that there would be not just change, but virtual revolution—so that the downward spiral of nearly two decades could be reversed quickly. But the new junta was composed of men like Minh who were sympathetic to their American ally and to their own people, men willing to talk realistically about the problems around them. Essentially men of an older order who believed in the traditions by which they had risen to the top, they were anything but revolutionaries. Moreover, the system was so corroded and the Army so riddled with ineptitude that any reforms of Diem's successors were largely neutralized by the residue. It was a time for greatness and brilliance, and these qualities were not forthcoming.

In the Seventh Division, for instance, Colonel Dong maneuvered his troops brilliantly for three weeks—and at the end of November he was relieved. Just why I never learned; perhaps General Dinh was afraid of him, perhaps the other leaders, who were aware of his close relationship with junior officers, feared that he might lead a revolt, perhaps he had offended one of the generals, perhaps there was jealousy over the Americans' enthusiasm for him.

My long tour of the Delta had been depressing enough, but

the removal of Dong hit me the hardest of all. It seemed that the old Vietnamese game was being played again, but it was much too late for that game. The times demanded talent, not pettiness. When I went out to Colonel Dong's house to see him, I learned that he had been posted to Formosa as a military attaché. It was an unhappy visit, for he was profoundly depressed about the state of the war.

In Saigon there were the first stirrings of political activity. Day after day ships were unloading political prisoners from the island of Poulo Condore who had finally been freed from detention and torture. At Xa Loi, thousands of Buddhist pilgrims paid homage daily at the pagoda. Through the events of the past six months the Buddhists had emerged as the most powerful political force in the country; it was they rather than the military who were widely credited by the population with having brought down the Government. "It appears that having tasted the excitement and controversy of public life, the [Buddhist] leaders are not going to take a back seat," I reported to the *Times*.

As I began to write my final wrap-up piece before leaving the country, I had never been so pessimistic about Vietnam's future. I suppose that the only thing that made me at all hopeful was the fact that I was an American, and therefore not as detached and coldly analytical as a neutral observer might have been. Many American friends whom I greatly respected, still believed that there was a chance to save the country, and this assuaged my pessimism somewhat.

Finally there came the moment to say good-bye. There had been a ritual to leaving the Congo; a correspondent there bought drinks, took people to dinner and tried not to gloat over his good fortune to those who had to stay on. But though I was going back to a good assignment, and though I felt in need of a rest after thirty months in the Congo and Vietnam, America had no great attraction for me. A tough American adviser had once surprised me by saying, "The paddies get to you," but now I discovered that it was true.

On the morning of December 9 we gathered at the airport. As we stood there saying good-bye, I thought for a moment of the scores of VIP's I had seen at Tan Son Nhut reading their proud statements; I remembered the many early mornings when we had come out before five o'clock to have breakfast with Ivan Slavich's armed helicopter units prior to going out on a mission; I remembered the times I had attended the memorial services for dead Americans on the same airstrip.

The Air Vietnam stewardesses looked the same as ever; they wore the same native costume and spoke in the same precise way, and I remembered thinking, when I landed there fifteen months before, what an incongruous introduction they were to a war.

In Hong King I was met by Seymour Topping, our new chief correspondent in Southeast Asia, who had just arrived after serving as bureau chief in Moscow. As much as any man could, Topping knew how I felt; twelve years before he had been a young AP correspondent who was pessimistic at a time when the American mission was optimistic about the outcome of the French Indochina war.

Topping told me that he had been in Saigon in 1951 when young Congressman John F. Kennedy had arrived on an overseas tour. After being received by all the official and optimistic greeters at the airport, Kennedy had asked to meet Topping, and then had come to Seymour's apartment later that day to get the unofficial story. On his return to the United States, Kennedy had made speeches that were critical of U.S. policy in Indochina, speeches that were not popular with the American government or with the Congressman's constituents.

In twelve years, I thought, the situation had not changed much—only the faces.

XIX

No Westerner can return from Vietnam a proud or satisfied man. If he has any conscience at all he goes home with a profound sense of inadequacy, along with whatever scars and sympathies and experiences he has acquired. The failure of the West in Indochina has been unnecessary, expensive and bloody; in Vietnam, Caucasians have staked their prestige and then showed only their worst and clumsiest side, as if anxious to confirm a Marxist caricature.

Whatever the capacity in which he has served, an American today comes back from Vietnam anguished, sad and more than a little bitter: bitter toward the Vietnamese (the easier target), bitter toward his fellow Americans in Southeast Asia, and then, after exposure to his fellow countrymen in the United States, most of all bitter toward them. On his way through this affluent land (America 1964 is overwhelming to anyone who has been to remote parts of the world for nearly three years), the returning traveler is asked or told:

"It sounds like a rat hole out there to me."

Or, "I hear they won't fight."

Or (from a bearded young integration worker in Mississippi), "I enjoyed your coverage of America's other colonial war."

Or, "Is there going to be a war out there?"

It is hard to reconcile the affluence of our society with the sights of Vietnam; the contrast is staggering. But what is more difficult to adjust to is America's indifference and ignorance, and so, many people coming back from Vietnam go through a period of bitterness during which they prefer the company of those who have been in Vietnam and know the country and care about it. When you meet these friends, now frustrated by a quieter, less committed life, everyone talks about going back to Vietnam. But very few do; it is hard to return, and there is not that much to go back to.

We live in a busy and complicated world; slowly other challenges and interests arise, and after a while you're able to forget something of what you have seen.

The months since I left Vietnam have not been happy ones for that country; neither have they been surprising. The later the date of an insurgency, the greater is the tide one has to turn, and the more limited is the capacity to turn it. The awaited miracle is still awaited. Vietnam does not lend itself to big miracles, only small ones: a badly hit helicopter making a safe landing, an ambushed Government force being rescued. Vietnam offers itself to whichever side pays a higher price, faces reality more readily, understands the nature of the conflict better and spends longer hours in the rice paddies and in teaching young peasant children how to read. But these are not miracles.

Over and over again I have been asked by people who have never been to Southeast Asia: Why don't they see it our way? Why don't they put aside their differences and fight in a common cause against a common enemy? But we have never been able to show the Vietnamese that the cause *is* common. We have never fully convinced them that *our* enemy is *their* enemy—in part because we have never understood their enemy.

As I write, there is political instability in Saigon. That is nothing new; there has been political instability there, accelerating and abating and accelerating again, since 1946, when the French Indochina war began. The only difference today is that in the past the unrest was below the surface; it could not readily be seen by the foreign eye. But it was real enough; it corroded the soul of a nation and it fomented a revolution that is still going on. But it took place in the hearts, and not until recently in the streets; and so, it was not the type of thing of which diplomacy is made.

After I had left Saigon, the generals' coup was overthrown at the end of January by the bloodless Nguyen Khanh coup. In effect this was a step forward in the political sophistication of the military. Khanh, ten years younger than the other generals, represented a new generation, and his goals were similar to those of the young officers whose coup the generals had thwarted. At this late date some younger ideas had come to the surface.

The generals, said Americans who were there at the time, seemed tired and lethargic, unable to respond to the urgency of the awesome challenges they had inherited. They had brought a certain amount of political stability to the country simply by overthrowing the detested Government, whereas Khanh brought youth and vigor. But in the fragile balance of post-Diem Vietnam, of newly won freedoms, of reluctance to return to the men and the ways of the past, Khanh's sudden power grab awakened old fears. The Buddhists and other new groups were eager to protect their new strength and influence. Lodge, who had understood the complexity of Vietnamese politics better than any American, was gone, and Taylor had taken his place. Following the naval incident in the Tonkin Gulf, Khanh, encouraged by the Americans, moved to establish total power with a very strong central government. Riots started again in the streets; the result was not that Khanh became stronger, but that his government fell.

On August 7, 1964, Peter Grose, the acute *New York Times* reporter in Saigon, wrote:

> How did this disintegration come about? Observers on the scene think that in sum it was the result of an attempt to impose a neat, American-style solution on an Asian society in disarray. General Khanh's offensive went too far

too fast, according to Vietnamese and foreign observers;
it ignored the basic motives of self-interest that propel
religious, political and social groups of this country. These
observers felt that insofar as United States policy makers
encouraged General Khanh in his bold moves to centralize
power, they bear a major responsibility for the present
situation. The risk they encouraged was not, in the view
of these observers, well calculated.

The opinion of these sources is that the Americans made
the basic error of assuming that the primary interest of the
Vietnamese people is the same as the primary interest of
the American mission in Vietnam: defeat of the Vietcong
insurgency.

Since the riots had succeeded in toppling Khanh's government, the Buddhists were stronger than ever. They enjoyed
their new power and felt that they had a virtual veto over any
government. Military rule soon ended and a caretaker civilian
government was established under Tran Van Huong, a widely
respected civil servant with a reputation for stubbornness and
honesty. Again the Buddhists challenged Huong's right to run
a government in which they were not the dominant factor;
they also claimed that there were too many Diem holdovers—
mostly civil servants—in his Administration. Huong replied
that the Buddhist grievances against Diem had been justified,
but that the ones against him were not and that his regime
should be given time to prove itself. Once more there were
riots in Saigon in late November 1964, but Huong stood firm.
Though Khanh, now commander of the Armed Forces, sulked
in the wings, Huong was momentarily strengthened when
other young officers rallied to his side.

During this period the Buddhists were making a strong bid
for control. With the fall of the Diem government they had
become the most powerful segment of the population. They
were popular because they had largely been responsible for
bringing down a hated government, and their leadership was
skillful. But Diem had also been highly acclaimed in his early
days, not because of his character or ability to govern, but
because his first acts—the crushing of the gangster sects, for
instance—had met popular response. How long the Bud-

dhists' popularity would last if they went too far was a crucial question. Were they headed for political nihilism, and if so, would they be able to retain their following? Some Americans believed that one of their advantages was the war weariness felt by many Vietnamese.

In January they were able to provoke demonstrations which shook Huong's government, and General Khanh and the military returned to power in a bloodless coup. For the moment the Buddhists relaxed the tension, but their power seemed very real. The question then became whether Khanh and the young officers would be able to work out some sort of rapprochement with the Buddhists. If this was accomplished, it would bring Vietnam some needed political stability; if not, it appeared likely that some sort of final showdown between the Buddhists and the military would eventually take place.

What has been taking place in Vietnam in the last few months is what Ambassador Lodge has called the "process of political evolution." South Vietnam has never had a chance to evolve naturally; there have been no stable institutions or elections through which such a progression could take place. But the relatively crude political maneuvering that has been occurring recently, in which varying groups jockey for place, is the first glimmering of the democratic process. If the Vietnamese government and the Americans are lucky, there may be a vague grouping which will hold the disparate interest factions of the country in delicate balance: Buddhist, Catholic, young officers, old-guard traditionalists, Delta Vietnamese, central Vietnamese and refugees. But such beginnings are taking place at a very late and desperate date.

In the countryside the situation remains grim. Occasionally Government units have stood and fought with remarkable tenacity, and American officers report that they are enjoying increased success in getting a hearing for their ideas. But many of the techniques of the past remain: the large, fraudulent operations; the commitment of troops to indefensible points. Moreover, an insurgency is not like the war in Korea, where a force evicted from a position one day could return the next and recapture the territory. In the infinitely complex Vietnamese war, there are a large number of factors which tend to produce a spiral; this downward spiral produces its own momentum, and it is far easier for this movement to accelerate than it is to slow it down, much less reverse it.

And so, as this is written, it is very late in Vietnam. It was very late in 1951 when the French stayed on; it was later in 1954 when the war was finally over; it was later still in 1961 when Taylor made our last-gasp commitment; and it was even later in 1963 when that last gasp failed and Diem was overthrown. What is there to recommend at the end of that long road down which we have traveled for years and years when the policy was: *There is no place else to go?* How do you find somewhere else to go now?

The basic alternatives for Vietnam are the same now as they were in 1961; they are no different, no more palatable, no less of a nightmare.

First, there is a great deal of talk about the possibility of a neutral Vietnam. But under present conditions this is out of the question. There is not the remotest possibility of neutrality in the sense that Switzerland, Austria, India or even Laos are neutral—which is these countries' way of saying that they wish to be neither a battlefield nor a participant of either side in the Cold War. The first step toward a neutral Vietnam would undoubtedly be the withdrawal of all U.S. forces in the country and a cutback in American military aid; this would create a vacuum so that the Communists, the only truly organized force in the South, could subvert the country at their leisure—perhaps in six months, perhaps in two years. There would simply be no force to resist them, and if Hanoi offered us and the South Vietnamese a neutral solution, it would only mean a way of saving face for the United States.

What *about* withdrawal? Few Americans who have served in Vietnam can stomach this idea. It means that those Vietnamese who committed themselves fully to the United States will suffer the most under a Communist government, while we lucky few with blue passports retire unharmed; it means a drab, lifeless and controlled society for a people who deserve better. Withdrawal also means that the United States' prestige will be lowered throughout the world, and it means that the pressure of Communism on the rest of Southeast Asia will intensify. Lastly, withdrawal means that throughout the world the enemies of the West will be encouraged to try insurgencies like the one in Vietnam. Just as our commitment in Korea in 1950 has served to discourage overt Communist border crossings ever since, an anti-Communist victory in Vietnam would serve to discourage so-called wars of liberation.

The only other possibility—for blocking or bombing the so-called Ho Chi Minh trail would not effectively alter the balance of power in the South—is the one that every American President has shied away from for more than twelve years: the commitment of U.S. combat troops to South Vietnam. This most difficult of options would undoubtedly be even more frustrating than Korea; there we were fighting a uniformed, identifiable enemy which had crossed a border, in terrain which had a front. In Vietnam, however, Caucasians would be killing South Vietnamese on their own soil in a political war. If only 5 percent of the population in the South is committed to the Vietcong, the arrival of U.S. combat units would probably make enemies out of fence-sitters; certainly the guerrillas' cause would become a broader and more popular one. Whatever military gains brought by U.S. troops might soon be countered by the political loss; the war would begin to parallel the French experience. It would be a war without fronts, fought against an elusive enemy, and extremely difficult for the American people to understand. The misconceptions, misinformation and lack of candor displayed by American officialdom in the past in Indochina does not give anyone confidence that our government would explain the conflict. (Even as late as December 1, 1964, when Taylor was home, he met with the President and other high officials. As the meeting was breaking up and the reporters were coming into the room, Charley Mohr heard McNamara tell President Johnson: "It would be impossible for Max to talk to these people without leaving the impression that the situation is going to hell.")

So for the moment we are caught in the quagmire. Neutralization would only delay the inevitable momentarily, we would dishonor ourselves and our allies by pulling out, and, despite the fact that we are deeply involved in a very real war, we should think and prepare for a long, long time before going in with our own troops.

It is, of course, a Vietnamese war, though it is true that it could not continue for very long without the American military commitment. But neither could it go on if it did not have the support of a certain range of Vietnamese people. If and when it becomes a hopeless war and a hopeless cause, it will not be the Americans who know this first; it will be the Vietnamese, who have now lived without peace for over nineteen years. After three years, less than the equivalent of a combat battalion of Americans has died; Vietnamese by the hundreds and occasionally by the thousands die each month. If the war becomes intolerable, it will be the Vietnamese who will and must decide that almost anything—even being ruled by a Communist government in Hanoi—is better than endless bloodletting. What would trigger this decision no one knows: perhaps a neutralist coup by young officers willing to negotiate; perhaps the complete domination of the Delta by the Vietcong.

In the meantime we are committed to playing our part of the bargain as best we can, in a desperate hope that we have learned some of the lessons of Indochina in time to use them in Vietnam. Just conceivably, at this late date the dissenting forces in the country will band together when the imminent threat of a Communist take-over finally makes the enemy a common enemy; fear sometimes succeeds where all other motivations fail. If various political factions could unite, there might be a strong enough base for a viable military approach to a solution. But only an improvement in the military situation can make real negotiations possible.

But after nineteen years of Western mistakes, these hopes are very frail. Probably the lessons will not be learned in time for Vietnam. Perhaps at this moment we are gaining the knowledge necessary to deal with a situation in Thailand, or Angola, or a small republic in South America—some country where it is not yet too late, where now there is only a quiet crisis and still some flexibility. Perhaps we should be glad that so far Vietnam is the only country in which the West became the stubborn prisoner of its colonial past and a colonial war. We should remember that the French did not repeat their mistakes in French West Africa, that they did get out of Algeria just in time, and that the British dissolved their empire with remarkable skill.

Throughout the world the chickens are coming home to roost, and for better or for worse, the responsibility for their roosting rests with the United States. The presidency does not lend itself to the study of quiet crises: there are too many noisy ones at hand. Right now the President has a hundred Vietnams: there is Mississippi, the gold balance, Cuba, poverty, Britain and the Common Market, De Gaulle and the MLF, the Congo, the USSR—the list is endless. Mr. Johnson is a fire chief with too many blazes to put out, and too little time to worry about spots where at the moment there is only a little smoke—where the status quo is now tolerable to the United States but intolerable to the population of that country. In 1951—perhaps the year the war was really lost—who was listening to the quiet voices from Indochina?

Thus the problem is partly a matter of deciding what our global commitments and our priorities are. What is the range of our self-interest and security? Is every country not yet inside the Communist Bloc a part of the United States' responsibility? Is each country on the continent of South America worth fighting for, or do only some of them have the resources and strategic location that make them worth the challenge? In what case is there a common interest between the two countries to make a commitment plausible and potentially successful? Before we ever plant the flag again, we must make sure that grounds for mutual self-interest exist, that the situation has not deteriorated beyond control and, above all, that we are wanted.

It is very hard to give aid effectively in the underdeveloped world. In Western Europe we were dealing with nations which had something in common with us ethnically, socially, culturally and morally—countries where the forces which bound men together were stronger than those which divided them, and where there was a broad basis of mutual self-interest with the United States. The motivation was there; we did not have to seek it—indeed, it sought us.

This is not true of Vietnam, nor is it likely to be true of any country where insurgencies occur in the foreseeable future. The things that motivate us are not likely to mean very much to illiterate, frightened and hungry peasants. The common interest between such a society and the United States is not an easy or natural one, but it does exist, and it behooves us to be smarter and better prepared to find that communality. To find a common purpose, something that we can offer underdeveloped societies that is more subtle and more rewarding than Communism's obvious appeal to a man who has nothing, we must know what his needs and motivations are and adjust ourselves to these, instead of shaping that man's government to our global aims and expecting him to adjust to us. Obviously we cannot simply translate our technology to a different environment, any more than we can easily transfer replicas of those institutions which motivate and stabilize the United States—the two-party system, the free ballot and the free press—to less fortunate lands with little political tradition or education and with a debilitating climate.

I believe that Vietnam is a legitimate part of that global commitment. A strategic country in a key area, it is perhaps one of only five or six nations in the world that is truly vital to U.S. interests. If it *is* this important, it may be worth a larger commitment on our part, but if so, we should be told the truth, not spoon-fed clichés as in the past.

What happens next in Vietnam will be determined on the basis of our real and attainable aims. But what are they? There has been too little planning in Washington and too much of a tendency simply to react to a crisis, regardless of its application to us.

The situation in Vietnam is not necessarily an indication that the most powerful, dynamic and developed country has nothing to offer a frail new nation; nor does it mean that the Communists have the answers and right approach for this part of the world and that therefore they will eventually win Asia. We do have something to offer these emerging nations. We can get things done; given a problem, we react well. We are prosperous; we have food, medicine and willing technicians of every sort to export. We do not demand servitude, and in comparison with our enemies, we are not doctrinaire. We want stability for these people, whereas the Communists actively provoke inconstancy. So, we cannot abandon our efforts to help these people, no matter how ungrateful they may seem, or how frustrating the task is for the giver, or how often we are accused of being soft or liberal. It is not a question of being liberal or conservative, or soft or tough; it is a question of being effective. Napalm is powerful, all right; both we and the French had plenty of napalm in Vietnam, but it was not enough. All the fine speeches and all the tough talk notwithstanding, they are not likely to deter our enemy, who are moving at night and live in the rice paddies, who know the war better than we do, who are more patient and subtle than we have been, and who are willing to pay a higher price. We had better get smart.

In Indochina a colonial war turned the nationalism of a proud people against the West and into the hands of a very real enemy. That was the beginning of the downward cycle, for in those years when the Western nations were powerful they might have channeled this nationalism into a relatively neutral force. Thereafter, other mistakes fell into place. Given a policy which was based in theory on our requirements to maintain international security and what we felt were the needs of the Vietnamese people, we always took the simplest path—our requirements. If there was a body of growing opposition to the regime, it was quickly passed off as being nothing but Vietnamese intellectuals; this despite the fact that we hail the very same kind of dissent by similar groups in Eastern Europe as the top of an iceberg, for there it fits our view of the world, and so it is convenient to pay more than lip service to it.

It is a quiet indictment of the American-Ngo decade that today the most powerful political force in the South is the Buddhists, a group that has risen to power more or less indifferent to the main thread of our policy—the prosecution of the anti-Communist war—and indeed has won much of its popularity because it challenged the Government we supported.

The American mission in Vietnam started out with the highest hopes and idealism. It failed for a number of reasons: not for lack of its own good intentions, not for lack of long working hours and patience (too much patience on occasion), but because the legacy of mistakes was too large, because the die had been cast long, long ago, because the United States was unable to face reality in Indochina, and because we responded with clichés to desperately complicated and serious challenges.

So far, our country's first major effect at counterinsurgency has failed. We are new at the game; the enemy is not. We are rich, therefore ironically at a disadvantage in foreseeing, judging and helping to alleviate the hardships of the poor and underprivileged. When grievances do not exist, wars do not start. But the underdeveloped world is filled with oppression, and there will almost surely be more wars of this kind.

So it becomes a matter of national self-interest to discover what we can offer in the future. Bombers and helicopters and napalm are a help, but they are not enough. When their advice was ignored, the American generals in Saigon fell back on their clichés; the enemy, they said, succeeds because of terror. But there is more than terror to the Vietcong's methods, though it is cleverly and judiciously and ruthlessly employed. Can the guerrillas really create more terror than Government troops with howitzers, armed helicopters, armored personnel carriers and bazookas? The Vietcong's control is based on far more than just terror. If our generals really believe their own slogans about terror, heaven help us; if they don't but are passing them on to the people in the United States, heaven help *them*. For unless we understand the source of the enemy's success, we will never combat it successfully.

Describing Hanoi in the spring of 1955, Graham Greene wrote:

> But the peasant doesn't miss the café, the restaurant,
> the French or American film—he's never had them. Per-

haps even the endless compulsory lectures and political meetings, the hours of physical training, are better entertainment than he has ever known.

We talk so glibly of the threat to the individual, but the anonymous peasant has never been treated so like an individual before. Unless a priest, no one before the Commissar has approached him, has troubled to ask him the questions, or spent time to teach him. There is something in Communism besides the politics.

There is something to the Vietcong besides the terror, something more to winning a revolutionary war than helicopters. In writing this book I became more and more haunted by the historical implications of the French Indochina war and the warped legacy it left us. I am certain now that only a miracle could have saved us in 1954; heirs to such uneven odds, we found ourselves caught in a limited, ineffective and almost certainly doomed holding action. Yet in the early fifties the people in America were subjected to constant statements from Paris and Washington about the West's battle to save Southeast Asia from the Communists. But the war was taking place in Vietnam, what was at stake were the lives of Vietnamese people, and to them the names seemed wrong; it was not a matter to them of the West against the Communists, but of themselves against the colonialists. It was a classic example of seeing the world the way we wanted to, instead of the way it was.

As I wrote this book, stories out of Vietnam received more and more space in the *Times*—moving from the bottom of the front page to the top, and then gradually over to Column Eight—and the number of crash crisis meetings on what to do about the country increased in frequency and duration. During this time I have also been asked what we should do over and over again by friends. But how do you answer questions about the difficulty of inheriting such vast global responsibilities so quickly? Were the key years in the late forties? Where were today's policy makers in 1946? Did they have a fair chance at shaping the origin of a crisis? It is no answer at all to say that the West should have asked itself that question in 1946—when Robert McNamara was a brand-new thirty-year-old "whiz kid" at Ford, ready to make his mark, and Lyndon Johnson was a young Congressman from Texas eying a Senate seat and thinking that international affairs meant Mexico, and twenty-seven-year-old McGeorge Bundy was working on the Stimson papers and about to become an instructor at Harvard.

Today there are quiet crises going on elsewhere in the world. The lesson to be learned from Vietnam is that we must get in earlier, be shrewder and force the other side to practice the self-deception. I read recently in a story about the Congo that South African and Rhodesian mercenaries had been hired to put down the Katangese rebels. Hiring South African mercenaries to bring peace to the Congo is something like the mayor of New York summoning the Mississippi Highway Patrol to quell riots in Harlem, and I thought that perhaps seven or eight years from now, when we are wondering when the second and fateful stage in the Congo began, hindsight may show that it was back in 1964, when Vietnam and the MLF were our main concerns.

I did not feel any better a few days later when I read an interview with Major Hoare, the South African who commands those mercenaries and who is undoubtedly a capable soldier (but whether the major should be in a position to implement the West's policy in the Congo is another question). There was suddenly the kind of lip service which marked two decades in Indochina. "A military solution," said Major Hoare, "is not enough. There must be some sort of political solution as well."

This is where I came in.